Legal Frameworks of Human Resource Management Reform

Perfecto Gatbonton Aquino, Jr.
https://orcid.org/0000-0001-6352-7916
Duy Tan University, Vietnam

Mercia Selva Malar Justin
Christian Management Institute, India

Revenio Cabanilla Jalagat, Jr.
Al Zahra College for Women, Oman

IGI Global
Scientific Publishing
Publishing Tomorrow's Research Today

Vice President of Editorial	Melissa Wagner
Director of Acquisitions	Mikaela Felty
Director of Book Development	Jocelynn Hessler
Production Manager	Mike Brehm
Cover Design	Jose Rosado

Published in the United States of America by
IGI Global Scientific Publishing
701 East Chocolate Avenue
Hershey, PA, 17033, USA
Tel: 717-533-8845 | Fax: 717-533-7115
Website: https://www.igi-global.com E-mail: cust@igi-global.com

Library of Congress Cataloging-in-Publication Data

No LCCN (CIP Data Pending)
ISBN13: 979-8-3693-5390-5
Isbn13Softcover: 979-8-3693-5391-2
EISBN13: 979-8-3693-5392-9

British Cataloguing in Publication Data
A Cataloguing in Publication record for this book is available from the British Library.

Table of Contents

Detailed Table of Contents

The legal reforms in the Human Resource Management (HRM) in employment protection, pension, wage laws, social security requirements and workforce compliance stipulations have become the major performance determinants, and the financial structure of modern economies. (Akbar, 2025) Previously perceived as regulatory interventions or welfare based interventions, these reforms have long since become considered financially material, and have both direct and indirect impacts on corporate cash flows, balance sheets, risk exposure and market values. The increasing labour costs, the presence of long-term employee benefits, and compliance costs all have more bearing on the decision-making process of managers, capital allocation, and the competitiveness of the firm (Bustamante, 2017).

The chapter is an in-depth analysis of the evolving legal frameworks that guide human resource management reforms in India, examining the nature of the influence of such regulations on workplace practices, labour rights, and corporate governance in one of the fastest-growing economies of the world. The present chapter, therefore, attempts to fill the gap between the theoretical perspectives of HRM and the practical implications of legal reforms in the continuously fluctuating economy, technology, and labour market. It shall be a ready reckoner for human resource professionals, policymakers, business leaders, and scholars interested in knowing how labour law and HRM interface in the Indian context.

The digital transformation of contemporary workplaces has accelerated the integration of advanced monitoring technologies and Human Resource Information Systems (HRIS), reshaping how organizations manage performance, administer HR functions, and ensure operational efficiency. While these systems offer unprecedented opportunities for data-driven decision-making, they also raise significant concerns about employee privacy, autonomy, and fairness. This chapter examines the evolution of employee privacy in relation to technological change, the development and limitations of existing data protection laws, and the growing ethical risks associated with algorithmic surveillance and biometric data collection. It argues that current legal frameworks are inadequate for addressing the complexities of digital monitoring and calls for comprehensive reforms that prioritize proportionality, transparency, and employee agency. This chapter provides governance strategies, organizational best practices, and future directions for safeguarding privacy in the digital workplace.

Artificial Intelligence (AI) is rapidly transforming Human Resource Management (HRM), offering enhanced efficiencies and innovative approaches in recruitment, performance management, and various HR functions. This chapter explores the integration of AI in HRM, examining the potential benefits, legal challenges, and ethical considerations associated with its use. Key opportunities include improved recruitment processes, data-driven performance evaluations, and personalized employee experiences. However, challenges such as compliance with data protection laws, addressing algorithmic bias, and maintaining transparency are critical. The

the importance of sustainability, effective legal regulations serve as critical tools for fostering ethical labor practices, diversity and inclusion, and employee well-being. This study examines global legal trends in HR sustainability, legal requirements for diversity, and the relationship between employment rights and well-being initiatives. Additionally, it highlights the importance of sustainable talent development, labor laws concerning environmental sustainability, and the integration of corporate social responsibility (CSR) into HR policies. Despite existing challenges such as enforcement gaps and resistance to change, the future of legal frameworks will likely evolve to address these issues through technological innovations and multi-stakeholder collaborations.

This chapter examines the intersection between secular Human Resource Management (HRM) legal frameworks and Biblical principles. While legal systems, like India's four Labour Codes, establish a necessary institutional "floor" for safety and wages, they often suffer from a "compliance gap" where profit precedes personhood. Through a review of 23 articles, the research reveals that whereas secular HRM is transactional, a Biblical approach is covenantal, rooted in the concept of Imago Dei, which recognizes inherent dignity beyond economic value. The study highlights a synchronization between global standards, such as ILO conventions, and scriptural tenets, framing fair compensation as a modern codification of Biblical stewardship. Ultimately, while the law prevents exploitation, Biblical principles provide the relational depth necessary for excellence. By shifting from compliance to sacred vocation, leaders can bridge the gap between "corner-cutting" and a flourishing culture.

Human Resource Management (HRM) reform has become a central policy and organizational concern in India as the country confronts economic liberalization, globalization, technological disruption, and significant demographic change. While mainstream strategic HRM scholarship often foregrounds managerial innovation, performance enhancement, and competitive advantage, this chapter argues that legal frameworks remain the most powerful institutional forces shaping employment relations and HRM practices. Focusing on the Indian context and informed by global comparative perspectives, the chapter examines the legal foundations of HRM reform through a historical, institutional, and regulatory lens. It traces the evolution of Indian labour and employment law from colonial regulation and post-independence protectionism to contemporary reform initiatives, with particular emphasis on the consolidation of labour legislation into four labour codes.

This research discusses the function of HR management reform as a mediating variable in the operations of civil service by analysing its impact on the effectiveness of decision making process in community based administration as a whole. It particularly explores how Reforms in HRM, related with strategic use of IT capabilities and adoption of AI based outcomes, to deliver a more flexible as well as efficient civil service workforce that would be able to solve complex community based problems. The infoldment goes along with into how AI-powered tools can delineate HR processes related with recruitment as well as sustainability appraisal to augment organisational efficiency as well as sustainability in community based sector entities. As well as, the along with of AI, within HRM through management information operations, optimises the decision-making process by making operations more precise and founded on information, leading to augmented recruitment, better long lasting operation and increased infoldment of staff.

Preface

INTRODUCTION

Human Resource Management (HRM) is undergoing profound transformation as legal frameworks across jurisdictions respond to globalization, technological disruption, demographic change, and evolving conceptions of work and dignity. Once viewed primarily as a compliance-driven function, HRM today sits at the intersection of law, ethics, strategy, and organizational governance. Legal reforms relating to employment protection, data privacy, artificial intelligence, gender equity, sustainability, and transnational labor standards increasingly shape not only how organizations manage people, but how they define fairness, accountability, and long-term value creation. Against this backdrop, *Legal Frameworks of Human Resource Management Reform* seeks to critically examine how law functions as a central institutional force in reshaping contemporary HRM practice.

This edited reference work brings together scholars from diverse disciplinary, geographic, and methodological backgrounds to explore the dynamic relationship between legal regulation and HRM reform. Rather than treating law as a static set of rules, the chapters in this volume conceptualize legal frameworks as evolving mechanisms that both constrain and enable organizational behavior. Across national and sectoral contexts, contributors interrogate how legal reforms influence managerial decision-making, workforce governance, employee rights, and organizational culture. Particular attention is given to emerging challenges such as digital surveillance, artificial intelligence, cross-border employment, and the persistence of structural inequalities that formal compliance alone cannot resolve.

The volume is designed to serve as a comprehensive resource for academics, policymakers, HR professionals, legal practitioners, and graduate students seeking to understand the multifaceted role of law in shaping HRM reform. By integrating theoretical perspectives with empirical insights and policy-oriented analysis, the book moves beyond prescriptive best practices to offer a nuanced understanding of how legal frameworks operate in practice. Collectively, the chapters underscore the argument that meaningful HRM reform requires not only regulatory compliance, but also ethical reflection, institutional coherence, and a commitment to human-centered governance.

CHAPTER OVERVIEW

Chapter 1, *Financial Impact of HRM Legal Reforms: Metrics and Methods*, examines how labor laws and employment-related legal reforms translate into financial consequences for organizations. By focusing on costs, risk exposure, and long-term liabilities, the chapter demonstrates that HRM legal compliance is financially material and integral to strategic decision-making.

Chapter 2, *Legal Frameworks of Human Resource Management Reform in the Context of India*, provides an in-depth examination of India's evolving labor law regime. It bridges theory and practice by analyzing how legal reforms shape workplace relations, labor rights, and corporate governance in one of the world's fastest-growing economies.

Chapter 3, *Privacy in the Digital Workplace: Reforming Data Protection Law for Monitoring and HRIS*, addresses the growing tension between technological efficiency and employee privacy. The authors critically assess existing data protection regimes and propose governance strategies to ensure transparency, proportionality, and employee agency in digitally monitored workplaces.

Chapter 4, *The Legal Challenges and Opportunities of Using AI in HR Functions*, explores the transformative potential of artificial intelligence in HRM alongside its legal and ethical risks. The chapter outlines compliance challenges related to data protection, algorithmic bias, and accountability, offering practical pathways for responsible AI adoption.

Chapter 5, *Impact of Globalization in HRM Reforms*, analyzes how global integration reshapes HR practices through cross-border labor regulation, cultural diversity, and global talent management. The chapter highlights the need for agile and ethically grounded HR strategies in an interconnected world.

Chapter 6, *Microaggressions, Power, and HRM Reform: Rethinking Gendered Labor Rights in India*, shifts the focus from formal legal violations to everyday workplace harms. Using microaggressions as an analytical lens, the chapter critiques existing HRM and legal reforms for their limited capacity to address entrenched gendered power relations.

Chapter 7, *Regulating the Private Sector: Opportunities, Risks, and Transnational Governance Pathways for HRM Reform*, examines legal and ethical challenges arising from workplace surveillance and digital governance. It advances a human-centric regulatory model that balances innovation with fundamental employee rights.

Chapter 8, *Role of Legal Frameworks in Promoting Sustainable HR Practices*, explores how employment law can advance sustainability, diversity, employee well-being, and corporate social responsibility. The chapter situates HRM reform within broader global sustainability agendas.

Chapter 9, *Compliance vs. Excellence: HRM Legal Frameworks vs. HRM Biblical Principles*, offers a distinctive normative perspective by contrasting secular legal compliance with faith-based ethical principles. It argues that while law establishes minimum standards, moral frameworks provide the relational depth necessary for organizational excellence.

Chapter 10, *Employment Law and HRM Reform in India*, provides a historical and institutional analysis of Indian labor law, with particular emphasis on the consolidation of legislation into four labor codes. The chapter reinforces the central role of law as a driver of HRM reform amid economic and technological change.

Chapter 11, *HR Management Reform Mediation in the Civil Service*, examines HRM reform in public sector and community-based administration. It highlights how IT capabilities and AI-enabled HR systems can enhance decision-making effectiveness and organizational sustainability in civil service operations.

CONCLUSION

Taken together, the chapters in this volume demonstrate that legal frameworks are not peripheral to Human Resource Management, but foundational to its reform and evolution. Across private and public sectors, national and transnational contexts, and emerging technological domains, law structures the boundaries within which HRM operates while simultaneously reflecting broader societal values and power relations. The contributors collectively show that HRM reform cannot be reduced to managerial innovation alone; it is deeply embedded in legal, institutional, and ethical systems.

This volume also reveals the limitations of compliance-driven approaches to HRM. While legal reforms establish essential protections and standards, they do not automatically produce fair, inclusive, or humane workplaces. Issues such as digital surveillance, gendered microaggressions, algorithmic bias, and globalization-induced inequalities require interpretive judgment, ethical leadership, and participatory governance that extend beyond the letter of the law. Several chapters therefore call for regulatory frameworks that are adaptive, transparent, and centered on human dignity.

We hope that *Legal Frameworks of Human Resource Management Reform* stimulates critical dialogue and future research on the role of law in shaping work and employment relations. By bringing together diverse perspectives and contexts, this book aims to support more informed policymaking, more reflective HR practice, and more just organizational outcomes. Ultimately, sustainable HRM reform depends on aligning legal innovation with ethical responsibility and a renewed commitment to the human foundations of work.

Chapter 1
Financial Impact of HRM Legal Reforms:
Metrics and Methods

Mohit Verma
https://orcid.org/0009-0005-3036-3894
O.P. Jindal Global University, India

Mansi Panwar
https://orcid.org/0009-0007-0470-8216
Devi Ahilya Vishwavidyalaya University in Indore, India

Manish Dubey
Shri Vaishnav College of Arts and Commerce, Indore, India

Mukhtaruddin Mukhtaruddin
Faculty of Economics, Universitas Sriwijaya, Indonesia

ABSTRACT

The legal reforms in the Human Resource Management (HRM) in employment protection, pension, wage laws, social security requirements and workforce compliance stipulations have become the major performance determinants, and the financial structure of modern economies. (Akbar, 2025) Previously perceived as regulatory interventions or welfare based interventions, these reforms have long since become considered financially material, and have both direct and indirect impacts on corporate cash flows, balance sheets, risk exposure and market values. The increasing labour costs, the presence of long-term employee benefits, and compliance costs all have more bearing on the decision-making process of managers, capital allocation, and the competitiveness of the firm (Bustamante, 2017).

DOI: 10.4018/979-8-3693-5390-5.ch001

1. INTRODUCTION

The legal reforms in the Human Resource Management (HRM) in employment protection, pension, wage laws, social security requirements and workforce compliance stipulations have become the major performance determinants, and the financial structure of modern economies. (Akbar, 2025) Previously perceived as regulatory interventions or welfare based interventions, these reforms have long since become considered financially material, and have both direct and indirect impacts on corporate cash flows, balance sheets, risk exposure and market values. The increasing labour costs, the presence of long-term employee benefits, and compliance costs all have more bearing on the decision-making process of managers, capital allocation, and the competitiveness of the firm (Bustamante, 2017).

Historically, HRM legal reforms have been considered more or less in the frames of the labour law or labour economics, and the focus on the employment rates, employee protection, and income distribution. Although these views will always be relevant, they can no longer be relied on (Zolak et al., 2025). Financially, HRM reforms influence operating margins, change the liability structures, and impact the exposure of the firms to the long-term risks, including the pension and litigation. Labour-related changes in law may have a significant impact on investors and analysts with regard to future profitability, stability of cash flow, and the risk of downside (Dibben et al., 2017). As a result, HRM reforms have become deeply rooted into the corporate finance analysis as opposed to the peripheral compliance concerns.

The increased focus on environmental, social, and governance (ESG) reporting and human capital disclosure has further enhanced the necessity of systematic methods of quantifying the financial impacts of HR-related change of law. Voluntary reporting systems and regulatory programs are also demanding that companies reveal workforce related data such as employee expenses, benefit liabilities, turnover and workforce stability. Sustainability reports and integrated financial reports emphasize the interdependence of human capital management and value creation on a long-term basis (Mahmoud & Othman, 2024). In the given context, the legal reforms of HRM cannot only determine the internal cost framework, but also affect the external view of the quality of corporate governance, social responsibility, and long-term sustainability.

Although their financial relevance may be clear, it is analytically difficult to directly attribute changes in the performance of the firms to the HRM legal reforms. HR reforms usually work via a number of channels and in an interactive sense (Kim & Cho, 2014). There are those that are immediate and measurable such as changes in payroll costs or employer social security payments in accordance with statutory changes. Indirect and behavioural others are those that involve a shift in the morale of the employees, productivity, retention, and organisational culture (Van Landuyt et al., 2017). In the long run, companies can also react strategically by reorganising operation, automate more, outsource labour-intensive tasks, or change the capital to labour ratio. These reactions may cloud the immediate financial effect of the initial legal reformation.

Further, the legal reforms in HRM are usually slow moving, transitional, phased, and delayed in behavioural reactions. E.g. the pension reforms can have a slow impact on the cash flows and cause significant change in the long-term liabilities and risk profile (Vermeeren et al., 2014). The reforms in employment protection might not have direct impacts on the hiring and firing decision within a few years but in the long-term. Consequently, short-term financial indicators may not reflect the overall economic impact of legal change and long-term results may be distorted due to other macroeconomic or industry-specific events occurring at the same time.

The legal HRM reforms are also institutional in nature, making causal inference even more complicated. The majority of the reforms are targeted at the jurisdictional, sectoral, or economy-wide basis, not the firms. (Budhwar & Varma, 2011) This renders it hard to build clean counterfactuals as regards the performance of the firms should they not have been reformed. Even the same legal environment can show heterogeneity in the behaviour of firms based on their size, industry, labour and financial structure, providing an extra level of heterogeneity to empirical analysis.

To address these issues, this chapter constructs an all-inclusive scheme of gauging the financial effect of HRM legal reforms. The framework clearly acknowledges the fact that no single measure can be used to measure the effect of reforms completely and thus it encourages the application of several complementary indicators. Measurements based on accounting, including payroll ratios, profitability measures, and employee-related liabilities, can give the insight on direct costs and balance sheet impacts. The expectations and perceived risk of investors are represented by market-based indicators, such as stock returns, valuation ratios, and cost of capital measures. The human capital performance indicators, including revenue per employee and human capital return on investment, can be used to associate legal reforms with productivity and value creation.

In addition to metrics, this chapter lays much emphasis on empirical procedures that have the ability to isolate reform effects. There are event studies, panel regressions, difference-in-differences, matched-firm and synthetic control methods, which discussing are seen as a tool to reinforce causal attribution. The methods have both benefits and drawbacks, and their validity relies on the availability of data, institutional background, and the study of reform. The chapter suggests that triangulation of methods and measurements provide the most plausible information.

The chapter ends by providing some practical advice to researchers, policymakers, and practitioners. It is a focal point of the best practices in metric selection and empirical design to the researchers. To the policymakers, it demonstrates the significance of considering HRM legal reforms based on not only employment results but also financial stability and firm competitiveness. It puts an increased pressure on managers and investors to incorporate HRM legal factors in financial analysis, risk management and long-term strategic planning.

2. HRM LEGAL REFORMS AND FINANCIAL TRANSMISSION CHANNELS

The legal reforms in Human Resource Management (HRM) determine the performance of firms via intricate financial transmission channels, which are both direct and indirect. These mechanisms should be known in order to choose the right performance measures, to develop empirical strategies, and to analyze the observed financial results (Wang et al., 2019). In this part, the author expounds the impact of HRM legal reforms on the financial reports, the risk-taking profile and strategic actions of firms and the rationale behind the use of multi-metric analytical framework.

2.1 Direct Financial Channels

Direct financial channels are executed by using the income statement, balance sheet and cash flow statement of the firm thereby giving their effects that are usually immediate and quantifiable.

Payroll and Compensation Costs: Reforms in legal regulations that touch on minimum wage, social security payments, severance compensations, pensions, or any other benefits that are compulsory to employees directly change the labour cost formation of firms. Rises in statutory wages or increases in the rate of employer contributions increase operating costs, which lower the operating margins and earnings before interest and tax (EBIT), especially in labour intensive sectors (Zolak et al., 2025). Reforms of pension and benefits can also lead to a rise in the deferred compensation costs which affect both the current expenditures and future cash flows liabilities. These impacts are normally evident in the payroll to revenue ratios, operating margins and operations cash flow.

Balance Sheet Liabilities: Pension-related reforms, post employment benefits, gratuities or any other scheme related to employees usually necessitate that the firms also identify or remeasure the long-term position. The accounting standards require that defined benefit obligations and other employee provisions be recognised at present value, that is, legal changes can result in an immediate adjustment on the balance sheet. A rise in liabilities involving employees impacts on leverage ratios, net worth and solvency ratios which could limit the borrowing capacity of firms (Singh & Sarkar, 2022). In severe situations benefit commitments unfunded can be similar to a claim of debt, which can affect compliance with financial covenants and capital structure choices.

Contribution and Tax Obligations: Alterations in the payroll taxes, social security payments, or required insurance plans by the employer affect the effective tax rates and net profitability of firms. Contrary to the corporate income taxes, the payroll-based taxes are not discretionary and profitability sensitive, and, therefore, they become especially heavy in economic recessions (Pillai & Sivathanu, 2022). Such commitments lower the free cash flows and can be crowding out investment expenditures, particularly among small and medium-sized companies with small financial cushions.

Administrative Costs and Compliance: New legal reforms of HRM tend to create new compliance, reporting and administrative demands. Companies can pay increased legal fees, human resources administration expenses, audit expenses, and expenses in keeping a record and internal controls. Reforms also make some cases more exposed to litigation or regulatory penalties which increases provisions and contingent liabilities. On a case-by-case basis, these costs may be petite and insignificant, but the sum may add up and have a tangible impact on overhead structures (Ntoumanis et at., 2024).

2.2 Indirect Financial Channels

Indirect financial channels work by way of expectations, perceptions and behavioural responses and such impacts are generally gradual, heterogeneous and more difficult to measure.

Productivity and Behaviour of the Workforce: Employee morale, job security and organisational commitment are motivating factors that can be affected by HRM legal reforms. The protected employment legislation, increases in benefits, or better working conditions can decrease the turnover and result in better accumulation of firm-specific human capital, which can boost the productivity and revenue development. On the other hand excessive inflexible labour laws can decrease managerial flexibility, performance incentives or dishearten hiring. The effects are not exhibited in direct cost changes but in the revenue per worker, value added per worker and long term trends of profitability (Demmke, 2020).

Capital Market Perceptions: HRM legal reforms are seen more as risks and sustainability by investors. Long-term obligation-enhancing reforms might be seen as having the effect of elevating fixed costs and decreasing operational flexibility, which leads to the negative valuation of firms. In its turn, the reforms aiming to make the workforce more stable, labour conflicts less frequent, or more ESG-oriented can be viewed as enhancing the quality of governance and long-term sustainability. These perceptions are observed through market-based measures of stock prices, valuation multiples and Tobin Q.

Cost of Capital: Both the cost of equity and the cost of debt can be influenced by changes in perceived operating risk, cash flow volatility or litigation exposure. Companies that have more labour rigidity or benefit commitment can be considered riskier and will attract a more premium charge by investors and charged by lenders in the form of an increase in the premium charged on borrowing. In the long run, increasing the cost of financing may also decrease the capacity to invest and also retard growth, incurring more financial effects, which HRM legal reforms may have, than its direct cost effects.

Strategic Investment Decisions: HRM legal restriction affects the long term strategic decisions of firms. In order to compensate increased labour costs or decreased flexibility, companies could raise capital intensity, use automation, outsource labour-intensive processes, or move production. Although these responses can be effective in enhancing efficiency, they entail adjustment cost and can change risk profiles and the competitive position of firms. Such strategic reactions make attribution difficult because seen financial results are a result of the reform and the self-generated responsiveness of the firm.

2.3 Implications to Measurement

Due to the co-existence of direct and indirect channels and mutual dynamism, no single measure can be used to account the entire financial influence of the HRM legal reforms. Accounting based measures are used to measure short term costs and balance sheet impact and may not reflect productivity changes or changes in valuation. Market-based metrics also have an impact on investor expectations, although it is also likely to be affected by macroeconomic conditions. Human capital measures give an understanding of behavioural reactions but can be reactors.

At that, to evaluate it adequately, a multi-metric framework, which is a combination of financial statement analysis, market-based indicators, and human capital performance measures, is needed. This would enhance attribution, increase comparability across organizations and countries, and a more comprehensive picture is obtained on how HRM legal reforms contribute to firm performance and financial stability.

3. KEY PERFORMANCE INDICATORS (KPIS) FOR MEASURING REFORM IMPACT

This part presents a developed framework of financial measurement of the HRM legal reforms organised into the cost-based, profitability-based, valuation based, capital market-based, and human capital-based metrics. The framework acknowledges that the legal changes in HR have impacts on the firms in various channels and with different time horizons, which is why the dependence on any single indicator is not enough (Akbar, 2025).

3.1. Measurements of Payroll elasticity and labour cost.

Payroll elasticity reflects the flexibility of labour expenses to the output, income or employment changes in the aftermath of the HRM law reform. It is especially applicable to the changes in the minimum wages, social security contributions, pensions, severance pay, and the statutory benefits. Some of the key indicators are the payroll-revenue ratio, labour cost per employee, payroll growth rate and the proportion of social security and benefits cost in the total compensation.

These indicators give the first-hand evidence of the direct cost effects of legal requirements. To illustrate, a rise in the statutory employer contributions is usually recorded in the increase of payroll-to-revenue ratio or the increase in the benefit cost share. Since these data can be observed in the financial statements, they are quite appropriate in short-term analysis and inter-firm comparison within the same regulatory setting (Ntoumanis et al, 2024).

There are however critical drawbacks of payroll-based metrics. They fail to capture behaviour modification like adjustments in effort, productivity or workforce composition. Besides, they are vulnerable to the periodical changes in demand and revenue that can easily hide the real impact of legal reform. Consequently, the payroll elasticity measures are to be considered along with the productivity and profitability indicators.

3.2 Profitability Indicators: ROA and ROE.

The common performance metrics of a firm are Return on Assets (ROA) and Return on Equity (ROE) that offers a larger scope of evaluation regarding the impacts of HRM legal reforms on profitability. ROA indicates the ability of the firm to make earnings out of the asset base under the circumstances where labour costs and employment constraints are altered. ROE on the other hand includes the leverage effects and also sensitive to the reforms that raise liabilities related to employees such as pension or post employment benefits.

The appeal of these metrics lies in their combination of both revenue side and cost side effects and the fact that they can be easily compared between firms and over time. The long-term downward trend in ROA after labour cost-increasing reforms can be a sign of low operational efficiency, whereas adaptation of ROE can demonstrate how the firms utilize leverage to cover the increase in labour-related costs (Martins, 2019).

However, accounting decisions, decisions on capital structure and macroeconomic factors affect the profitability measures. Unless this is properly checked, they can capture macro trends in the economy instead of being reform effects. ROA and ROE are therefore to the extent most informative when used along with econometric statistics which can isolate when and how far legal changes have occurred.

3.3 Metrics of Market Valuation: Q of Tobin.

Tobins Q, which is the value of a firm as a ratio of its market value and the cost of replacing the assets of the firm, is used to estimate what the investors expect about the future profitability and growth of the firm. The HRM legal reform could determine the value of the Q of Tobin based on the expected rigidity of the labour costs, less flexibility of the managerial abilities, or social governance and alignment with the ESG (Dibben et al., 2017).

Being a prospective measure, the Q of Tobin is especially applicable in evaluating indirect and long-term implications of HRM reforms that are not yet being exuded in accounting performance. As an example, changes that are seen to make the workforce more stable and lower labour conflicts can lead to valuation even when the immediate cost increases.

Nevertheless, Q is very sensitive of Tobin to sentiment in the market, interest rates and macroeconomic shocks. The attribution of causality cannot be therefore done easily unless where supported by event-study or difference-in-differences designs which take advantage of the timing of reforms. In this regard, valuation measures are complements of accounting-based measures and not substitutes.

3.4 Cost of Capital Metrics

Legal reforms in HRM have the ability to change risk profile of firms and hence the cost of capital. The weighted average cost of capital (WACC), credit spreads, interest coverage ratios and equity beta are the relevant indicators. Reforms which raise the long term labour immobility or pension commitments can raise perceived operating risk resulting in a higher demand in returns by the investors and lenders (Kim & Cho, 2014: Martins, 2019).

These measures can be applied directly to capital budgeting, valuation and strategic decision-making. The growth in the WACC which occurs after the HR reforms can significantly lower net present values of investments projects, affecting long term growth.

The key risk is the complexity of estimation and exposure to macro-financial factors. Reform effects at the firm may be overshadowed by changes in interest rates or market volatility. Thus, cost-of-capital indicators must be benchmarked and have control variables to provide sound interpretation.

3.5 Human Capital ROI and Efficiency Metrics.

Measures that are based on human capital make a clear connection between investment in the workforce and value generation. The excess generated per unit of labour cost is the Human Capital Return on Investment (HCROI) which is computed as:

Other performance measures are the revenue per employee, value added per employee and profitability adjusted by turnover. Such measures are a capture of productivity, behavioural reaction to legal reforms of HRM, providing information in addition to cost containment. (Ntoumanis et al., 2024)

The major asset of them is that they act as an interface between HRM and finance and allow evaluating whether increased labour expenses are compensated by productivity mprovements. Comparability is however, constrained by differences in measurement across firms and industries and the sensitivity to the structure of the organisation.

4. REFORM IMPACT: EMPIRICAL METHODS OF MEASUREMENT

HRM legal reforms have been associated with attributing changes in the performance of firms, a strong empirical problem because of simultaneity, gradual adjustment, and confounding macroeconomic factors. Strong empirical techniques are thus important in order to disentangle reform impacts and other factors. The given section will review the main approaches that were employed in the literature and discuss their appropriateness in studying the legal change related to HR.

4.1 Event Study Methodology

Event studies compare observed stock returns to predicted returns of asset pricing models within the context of particular abnormal stock returns at the time of announcement or actual implementation of HRM legal changes. This method is especially effective in the case of labour law reforms, pension reforms announcements, and the court decisions that significantly impact the employment requirements (Mahmoud & Othman, 2024).

The advantage of event studies is that it reflects the market responses instantly and gives the idea of the investors about the net present value implication of the reform. Due to the speed with which financial markets absorb the novel information, the abnormal returns within the event window are evidence of the change in the perceived cash flows, risk, or growth opportunities.

Event studies however, are based on an excessive degree of semi-strong performance of a market and are restricted to the short-term impact. They are unable to take the slow changes in productivity, labor structure, or capital structure. In addition, it can pollute estimates where there is overlap of events and information leakage of events, especially where there are long-run reforms that are expected or under discussion.

4.2 Panel Regression Analysis

Panel regression models capitalize on data on firms through time to estimate how much HRM legal reforms on average have affected them:

$$Performance_{it} = \alpha + \beta Reform_t + \gamma Controls_{it} + \mu_i + \lambda_t + \epsilon_{it}$$

This framework is versatile and can be scaled to enable the researcher to analyze several performance measures at the same time.

Panel regressions are especially helpful to examine the slow and unswerving influence including the adjustments in labour expenses or profitability due to the reforms of pension or employment security. Their major constraint is the issue of endogeneity. Reforms can be associated with unobservable economic conditions or politics which also affect firm performance creating bias in estimations unless countered by instrumental variables or quasi-experimental design (Pillai & Sivathanu, 2022).

4.3. Difference-in-Differences (DiD)

Difference-in-differences (DiD) involves a comparison of the level of outcomes in treated firms impacted by reform and a group that was not impacted by reform, pre-implementation and post-implementation. This method is a classic standard of policy evaluation, (when the parallel trends assumption is true).

DiD provides fairly robust causal inference and is appropriately designed to be applied when it comes to reforms related to particular sectors, firm sizes, or regions. It enables scholars to disaggregate the overall effects of reform and to control the same.

Nevertheless, DiD is susceptible to selection of control groups, and can be nullified by staggered or overlapping reforms (Fuenzalida & Riccucci, 2019). The current methodological innovations overcome these problems, though they should be carefully designed and checked by their strength.

4.4 Synthetic Control Methods

The synthetic control techniques form a weighted outlook of control firms or regions to estimate the counterfactual functionality of the treated entity. This method is specifically useful with large scale or economy-wide reforms in which there is one treated unit.

The simplicity of the process and its clarity are the primary advantages, whereby the counterfactual is clearly built using observed data. Synthetic control is particularly convenient in the analysis of long-term impact of reforms, e.g., in the analysis of pension reforms.

Weaknesses are data intensity and inability to infer statistics because standard significance testing is not so easy. However, synthetic control techniques have become eminent in the assessment of policies owing to their plausibility (Singh & Sarkar, 2022).

4.5 Matched Firm Analysis

Matched firm analysis enhances comparability because the treated firms are matched with the similar untreated firms using observable attributes, including size, industry, leverage, and pre-reform performance. This will minimize selection bias and increase the validity of the further DiD analysis.

Although matching enhances balance on observables it is unable to control the unobserved shocks and differences in behaviour and this restricts the ability to interpret causally. Equivalent quality is thus very vital and ought to have been evaluated with caution.

4.6 Sensitivity Analysis and Scenario.

The main use of scenario analysis and sensitivity analysis is ex ante analysis and not causal inference. Financial outcomes are modelled in response to alternate legal assumptions by the firms, e.g. contribution rates or benefit obligations change.

The techniques are useful in corporate planning and risk management, which puts an emphasis on exposure to legal and regulatory uncertainty (Dibben et al., 2017). But they are not causal and require a lot of assumptions which makes them not suitable when it comes to ex post analysis.

5. RELIABILITY OF METRICS TO ATTRIBUTING REFORM EFFECTS

One of the key areas of research is finding the measures that best reflect the effect of the reforms.

5.1 Most Reliable Metrics

Payroll-based measures are very reliable on wage, benefit reforms and contribution reforms because they are directly related to legal requirements. Balance sheet measures are most suitable in reforms of pension and long term obligation. The indicators of cost of capital are valid when they are used in conjunction with event studies or DiD frameworks that isolate market responses.

5.2 MPA Moderately Reliable Metrics.

ROA and ROE are informative when there is a high level of control and HCROI gives context-specific information on productivity. Tobin Q is useful when used with market based techniques.

5.3 Least Reliable Metrics

Standalone revenue, employment growth, which does not adjust to productivity and short-term measures of profitability, which does not use controls, are the least reliable.

6. MANAGERS, INVESTORS AND POLICYMAKERS IMPLICATIONS

Legal reforms in the Human Resource Management (HRM) are associated with far-reaching implications that go far beyond compliance. Their economic implications determine a strategic planning, capital allocation, valuation, and economic policy. The managers, investors and policymakers working at the intersection of financial performance and labour regulation should understand these implications.

6.1 Implications for Managers

The HRM legal changes are a strategic financial risk to corporate managers who need to incorporate them into the fundamental planning and decision-making strategies. Wage and employment protection, pension, and social security contribution labour laws have a direct impact on cost structure, predictability of cash flow and long-term obligations. The managers should then go beyond the concept of compliance mindset and bring in the HR legal risk as part of the financial forecasting, budgeting, and capital structure choices.

A major implication is on the balance sheet management. Reforms in pension and post employee benefits can raise the long term liabilities which are like debts that can impact leverage ratios and borrowing ability. Managers should expect these impacts in negotiating debt covenants, investing, or even mergers and acquisitions. Unexpected limitation on financial flexibility may occur as a result of failure to take into consideration employee related liabilities.

There is also a closer need to coordinate HR, finance, and legal functions in terms of HRM legal reforms. The choice of workforce composition, benefits and employment contracts should both be reviewed not only concerning the employee relations but also concerning the financial risk and perception of the investors (Van Landuyt et al., 2017). Put differently, a shift in the defined benefit towards defined contribution schemes might decrease the risk on the balance sheet at the cost of employee morale and retention. It is therefore necessary that strategic HR-finance alignment takes place.

Lastly, reforms can lead to structural and technological changes, including automation and outsourcing or variations in capital intensity. Managers ought to take a keen consideration before such responses can promote long-term productivity or rather shift the risk to other people. By introducing scenario analysis and stress testing within the enterprise risk management frameworks, the firms may navigate these trade-offs.

6.2 Implications for Investors

To investors, HRM legal reforms are becoming more and more realised as material valuation determinants, as opposed to soft governance determinants. Pension liabilities, labour rigidity and workforce liabilities may have a material impact on the expected cash flows, downside risk and cost of capital. This compels the investors to transform valuation models in an explicit manner to include these risks (Demmke, 2020).

Firm value should also be evaluated by equity investors, especially in regards to labour cost structure, benefits obligation and pension funding status. The companies in the jurisdictions with high protection of employment or generous statutory benefits may have increased fixed costs and reduced operating flexibility and should be incorporated in discount rates or cash flow estimates. On the other hand, long-term value creation can be facilitated by reforms that increase labour security or lessen labour conflicts.

The same applies to debt investors as well as credit analysts who must consider pension and employment related liabilities in the process of determining credit-worthiness. Poorly funded pension plans or inflexible labour agreements may put pressure on default, particularly when an economy is experiencing a recession. The agencies are more likely to manipulate the leverage and coverage ratios to indicate these responsibilities, which are important in pricing bonds.

6.3 Policymaker implication

The financial impact of HRM legal reforms to policymakers emphasizes the importance of considering policy in their entirety. In the traditional labour reforms, labour reforms have been measured mainly based on employment, wage distribution or worker protection. Although the importance of these outcomes is indisputable (Bustamante, 2017; Vermeeren et al., 2014), it is also crucial to pay attention to the impacts of reforms on the competitiveness of the firms, their investment behaviour, and financial stability.

Reforms that raise the cost of labour substantially or extend the duration of commitment can have unwanted effects on investment ability of firms, stimulating automation or offshoring or putting smaller firms, with smaller financial cushions at a disadvantage. On the other hand, the sustainable growth and innovations can be supported with well-designed reforms that promote productivity and stability of the workforce (Wang et al., 2019). Regulatory impact analysis therefore ought to incorporate firm-level financial analysis by policymakers.

It is also important that there are transparency and data accessibility. Comparability can be enhanced and evidence-based policymaking possible through harmonised accounting and disclosure standards regarding labour costs, benefits and human capital. Labour ministries, financial regulators and statistical agencies should work together and improve knowledge of the effects of reforms.

7. FUTURE RESEARCH DIRECTIONS

Further studies are needed to further enrich the knowledge on the financial implications of HRM legal reforms. Among the potential opportunities, it is possible to discuss the combination of HR reforms and automation, or the way in which labour regulation affects the choice of capital-intensive technologies by firms. The other key area is associated with ESG-motivated valuation impacts, discussing the notion of whether the labour protection is becoming more and more priced by the financial market.

Comparative studies of harmonised accounting data across different countries can be used to produce insight about institutional differences and policy effectiveness. Lastly, HRM legal reforms need to be evaluated in terms of their impact on innovation, growth of investments as well as productivity over the long term, beyond looking at short-term cost issues to consider their contribution to long-term economic sustainability.

8. CONCLUSION

The financial impact assessment of Human Resource Management (HRM) legal reforms, needs to take a step way outside of the limited cost accounting techniques to a multi-dimensional financial and econometric model. Although the most obvious impact of legal reform may be the alteration of wages, benefits or statutory contributions, it is important to note that such factors can be misleading because the impact of change is more enduring and far-reaching when it comes to individual firms (Budhwar & Varma, 2011). The HRM legal reforms affect operating costs as well as balance sheet structure, risk exposure, capital costs and long-run strategic behaviour.

It has been revealed in this chapter that the reforms of HRM can be implemented either via direct financial routes, including the payroll costs and employee related liabilities, or indirect routes, including the productivity, perceptions of the investors, and organisational responses. Consequently, reform effects can not be reliably measured using only one metric. Cost-based indicators offer efficiency in determining the instant effect, but they should be supplemented with profitability, valuation, cost of capital and human capital indicators to offer the comprehensive financial performance (Zolak et al., 2025). It is also important to note that reform effects are time-dimensional and usually emerge over time as well as are also interrelated with firm-specific strategies and macroeconomic environment.

Methodological rigor is paramount to having strong attribution of reform impacts. Difference-in-differences, event studies, and synthetic control methods are quasi-experimental designs that are used as the main tool in separating causal effects and alleviating endogeneity bias. Together with the proficiently chosen financial and market-based measures, the approaches provide the most plausible evidence on the influence that HRM legal reforms have on firm performance.

With the ongoing convergence of HRM with corporate finance, governance, and even ESG, the legal aspect of measuring the effects of legal reforms will have an increasing significance. To policymakers, stringent measurement aids regulation founded on evidence that would help strike a balance between worker protection and firm competitiveness (Akbar, 2025). To the managers and investors, it improves strategic decision making and assessment of risk. Finally, effective measurement structures are inevitable to comprehend financial implications of the HRM legal reforms within the current regulatory and economic environment.

REFERENCES

Akbar, M. S. (2025). Governance transformation through institutional conversion: From Section 42 company to authority. *Review of Education. Administration & Law*, *8*(2), 401–414.

Budhwar, P. S., & Varma, A. (2011). Emerging HR management trends in India and the way forward. *Organizational Dynamics*, *40*(4), 317–325.

Bustamante, A. R. (2017). Labor Relations Reform in 21st Century. *Latinskaia Amerika = América Latina*.

Demmke, C. (2020). Governance reforms, individualization of human resource management (HRM), and impact on workplace behavior—A black box? *Public Integrity*, *22*(3), 268–279.

Dibben, P., Brewster, C., Brookes, M., Cunha, R., Webster, E., & Wood, G. (2017). Institutional legacies and HRM: Similarities and differences in HRM practices in Portugal and Mozambique. *International Journal of Human Resource Management*, *28*(18), 2519–2537.

Fuenzalida, J., & Riccucci, N. M. (2019). The effects of politicization on performance: The mediating role of HRM practices. *Review of Public Personnel Administration*, *39*(4), 544–569.

Kim, N., & Cho, W. (2014). Agencification and performance: The impact of autonomy and result-control on the performance of executive agencies in Korea. *Public Performance & Management Review*, *38*(2), 214–233.

Mahmoud, M. M. H., & Othman, R. (2024). Effects of new public management reforms on human resource practices: A case study in Jordan. *Management and Labour Studies*, *49*(1), 149–176.

Martins, P. S. (2019). The Microeconomic Impacts of Employee Representatives: Evidence from Membership Thresholds. *Industrial Relations*, *58*(4), 591–622.

Ntoumanis, A. B., Jorge, S. O., Zagarese, E., Wunderlin, A., Stern, A. R., & Luiz, P. J. (2024). The Impact of Decree 70/2023 on Labor Regulation and Industrial Relations in Argentina: A Legal and Economic Analysis. *International Journal of Law and Public Policy*, *6*(2), 77–84.

Pillai, R., & Sivathanu, B. (2022). Measure what matters: Descriptive and predictive metrics of HRM-pathway toward organizational performance. *International Journal of Productivity and Performance Management*, *71*(7), 3009–3029.

Singh, P., & Sarkar, S. (2022). Human resource metrics for enhancing organizational performance: Case of Indian State-owned enterprises. *Management and Labour Studies*, *47*(2), 233–250.

Van Landuyt, Y., Dewaelheyns, N., & Van Hulle, C. (2017). Employment Protection Legislation and SME Performance. *International Small Business Journal, 35*(3), Vermeeren, B., Steijn, B., Tummers, L., Lankhaar, M., Poerstamper, R. J., & Van Beek, S. (2014). HRM and its effect on employee, organizational and financial outcomes in health care organizations. *Human Resources for Health*, *12*(1), 35. PMID: 28549434

Wang, M., Zhu, C. J., Mayson, S., & Chen, W. (2019). Contextualizing performance appraisal practices in Chinese public sector organizations: The importance of context and areas for future study. *International Journal of Human Resource Management*, *30*(5), 902–919.

Zolak Poljašević, B., Gričnik, A. M., & Šarotar Žižek, S. (2025). Human resource management in public administration: The ongoing tension between reform requirements and resistance to change. *Administrative Sciences*, *15*(3), 94.

Chapter 2
Legal Frameworks of Human Resource Management Reform in the Context of India

Shashank Mittal
https://orcid.org/0000-0002-8666-5323
JGBS, O.P. JIndal Global University, India

Majdi Anwar Quttainah
https://orcid.org/0000-0002-6280-1060
Kuwait University, Kuwait

Dilshad Jeffery
Qasim Ibrahim School of Business, Villa College, Maldives

ABSTRACT

The chapter is an in-depth analysis of the evolving legal frameworks that guide human resource management reforms in India, examining the nature of the influence of such regulations on workplace practices, labour rights, and corporate governance in one of the fastest-growing economies of the world. The present chapter, therefore, attempts to fill the gap between the theoretical perspectives of HRM and the practical implications of legal reforms in the continuously fluctuating economy, technology, and labour market. It shall be a ready reckoner for human resource professionals, policymakers, business leaders, and scholars interested in knowing how labour law and HRM interface in the Indian context.

DOI: 10.4018/979-8-3693-5390-5.ch002

INTRODUCTION

There are some recent labour law reforms that have come into being in India, including the Industrial Relations Code, Code on Wages, Social Security Code, and the Occupational Safety, Health, and Working Conditions Code, with their implications for HRM practices. Further, this chapter will present challenges in the implementation of these reforms across the diverse formal and informal sectors in India. The role of the HR departments in ensuring that compliance is adhered to, ethical labour practices and changes in the legal landscape will be reviewed. A discussion on how HRM reform will affect key areas such as employee relations, compensation and benefits, health and safety, labour rights, dispute resolution, and talent management will be done. In the background of global trends, technological changes, and post-pandemic recovery, the future trajectory of human resource management legal frameworks in India will be looked upon. The legal frameworks governing human resource management reform in India present an interplay of factors wherein historical evolution collides with regulatory changes and socio-economic factors. Different stages in the evolution of HRM in India include the policy on labour welfare in the 1930s and 1940s, the Factories Act in 1948, and post-liberalization in the 1990s when modern practices of HRM started to emerge. This background has been very important in setting up the current legal frameworks that guide HRM practices in the country. In any case, the opening up of the Indian economy since 1991 has brought about some degree of change in the way human resource management is conducted, which moved from an administrative to a more strategic and proactive role for the function of HRM-specific activities (Nandan et al., 2018). Such a change is itself influenced by the legal and regulatory environment in which employment is conducted. For instance, NPM reforms have brought into sharp focus the need for accommodation of new governance structures that reflect principles of efficiency and accountability in HRM policies. Such reforms have made many organizations rethink their HRM strategies in line with larger organizational objectives and the requirements of the law. Secondly, the legal framework underlying HRM in India is marked by enforcement and compliance challenges. It is thus obvious that the unorganized sector also employs a huge proportion of workers. Most of this participation takes place outside the ambit of formal HRM regulations, relating to job insecurity and inappropriate working conditions, according to Bharadwaj et al. (2022). This portrays a scenario that requires complete legal reforms that can establish superior methods of workforce rights, ensuring their correct implications in industries. Other than these matters, the involvement of technology in HRM practices, through electronic HRM, has become an essential area of concern. It is induced by the Government's policies and the demand for accreditation that the Indian higher education institutions have started adopting e-HRM, but the incidents of its barriers to implementation are very high. Hence, this shows that there is a need for legal frameworks that promote technology, yet simultaneously address certain challenges of the Indian context. Further, there is a talk of the role of organizational trust in creating and using HRM practices, especially in public sector organizations where trusting relations are a prerequisite to the successful implementation of HRM policies and strategies. These are the relational dynamics that have to be considered in the legal frameworks governing HRM so that the latter develop policies of trust and collaboration between employees and their management. In sum, it is the historical developments, economic liberalization, and compliance issues arising from a diverse workforce that remains as strong factors contributing to changing legal frameworks of HRM reform in India. Each of these factors causes a continuing requirement for reforms, especially to address the specific challenges to the Indian context of HRM, so that the legal structures allow not only for organizational objectives but also for the welfare of the employees.

The contemporary status of Human Resource Management in India is one of significant evolution and has been affected by economic growth, globalization, and technological modification. The integration of modern practices of HRM is quite aggressive, especially in sectors like IT, telecommunications, and BPO firms, which have been at the forefront in implementing some new forms of HR strategies to elicit improved performance and better satisfaction among employees. This transition towards modern HRM practices is not uniformly distributed across all sectors. Traditional industries, such as textiles or low-value-added manufacturing, still rely on previous HR methodologies. This points out the fact that a gap exists in the HRM practices of the Indian economy. The emergence of MNCs in the Indian context also played a strategic role in reshaping HRM practices. Such companies often benchmark the best practices in the local context to facilitate easy cultural assimilation and operational efficiency. However, this drifting away from traditional industrial relations frameworks to strategic HRM approaches has generated concerns that pluralist employment relations are lost to a unitarist model of employment relations, which does not adequately address the diversified needs of employees. This transition, therefore, calls for a re-evaluation of the existing laws that control the working environment in HRM and the extent to which they are in line with current practices and changing labour markets. Further, COVID-19 has subsequently underscored the need for reforms in the legal environment in which HRM functions. The pandemic forced organizations to provide flexible working conditions and the safety and health of employees, as noted by Sridevi 2024 and Adikaram et al. 2021 resulted in a review of their HR policies and practices during the pandemic period. These changes portend a number of legal implications, especially with regard to employee rights and workplace safety, and call for a serious revision of labour laws so that they are responsive to the new realities of the workforce. The integration of AI in HRM practices faces both opportunities and challenges that require adaptation by legal frameworks to the ethical and operational complexities brought about by technology.

These emerging developments create a growing need for legal reform in the HRM sector in India. As Meijerink and Keegan (2019) say, the existing labour laws, designed for an economically vastly different time, are unlikely to be well-placed to tackle the issues of modern employment relationships in gig economies and among SMEs. Any employment law reform should be directed towards an inclusive labour market, which is equitable in the treatment and protection of all categories of workers, irrespective of their employment status. Besides, since most organizations nowadays adopt policies on socially responsible human resources management, it would increasingly be necessary that legal frameworks keep pace to facilitate corporate sustainability goals and organizational citizenship behaviour on the part of employees.

The emerging contour of HRM in India is thus fast changing with the altered economic scenario, globalization, and technological revolution. However this evolution indicates an increasing trend of legal reform that ensures alignment of labour laws to the modern trends of HR practices and contemporary realities of the modern workforce.

EVOLUTION OF LABOUR LAWS IN INDIA

Labour law in India has undergone many changes since the country attained independence in 1947. The growth and development of these laws are indicative of the changing socio-economic scenario, besides attempts at satisfying the needs of both workers and employers in their respective interests and at the same time attempting to achieve economic growth. In the post-independence period, India launched a protective policy framework for labour rights impelled by the need to rectify the situation of exploitation of workers under colonial rule. For instance, one such cornerstone in this protective regime was the Industrial Disputes Act of 1947. The catch in such legislation was to regulate industrial relations with the purpose of job security. Very fast, however, this regime rigidly served to depress the labour force participation rates and to increase unemployment rates in the economy, according to a number of scholars (Amin, 2009; Bonsay et al., 2021). In fact, the stringency of these set of laws has been more or less considered one of the stumbling blocks towards industrial development as they deter the firms from hiring workers due to the headache involved in sacking labourers. (Gupta & Kumar, 2012; Fernandes & Pakes, 2008)

The economic liberalization that began in the early 1990s brought a paradigm shift in the development of labour law. That is, the abolition of the so-called "License Raj" and the acceptance of market-oriented reforms had been an attempt towards competitiveness enhancement and attracting foreign investment. Aghion et al. 2008 Meanwhile, its impact has been at best mixed regarding changes in labour laws. Whereas some states have moved to more flexible labour laws that enhance productivity and increase employment in certain sectors, the rigid laws hinder growth in other states (Dougherty et al., 2011; Hasan et al., 2003). Divergent state-level reforms have promoted disparate economic performance nationwide, and indeed, states with pro-employer reforms have posted higher industrial growth rates than states that have more restrictive labour legislation (Aghion et al., 2008; Dougherty et al., 2011).

Recent debates on labour law reform have revolved around the imperative to check the informalisation of labour, which has been on a secular increase since the 1980s. The increasing trend of unorganized sector employment and the growing use of contract labour point to a shift toward flexible or precarious work arrangements. As scholars have noted, this is partly because of inflexible labour laws, which have led employers to create informal arrangements that would circumvent such legal restrictions (Goldar & Aggarwal, 2012; Maiti, 2012). It also implies that the relatively less restrictive labour laws of some states have enabled their economies to respond more effectively and efficiently to changes in the global economy, to which, in turn, their elasticities of labour demand are positively related. Evidence also exists to suggest that more flexible labour laws have positioned certain states better to respond to changes in the global economy, thereby increasing their elasticities of labour demand (Dougherty et al., 2011; Das et al., 2014).

The Supreme Court of India has also interpreted labour laws on numerous occasions in such a way that changes in enforcement have been affected in consonance with the changing economic environment. For instance, the decisions of the court have allowed growing use of contract labour, that has been increasing in most of the industries today (Dougherty, 2009). This judicial interpretation shows that labour law in India has been dynamic; legal frameworks have been continually revised by socio-economic realities. Conclusion The historical development of labour law in India has thus been marked by a constant balancing act between worker protection and the imperatives of economic growth. While the early post-independence laws worked to protect labour rights, subsequent reforms have sought to balance these protections with imperatives for flexibility in a dynamically changing economic environment. The continued debate on labour law reform underlines the fact that legal institutions must evolve to meet new challenges if both worker welfare and industrial competitiveness are to be assured in today's world.

THE NEW LABOUR CODES – A GAME CHANGER?

The four new labour codes indicate a massive upheaval in the large domains of employment practices, wage structures, social securities, and even occupational safety across sectors. These will be aimed at streamlining labours legislations, adding to the protection of workers, and responding to the contemporary labour market realities. The new labour codes would usher in modernity in labour practices by bringing in flexibility along with inclusiveness to the workforce. The codes, for instance, encourage formalization in employment relationships highly relevant for sectors largely reliant on informal labour in industries such as agriculture and construction. It is also expected to enhance wage structures by adopting appropriate remunerations and benefits to all workers concerned in the application of codes and thereby assuage wage differentials. What's more, the emphasis that the same codes put on corporate social responsibility emphasizes remuneration and working conditions that are considered to be at par with global standards on employee rights. According to Kubasinski & Sławińska (2021), the fact that wage theft could be tackled with provisions that guarantee employees would be paid on time is very important. The aforementioned measure in this regard seems to be most effective in the industries where labour exploitation has higher rates such as agriculture, where workers mostly face issues of delayed and ineffective compensation. These codes also try to sort out the issue of the gender wage gap prevailing in most labour markets for quite a long time. It ensures equal pay for equal work for an equitable structure of wages across demographics. Thus, the codes enhance social security provisions immensely by incorporating them into the complete coverage of employment structure in health, maternity, and unemployment benefits. The integration is badly needed in areas like agriculture, where labourers are denied even basic social security. The codes also emphasize that the contribution to social security funds by an employer would help the employees to secure themselves when they fall into situations like job losses and health crises.

Also, codes inspire the establishment of grievance redressal mechanisms, which would be very fundamental in addressing complaints from workers on social security entitlements. This is in particular relevance to those sectors where workers may not be conversant with their rights or could be facing challenges in claiming their benefits. As would be seen in the development regarding the focus on social security, the morale and productivity of the worker are generally enhanced as the workers feel secured in their employment.

Occupational safety is one of the fundamental elements contained within the new work codes, to a large degree of awareness about health and safety issues at work. Codes demand more rigorous compliance with OHS in high-risk sectors, like the construction and agriculture sectors. It includes training programs on safety issues, along with periodic inspections to follow the standards of safety.

The codes also consider improving the training and competency of occupational safety professionals, highly linked with effective risk management and accident prevention. The improvement in the qualification of occupational safety specialists, the codes intimate, would create a safety culture that upholds the health and well-being of workers by reducing workplace accidents. The codes also encourage the usage of technologies and data analytics in order to monitor workplace safety, possibly leading to a more proactive approach to the prevention of occupational hazards.

These four new labour codes in brief will bring sea change in the pattern of employment, wage structure, social security, and occupational safety. All this-development encouraging formal employment, topping up social security protection, prioritizing occupational safety- is aimed at rendering the labour environment more fair and secure. In how far these codes are implemented effectively depends upon the seriousness of the commitment of employers and government agencies in upholding rights and welfare concerning workers.

HUMAN RESOURCE MANAGEMENT CHALLENGES IN THE INFORMAL SECTOR OF INDIA

The informal economy of India, where the greater share of the workforce population is concentrated, poses its own set of challenges insofar as applying labour legislation and human resource management practices are concerned. Employment in the informal sector, which accounts for more than 80% of total employment, is done mostly outside the ambit of formal labour laws and regulations, hence making the conditions of working precarious or inadequate for workers' protection. The same arguments are presented by Bharadwaj et al. (2022), "The Effectiveness of Indian Labour Laws in Protecting the Rights of Workers: A Quantitative Perspective of Indian Labour Law" (2023), and Maiti (2012). This only goes to reveal that the inability to regulate this sector in the right manner has been at a great cost; for example, most workers in this category are denied the minimum wage, facilities, and a working environment that is not conducive. Indeed, in "The Effectiveness of Indian Labour Laws in Protecting the Rights of Workers: A Quantitative Perspective of Indian Labour Law", 2023; Kerswell & Pratap, 2015 have agreed that many underdeveloped nations face the reality of underregulated informal economies where labour laws remain unimplemented. Formal institutions' failure to enforce labour laws has led to an increase in informal institutions, acting as labour-regulating alternatives, which complicates the context of HRM. In this regard, it is supported that the context of HRM becomes increasingly complicated. Darwish et al. (2023)

The problems of HRM in the informal economy are not unidimensional. The issue of transient labour, where employment is seasonal and contractual, makes talent management and employee engagement challenging. The informal sector is not only characterised by 'amorphous' HRM but also troubled by a lack of prescribed mechanisms for resolving employee grievances and labour standards (Cooke & Saini, 2015). All these difficulties are further compounded by the inadequacy of public institutions for grievance redressal, as workers in the informal sector are at the mercy of the goodwill of employers for their welfare. Cooke & Saini (2015) also support this claim. In India, the political and economic environments add to the complication by requiring that labour laws be seen as a burden to be circumvented by promoting non-observance and informalization of labour practices. Kerswell & Pratap (2015) also confirm this.

The characteristics of an informal economy also give rise to significant wage gaps between formal and informal workers, to a great extent caused by the impact of education, skill, and accessibility to different resources. The human capital theory suggests that this wage gap caused by such a difference in qualifications is perpetual and hence a matter of grave concern for a human resource management professional who aims to foster equality in the workplace. Most times, informal sectors depend on informal HRM practices that do not apply strategic HRM for employee satisfaction and retention. In this aspect, Melhem (2024) claimed.

Conclusion: Application of labour laws in an informal economy in India is quite difficult, thus affecting HRM practices hugely. The absence of institutional supervision, coupled with the temporary nature of employment in the informal sector and the non-existence of any systematic method of HRM, has made workers very vulnerable and their rights mostly unprotected. These challenges create the need for a collaborative approach by policymakers and HRM practitioners in devising inclusive strategies that take into account the peculiar character of the informal sector while advocating a voice for the rights and welfare of workers.

COMPLIANCE AND CORPORATE GOVERNANCE

The various facets of the role played by human resources departments in ensuring compliance, transparency, and good corporate governance have critical dimensions in today's corporate world. Human resource departments are found to be the backbone for ensuring that organizations pursue legal standards and ethical practices. Synthesis has discussed the role of HR in these analytical areas derived from several scholarly sources. For instance, human resource departments should be at the forefront of enforcing compliance with the law in organizations. For example, they are supposed to be updated on any change regarding labour laws and regulations. They can only achieve this by highlighting how HR professionals remain at the centre of introducing and implementing policies which place organizations in strict compliance with the law, therefore maintaining the level of compliance baek & choi, 2020. This proactive monitoring is especially required in legal environments that are not only complex but also highly susceptible to change. In the study, for instance, the importance of HRM in negotiating legal responsibilities in particular contexts-such as private equity investments in China-is underlined. Indeed, greater integration of technology in human resource practices has been proven to positively influence compliance with the law by making recruitment processes more transparent and equitable, hence meeting threshold legal requirements set up by Purba (2024).

On the other side, apart from the legal perspective, human resource departments play an important role in ensuring organizational transparency. Among employees and stakeholders, transparency is a deal way out when it comes to credibility; how it works in an organization or company can largely be manipulated through HR practices. For example, their study refers to how transnational labour governance would create transparency and accountability at higher levels of organization across the board. In further clarification, more emphasis on corporate social responsibility within human resource practices brings in more transparency. Indeed, as observed, CSR has become so imperative in HRM that in other parts of the world, for instance, the Gulf Cooperation Council, the legal requirements make it binding upon corporations' practices to be transparent. Aligning the HR practices with CSR contributes not only to increased transparency but also adds to the positive corporate image. Human resources departments are a promoter of good corporate governance. Good governance frameworks necessitate that an organization operate within ethical bounds and at the same time uphold the legal standards. This is further instigated in the realm of HR by the findings of, who present the argument that HRM is one of the most privileged sites for understanding the interplay between legal compliance and corporate governance. They indicate that HR practices may serve to reinforce or undermine governance structures, depending on how they are implemented. Also, introducing compliance officers into organizations, as noted by, further stresses the role of HR in governance because these officers ensure legality and ethical standards are complied with (Tošić, 2023).

On the whole, it is HR that is instrumental in ensuring legal compliance and guaranteeing transparency to enhance good corporate governance. Their many-faceted role involves monitoring legal changes, instituting practices that ensure transparency, and reinforcing governance structures. As societies continue to press organizations to face increased legal requirements and social concerns, HR's strategic presence in this regard will increasingly be required for sustainability.

EMPLOYEE RELATIONS AND DISPUTE RESOLUTION MECHANISMS

Legal reforms in India bear significantly on employee relations, grievance handling practices, and dispute resolution mechanisms in different industries. In this light, the 1947 IDA has been regarded as a basic precept that seems to undergird these situations. The efficacy of labour laws, with regard to judicial efficiency and the prevalence of informal employment, has received critical attention. The state-level amendments to IDA significantly impact the nature of employment, with a resultant tilt on the formal and informal sector contributions towards shaping the dispute resolution landscape. In essence, this legal framework, according to Fagernäs, 2010, sets the tone not just in terms of workers' rights but also in terms of how grievances will be handled inside organizations. When it comes to grievance handling, structured procedures have to be followed to ensure satisfaction and trust among employees. In this regard, Geetika et al. (2014) conducted a study at a power distribution company in India and revealed that an organization generally follows the Model Grievance Procedure, which always emphasizes the fact that the investigation of employee grievances should be prompt and full. Their study showed that good grievance handling is positively related to a higher degree of employee satisfaction and as such procedural justice is considered the prime aspect of industrial relations. On the same note, present an argument that collective bargaining plays an imperative role in handling industrial disputes by advocating for a grievance handling process that is fair and on time, concerning the rights of all parties. This is based on the idea of a well-structured grievance mechanism being related to better organizational performance and greater employee trust. The Indian telecommunication industry is a relevant case study involving the evolution of dispute resolution machinery. With the induction of ombudsman system, as had been discussed by, there is a considerable shift towards ADR within the sector. It is designated to offer a higher authority for the consumers with an aim to smoothen the dispute resolution process by hearing their grievances. The legal framework of ADR in the telecommunication sector is still evolving, reflecting a wider trend toward integrating informal and formal mechanisms for effective dispute resolution. Technology also plays an important role in dispute resolution. Traditional approaches to dispute resolution have been revolutionized by the integration of ODR mechanisms, with increased access and efficiency. Emphasize the fact that with the use of information technology in dispute resolution, there is a potential to create more efficient grievance-handling and dispute-management processes (Lodder & Zeleznikow, 2010). This techno-shift has important consequences for e-commerce and for consumers where traditional methods may not serve their purpose. In conclusion, the legal reform in the form of Acts of Parliament significantly influences employee relations and might have wide ramification for approaches to grievance handling and dispute resolution at the workplace or within various industries. The interface of the formal legislation and collective bargaining and technological advancement indeed provides a multi-factoral environment that dictates the course of grievance management and dispute resolution. The case studies from the different sectors point toward structured procedures, the role of ADR, and how technology forms the basis for an industrially harmonious environment.

HEALTH, SAFETY, AND WELL-BEING IN THE WORKPLACE

The various statutes and regulations thus have legal obligations for occupational health and safety in the Indian context with aims at safe working environments across different sectors. The major law comprises the Factories Act, of 1948, and the Occupational Safety, Health and Working Conditions Code, of 2020, laying responsibility on every employer to ensure a safe workplace, take risk assessments, and implement safety measures in order to minimize hazards. These also identify that employers are under obligation to train employees for correctly observing standards aimed at maintaining safety culture in their organizations.

Overall, HRM has played a major role in enforcing these legal requirements and considering the safety of their working places. HRM strategies include developing and implementing policies on safety, training programs, and several initiatives that are undertaken to develop a culture of safety among the employees. For instance, HRM can arrange frequent safety training; it can also undertake safety audits and involve employees through safety committees for building their awareness and participation in OHS practices. HRM is also responsible for the infusion of occupational health issues within the broader policies of the organization to align the wellbeing of the employees with business objectives.

More importantly, effective channels of communication and mechanisms for feedback flow will assist HRM significantly in enhancing the workplace and guaranteeing its safety. That is, such systems allow identifying hazards early enough to allow the implementation of corrective measures in good time (Oyewole, 2024). Further, through technology, HRM could monitor the observance of safety regulations and reporting incidents that would boost accountability and, therefore see to it that there is also transparency in the company. According to Yassi et al. (2011), the management of occupational health and the safety management system within the organizational system sees to it that workplace accidents and injuries are minimal since the safety measures are systematically followed and continuously improved.

In other words, the Indian legal framework on occupational health and safety places more responsibilities on employers, which could be tactfully handled through strategic HRM practices. It could therefore make enormous contributions toward ensuring the safety of all categories of employees by prioritizing safety training, safety culture, and compliance with legal standards.

GLOBAL TRENDS AND INDIA'S HRM LANDSCAPE

The fast-changing landscape of HRM in India has resulted from global trends, as well as from local dynamics. While organizations are struggling hard to keep pace with the complexities brought about by globalization, technological advancement, and changing expectations of the workforce, a few trends have emerged that will continue to shape the face of HRM practices in India. First, global influence on HRM practices is proving increasingly influential for Indian firms. That is, Indian HRM is more likely to be influenced by US-style HR practices that emphasize individual performance and meritocracy, yet the effectiveness of these practices is more in tune with Japanese-style HR practices that emphasize collective harmony and long-term employment. Accordingly, Indian organizations face the dual influence of having to balance global best practices with local cultural nuances, which further complicates how HRM strategies are crafted to be effective and also culturally congruent. Beyond this, the digital revolution is certainly altering the pattern of HRM practices across the globe, and India is no exception. In this regard, the integration of ICT in human resources management processes will be so vital in driving higher operational efficiency and employee engagement. The digital tools adopted, such as e-HRM systems, by organizations make the processes of HR more functional and facilitate proper data management in the organization to increase the enthusiasm at work. This will increase the precision of the HRM practices and also enable workforce agility toward the rapid changes in business processes.

Apart from the technological changes, the focus on sustainability and corporate social responsibility has been increasingly shaping the contours of the HRM practices. Increasingly, the organizations are looking to sustainable HRM practices to reduce the social and ecological impact of their operations. The trend in business is particularly relevant in the Indian context, as there has been a growing awareness of the need for ethical practices in contributing to the good of society while reinforcing the performance of organizations. By incorporating sustainability into the HRM strategies of Indian firms, there will be improved reputation by the firm, attraction of more talent, building employee loyalty. Further, globalization is changing the talent management landscape, where organisations in India are reshaping the way workforce development takes place. Organizations face issues on cultural diversity, compliance, and talent acquisition with globalization. Organisations should, therefore, make sure that their strategies are sensitive to local contexts and leverage off best global practices while managing talent globally. This means that one will need a greater understanding of the local labour market, cultural expectations, and legal frameworks to ensure sufficient integration and retention of talent. Last but not least, the changing nature of the demographic profile of any organization, the millennial and Gen Z ascendancy in particular, is really stretching the supervisory limits of HRM policies. The younger generation believes in work-life balance, career development opportunities, and organizational culture. Indian organizations should therefore adopt such HRM practices that will create engagement and diversity to include giving employees a supportive and dynamic work environment to woo and hold such employees. The last but not least is the emergence of the patterns of HRM in India flowing out of the conflux of global trends, technological advances, and local cultural dynamics. But in addressing such changes, organizations need to move towards flexible and innovative HRM strategies that are aligned to both global best practices and local expectations. This approach would not only guarantee improved organizational performance but would also make the work environment more sustainable and inclusive.

FUTURE DIRECTIONS FOR HRM REFORM IN INDIA

The future of labour law reform in India is certain to be vastly influenced by economic, demographic, and technological changes. As India struggles to get along with the labour market problem, the ramifications on HRM continue to be fundamental, with a need to reassess practices and policies instituted. Economic change, especially resulting from globalization and deregulation, has been responsible for a more lively labour market. By contrast, research relating labour market flexibility-in particular, labour laws to productivity and employment growth is remarkably sparse. There are indications, however, that the deregulation of industries in the 1980s and 1990s did indeed lead to faster growth in those states whose labour laws were more pro-employer, implying that labour market flexibility increases productivity and employment opportunities (Fagernäs 2010, Dougherty et al. 2011). However, the rigidity of the prevailing labour laws has often been blamed for growth retardation, especially in the organized sector, with high labour costs and strict hiring and firing laws acting as a disincentive to hire people (Maiti, 2012; Gupta & Kumar, 2010). The case for reform is further underlined by the fact that economic growth in India has not been employment-intensive, indicating a mismatch between labour supply and demand (Upender, 2011).

Demographically, the country is at the threshold of a big transition as the working population is bourgeoning-a period aptly described as the demographic dividend. However, unless proper reforms are enacted, this boon threatens to become a demographic disaster according to Chhibber (2021) and James (2011). The rate of female workforce participation is still low, and dealing with this challenge is of essence in the full realization of the demographic dividend gains. Further, the issues of informal employment and precarious work conditions call for labour law reforms able to effectively balance the protection of vulnerable workers with the promotion of economic growth in the process.

Changing employment nature because of technological advancement is leading towards nonstandard employment forms, including gigs and contract works. This predisposes labour laws to a rethinking in how they adapt to emerging new forms of employment. More importantly, perhaps, integration of technology in the HRM practices can enable better facilitation of flexible work arrangements, but at the same time, worker's rights and protection issues crop up in the context of an increasingly digitizing economy.

Thus, the interplay of economic, demographic, and technological factors are likely to define the future course that labour law reform will take. From the viewpoint of HRM, this means further flexibility of the labour market while ensuring that workers' rights are taken into consideration in keeping with changing legislations. Therein lies the challenge of balancing economic growth with the need for social equity, more so in view of the overwhelming demographic diversity of India.

CONCLUSION

It is imperative to underline that changing legal frameworks underpin a remodelling of HR practices in India, bringing them at par with global standards while considering challenges unique to the Indian workforce. Regulatory reforms usher in this transformation through a fine balance between strengthening worker protection and economic growth, building inclusive workplaces, and promoting work culture toward wellness.

The Indian legal landscape increasingly highlights modernization labour laws in view of the growing demands brought about by the digital economy, automation, and globalization of business. This would encompass reforms around flexibility in hiring, enhanced laws for data protection, and fair wages. In addition, the legal frameworks are slowly but surely catching up on issues related to gender equity, workers' rights, and social security in order to make the workplace inclusive and diversified. Equally, this change is reflected in attempts at formalizing the gig economy and, therefore, its benefits to bring in inclusivity for informal workers. As much as regulatory compliance is an important issue, it is also about innovating talent management, recruitment, and retention through HR reforms. The balancing of complex legal structures with innovation and employee empowerment is itself a challenge before any business. Besides this improvement, bureaucratic delays, regional disparities, and gaps in enforcement remain challenges. The future course of HR reforms is going to be essentially the implementation of legal frameworks that effectively address these issues.

The unending HR management reforms in India aim to ensure that business competitiveness goes hand in hand with legal frameworks that protect employee rights and provide a long-term, sustained growth pattern. The role of HR reforms is going to be very significant in shaping a balanced, equitable, and future-ready workforce in India while it continues to rise economically.

REFERENCES

Adikaram, A., Naotunna, N., & Priyankara, H. (2021). Battling covid-19 with human resource management bundling. *Employee Relations*, *43*(6), 1269–1289. DOI: 10.1108/er-08-2020-0390

Aghion, P., Burgess, R., Redding, S., & Zilibotti, F. (2008). The unequal effects of liberalization: Evidence from dismantling the license raj in india. *The American Economic Review*, *98*(4), 1397–1412. DOI: 10.1257/aer.98.4.1397

Amin, M. (2009). Labor regulation and employment in india's retail stores. *Journal of Comparative Economics*, *37*(1), 47–61. DOI: 10.1016/j.jce.2008.07.001

Bharadwaj, V., Sharma, V., & Bhatnagar, A. (2022). Covid-19 and manufacturing industries in india and role of human resources management. *Business and Management Research*, *11*(1), 15. DOI: 10.5430/bmr.v11n1p15

Bonsay, J., Cruz, A., Firozi, H., & Camaro, A. (2021). Artificial intelligence and labor productivity paradox: The economic impact of ai in china, india, japan, and singapore. *Journal of Economics Finance and Accounting Studies*, *3*(2), 120–139. DOI: 10.32996/jefas.2021.3.2.13

Chhibber, A. (2021). India's demographic dividend or disaster? mismanaged factors of production—Land, labor, infrastructure, cities. *Journal of Infrastructure Policy and Development*, *5*(1), 1253. DOI: 10.24294/jipd.v5i1.1253

Cooke, F., & Saini, D. (2015). From legalism to strategic hrm in india? grievance management in transition. *Asia Pacific Journal of Management*, *32*(3), 619–643. DOI: 10.1007/s10490-015-9417-0

Darwish, T., Singh, S., Batsakis, G., & Potočnik, K. (2023). Cross-country analysis of hrm parameters in emerging markets: An assessment of measurement invariance. *British Journal of Management*, *35*(2), 692–705. DOI: 10.1111/1467-8551.12730

Das, S., Raychaudhuri, A., & Roy, S. (2014). Trade and labor demand in an emerging market economy: An analysis for indian manufacturing during 1991–2010. *Journal of Developing Areas*, *48*(3), 353–379. DOI: 10.1353/jda.2014.0043

Dougherty, S. (2009). Labour regulation and employment dynamics at the state level in india. *Review of Market Integration*, *1*(3), 295–337. DOI: 10.1177/097492921000100303

Dougherty, S., Robles, V., & Krishna, K. (2011). Employment protection legislation and plant-level productivity in india.. https://doi.org/DOI: 10.3386/w17693

Fagernäs, S. (2010). Labor law, judicial efficiency, and informal employment in india. *Journal of Empirical Legal Studies*, *7*(2), 282–321. DOI: 10.1111/j.1740-1461.2010.01179.x

Fernandes, A. and Pakes, A. (2008). Factor utilization in indian manufacturing: a look at the world bank investment climate surveys data.. https://doi.org/DOI: 10.3386/w14178

Geetika, G., Ghosh, P., Rai, A., Joshi, J., & Singh, P. (2014). Measuring workers' satisfaction with grievance-handling procedure: Study of a power distribution major in india. *Asian Journal of Management Cases*, *11*(2), 139–157. DOI: 10.1177/0972820114538347

Goldar, B., & Aggarwal, S. (2012). Informalization of industrial labor in india: Effects of labor market rigidities and import competition. *The Developing Economies*, *50*(2), 141–169. DOI: 10.1111/j.1746-1049.2012.00162.x

Gupta, P., & Kumar, U. (2010). Performance of indian manufacturing in the post reform period. SSRN Electronic Journal. https://doi.org/DOI: 10.2139/ssrn.1608663

Gupta, P. and Kumar, U. (2012). Performance of indian manufacturing in the postreform period., 225-252. https://doi.org/DOI: 10.1093/oxfordhb/9780199734580.013.0008

Hasan, R., Mitra, D., & Ramaswamy, K. (2003). Trade reforms, labor regulations and labor-demand elasticities: empirical evidence from india.. https://doi.org/DOI: 10.3386/w9879

James, K. (2011). India's demographic change: Opportunities and challenges. *Science*, *333*(6042), 576–580. DOI: 10.1126/science.1207969 PMID: 21798938

Kerswell, T., & Pratap, S. (2015). Informality in automobile value chains in india. *Working USA*, *18*(4), 533–553. DOI: 10.1111/wusa.12211

Kubasinski, S. and Sławińska, M. (2021). Research on corporate social responsibility (crs) in terms of work safety. European Research Studies Journal, XXIV(Special Issue 5), 626-636. https://doi.org/DOI: 10.35808/ersj/2755

Lodder, A. and Zeleznikow, J. (2010). Enhanced dispute resolution through the use of information technology.. https://doi.org/DOI: 10.1017/cbo9780511777554

Maiti, D. (2012). Precarious work in india. *The American Behavioral Scientist*, *57*(4), 507–530. DOI: 10.1177/0002764212466247

Meijerink, J., & Keegan, A. (2019). Conceptualizing human resource management in the gig economy. *Journal of Managerial Psychology*, *34*(4), 214–232. DOI: 10.1108/jmp-07-2018-0277

Melhem, M. (2024). Navigating hrm practices in the indian institutional context: Multinational vs domestic enterprises in comparative perspective. *Review of International Business and Strategy*, *34*(4), 495–515. DOI: 10.1108/ribs-12-2023-0142

Nandan, S., Halkias, D., Thurman, P., Komodromos, M., Alserhan, B., Adendorff, C., & Seaman, C. (2018). Assessing cross-national invariance of the three-component model of organizational commitment. *EuroMed Journal of Business*, *13*(3), 254–279. DOI: 10.1108/emjb-09-2017-0031

Oyewole, A. (2024). Human resource management strategies for safety and risk mitigation in the oil and gas industry: A review. *International Journal of Management & Entrepreneurship Research*, *6*(3), 623–633. DOI: 10.51594/ijmer.v6i3.875

Purba, Y. (2024). Implications of technological evolution on human resource management strategies and legal compliance. *Jurnal Minfo Polgan*, *12*(2), 2686–2692. DOI: 10.33395/jmp.v12i2.13337

Sridevi, J. (2024). The implications of the covid-19 pandemic on hrm practices in indian manufacturing industry., 578-588. https://doi.org/DOI: 10.2991/978-94-6463-433-4_44

Upender, M. (2011). Differential output elasticity of employment during post-economic reform period in the indian economy. *The Singapore Economic Review*, *56*(02), 189–202. DOI: 10.1142/s0217590811004249

Yassi, A., Bryce, E., Breilh, J., Lavoie, M., Ndelu, L., Lockhart, K., & Spiegel, J. (2011). Collaboration between infection control and occupational health in three continents: A success story with international impact. *BMC International Health and Human Rights*, *11*(S2). Advance online publication. DOI: 10.1186/1472-698x-11-s2-s8 PMID: 22166059

Chapter 3
Privacy in the Digital Workplace:
Reforming Data Protection Law for Monitoring and HRIS

Mohan Kumar
https://orcid.org/0000-0002-5171-0892
Faculty of Commerce and Management, SGT University, India

Ali Najeeb
https://orcid.org/0000-0003-4663-9347
Qasim Ibrahim School of Business, Villa College, Maldives

Himanshi Rajora
https://orcid.org/0000-0001-5686-3030
JGBS, O.P. Jindal Global University, Sonipat, India

Pooja Rani
Department of Economics, Maharshi Dayanand University, Rohtak, India

ABSTRACT

The digital transformation of contemporary workplaces has accelerated the integration of advanced monitoring technologies and Human Resource Information Systems (HRIS), reshaping how organizations manage performance, administer HR functions, and ensure operational efficiency. While these systems offer unprecedented opportunities for data-driven decision-making, they also raise significant concerns about employee privacy, autonomy, and fairness. This chapter examines the evolution of employee privacy in relation to technological change, the development and limitations of existing data protection laws, and the growing ethical risks associated with algorithmic surveillance and biometric data collection. It argues that

DOI: 10.4018/979-8-3693-5390-5.ch003

current legal frameworks are inadequate for addressing the complexities of digital monitoring and calls for comprehensive reforms that prioritize proportionality, transparency, and employee agency. This chapter provides governance strategies, organizational best practices, and future directions for safeguarding privacy in the digital workplace.

INTRODUCTION

The rate of the digitalization of the work has increased significantly in the last twenty years, changing the organization setting, the ways of managing it, and the character of employment relationships. Advanced Human Resource Information Systems (HRIS) and AI-driven analytics are just some of the technologies that have offered employers potent recruitment, performance, attendance, security, and engagement management. The emergence of remote and hybrid working systems that have developed in the wake of global disruptors, such as the COVID-19 pandemic has further escalated the usage of digital monitoring technologies, including keystroke loggers, productivity trackers, biometric authentication platforms, and real-time analytics platforms (Moore, 2022). These tools were initially specialized and have now been incorporated into the normal operations of the workplace. Although these systems bring certain benefits to the organizations, increasing their productivity, bringing transparency to the workflow, and providing cost-effectiveness, they also put the traditional limits of privacy and autonomy into question.

The most controversial issue concerning the use of data within a data-intensive workplace is the question of the protection of employee privacy. In the past, the privacy rules presupposed a distinct division of work and personal life with the little monitoring except the attendance and direct supervision. Nonetheless, new technologies allow tracking the behaviors and emotions of employees, communication patterns, and even physiological indicators in real-time and granularly (Ball, 2021) (Mohit Yadav & Rangnekar, 2016). This change has questioned traditional beliefs of consent, surveillance and power imbalance in the employment relationship. In addition to this, the growth of online data traffic through cloud infrastructure and 3rd-party providers have created new vulnerabilities such as unauthorized access to data, algorithmic discrimination, and improper secondary use of employee data.

Current privacy protection laws, including the European General Data Protection Regulation (GDPR) and other national privacy laws, are trying to mitigate these issues but tend to be technologically outdated (Bennett and Raab, 2020). Numerous of these laws were designed in the consumer-facing context, and are hard to implement in the workplace, where consent is complicated by hierarchical power relationships. The chapter holds that the modern data protection legislation should be redefined to reflect the new realities of digital monitoring and HRIS systems. This will need not only legally changes but also organizational governance systems, ethical standards and participatory systems giving employees powers.

The chapter examines theoretical, ethical, legal, and practical aspects of privacy at the work place in the digital age. It examines the history of employee privacy, discusses the existing monitoring technologies, evaluates the existing legislation on data protection, highlights the main gaps, and suggests the reform to provide fairness, transparency, and accountability. Finally, it brings out the necessity of a humanistic strategy that addresses the needs of organizations and rights and dignity of employees.

UNDERSTANDING THE DIGITAL WORKPLACE

Digital workplace can be defined as an organizational ecosystem in which communication, collaboration and management of resources are becoming more dependent on a combination of integrated digital technologies. It includes cloud-based solutions, virtual teamwork, AI-based workflow solutions, mobile devices, and digital human resource solutions (Davis, 2020)(Kumar, Nain, et al., 2025; Kumar, Yadav, et al., 2025). The digital workplace is not just a collection of tools but a socio-technical space that forms the work pattern, relationship and expectation as organizations transform into a more modernized form. Centrality of data is one of the characteristics of the digital workplace. Each and every interaction, emails, chat messages, keystrokes, time of login, meeting attendance, and task execution can be recorded and converted into operational intelligence. HRIS systems enable companies to keep track of the life cycles of employees (recruitment to retirement), whereas enterprise software gathers behavioral and productivity data. It is a continuous process of datafication of work, which allows organizations to detect inefficiency, customize employee development, and predict future performance trends (Choudhary et al., 2021)(Wang, 2021). Nonetheless, the identical abilities generate unparalleled insight into the behaviors of employees.

The physical space of the work place has also been reinvented by technological innovation. Hybrid and remote work formats have broken up the space limits in terms of which people used to practice surveillance, and this practice has spread into the domestic space. An example is that the employers can install activity-tracking software on personal devices, make webcams mandatory during meetings, or track work hours using VPN logs (Moore, 2022). Such practices express themselves deeply on the issue whether employers ought to have access to the private spaces, even indirectly.

Digital workplace is also being typified by rising automation. AI will help in screening resumes, communication patterns, attrition prediction, as well as identifying high potential employees. The combination of real-time analytics also makes it possible to have algorithmic management, where algorithms inform decisions regarding performance, tasks to be allocated, and disciplinary actions (Mateescu and Nguyen, 2019)(Nguyen et al., 2025). The model is reflective of what platform companies like Uber and Amazon have done, which is to continually assess workers with automated systems. Although it has its efficiencies, the digital workplace creates asymmetries between the employer and the employee. The employers have much more knowledge on the monitoring tools utilized, the information gathered and the use of data. Employees might not even be aware that they are being shrivelled or that algorithmic evaluations can be used. Such imbalances of power highlight the need to have open and just systems of governance so that the digital workplace technologies do not undermine the autonomy and dignity of workers.

EVOLUTION OF EMPLOYEE PRIVACY CONCEPTS

The privacy of employees has been changed tremendously due to the changes in work environment, management and technologies. The physical space and immediate supervision formed the basis of the traditional models of employee privacy. Supervisors observed, interacted and used performance measures that involved human judgment. The issues of privacy were in the form of locker checks, phone monitoring, and confidentiality of personnel files (Westin, 1967)(Trivedi et al., 2023). Nonetheless, with the digitization of the workplaces, the extent of the privacy extended to informational and psychological levels. The initial significant change was the emergence of computerization in the late 20th century. The digital record keeping established new types of personal data including electronic communications, computer use logs, and attendance records. With the use of email systems and intranet platforms in organizations, the privacy debate that concerned the workplace was whether the employer had the right of reading emails or monitoring internet activities. The courts tended to rule in favour of the employers reaffirming the fact that the work resources were part of the organization (Schwartz, 1999).

The second significant change was due to the emergence of mobile technologies and remote employment. The use of Smartphones significantly eroded work and life boundaries, and people could always be connected. The wearable technologies also brought about new biometric data like heart rate and movement patterns, which were utilized by some employers in their wellness programs or in workplace safety programs (Ajunwa, 2020). These changes shifted the physical concept of privacy to a relational one, which was influenced by the ownership of data, consent, and power.

The third and most radical change is the present-day age of algorithmic surveillance. Digital footprints can be used to determine personality traits, stress, collaboration and even emotional states using AI systems. Surveillance has turned out to be environmental, constant and anticipatory. Instead of just documenting the behaviors, systems have become able to make inferences on forthcoming behaviors, including turnover threat or performance possibility (O'Neil, 2016)(Yadav et al., 2025). This anticipatory aspect brings more serious issues to the question of fairness, prejudice, and independence. Employee privacy has been evolving in line with changes in the wider society. With the expansion of the general knowledge of the rights of the digital era, employees start perceiving privacy as a key component of dignity, freedom, and psychological security. The young generations coming to the working age desire more transparency and control over their personal information than the previous generations (Ball, 2021). Therefore, the history of workplace privacy is not merely the history of technology but the history of culture and organization.

HRIS AND EMPLOYEE MONITORING TECHNOLOGIES

HRIS are the most important systems in the management of the modern workforce. They facilitate recruitment, payroll, performance management, training, attendance tracking and employee engagement. By so doing, they are accumulating huge amounts of structured and unstructured employee data, which may be incorporated with other enterprise systems. The HRIS has grown beyond the administrative functions to predictive analytics and AI-inspired decision-making, which has changed the essence of monitoring employees (Stone et al., 2015).

Monitoring technologies of employees are on a vast spectrum. Simple devices such as time tracking software, email monitoring and access control systems can be used. More sophisticated systems include keystroke monitoring, screen capture software, geographical location tracking and productivity scoring on the basis of activity. Biometric systems, like fingerprint systems, facial recognition system and voice authentication systems are becoming more popular as a means of access control and attendance tracking. These systems create a new level of privacy threats since biometric information is very sensitive, irreversible, and prone to abuse (Ajunwa, 2020)(Kumar, Dagar, et al., 2025; Kumar, Nain, et al., 2025). The most recent frontier is AI-driven surveillance devices. These consist of sentiment analysis solutions that understand the mood of employees using patterns of communication, machine learning solutions that rank productivity, and predictive models that detect high-risk behavior or disengagement. Some sectors have AI systems to track the fatigue of drivers, the movements of workers in the warehouse, or the tone of voice of customer service agents (Mateescu & Nguyen, 2019).

Remote monitoring tools have become relevant as a result of the emergence of hybrid work. Monitoring software which records mouse movement, keyboard action, or web camera shots purports to be accountable but is frequently intrusive to privacy. There are platforms which will label workers as active or idle, automatically creating performance metrics. These breaches blur the professional and personal spheres, and there have been criticisms that these tools encourage a culture of mistrust (Moore, 2022).

Companies use justification of monitoring technologies due to different reasons: security, productivity, compliance, quality assurance, and regulatory requirements. Nonetheless, the disproportionate monitoring may cause the loss of morale, the rise of stress, and the destruction of psychological safety. Workers who are regularly surveilled will also complain of feeling distrusted, dehumanized or pressured to perform in a way that will satisfy monitoring apparatuses as opposed to contributing to better performance (Ball, 2021).

The emergence of surveillance technologies emphasizes the importance of legal regulations and ethics that restrict inappropriate surveillance, transparency, and dignity of employees.

LEGAL FRAMEWORKS GOVERNING EMPLOYEE DATA PRIVACY

The laws that regulate the privacy of employee data are markedly different in different jurisdictions. Nevertheless, the majority of the laws strive to reconcile the interests of employers, including the security and efficiency, with the right of employees to privacy and autonomy. Nevertheless, it has not been enough since technological innovation has largely been ahead of the regulatory responses, leading to a patchwork and uneven protection. The General Data Protection Regulation (GDPR) has been considered the most extensive privacy regulation. It is applicable to processing of data within the workplace and incorporates the following principles: transparency, purpose limitation, data minimization, and accountability (Voigt and Von dem Bussche, 2017). The inequality of power between employers and employees in the employment relationships is recognized in GDPR as consent is not considered a legitimate source of law. Rather, it should be processed based on a legitimate interest, a necessity of the contract or a legal requirement. Nevertheless, the lack of clarity regarding what is meant by legitimate interest frequently enables employers to rationalize a vast range of surveillance (Bennett and Raab, 2020).

Beyond the EU, the law is different. The US does not have a federal privacy legislation, as it falls back on industry-specific policy and state privacy laws. In the U.S., the majority of states encourage a wide scope of monitoring at the workplace, where the provision of notice and proportion is minimal (Schwartz, 1999). The California Consumer Privacy Act (CCPA) and its new version, the CPRA, has more rights but fewer protections than GDPR. The Personal Information Protection and Electronic Documents Act (PIPEDA) of Canada demands a meaningful consent, and the workplace scenario makes it difficult to apply it (Dabrowski, 2019). The Privacy Act of Australia has exemptions on employee records, which has exposed a lot of workers. Other Asian jurisdictions are different: Singapore has a PDPA that focuses on consent and the Personal Information Protection Law (PIPL) in China includes strict compliance requirements but allows a wide scope of government access to data.

The workplace privacy is also influenced by labor law, particularly in countries where collective bargaining is highly practiced. In Germany, the monitoring technologies are to be approved by works councils. Nevertheless, employees in the areas where no collective representation exists have lesser chances to affect the monitoring decisions.

The courts have started to deal with workplace privacy cases; however, the decisions are not consistent. Courts uphold prerogatives of employers to monitor working resources, whereas others emphasize the requirements of employees to their privacy, particularly in personal devices and off-site settings (Moore, 2022).

In general, existing legal systems offer partial and biased protection, which is not able to keep up with the changing technologies and realities of the workplace.

ETHICAL ISSUES AND RISKS IN A DIGITALLY MONITORED WORKPLACE

The ethical implications of digital monitoring in the workplace extend far beyond basic legal compliance. While regulatory frameworks provide minimum standards for employee data protection, ethical considerations delve deeper into the moral responsibility of organizations to respect human dignity, autonomy, psychological well-being, and fairness. The intensification of surveillance technologies-particularly AI-powered tools—raises urgent ethical questions concerning the nature of control, transparency, and the balance of power between employers and employees (Ball, 2021). One of the most prominent concerns is the erosion of autonomy. Employees subjected to constant tracking may feel as though they are no longer in control of their own work environments, decisions, or behaviors. Autonomy is foundational to intrinsic motivation, creativity, and job satisfaction, as demonstrated in the self-determination theory proposed by Deci and Ryan (2000). Excessive surveillance can diminish an employee's sense of agency, leading to a mechanized work culture that discourages innovation and independent thought (Ajunwa, 2020). In such environments, performance may improve in the short term due to pressure, but long-term productivity and well-being often decline as stress accumulates and disengagement rises.

Algorithmic decision-making represents another ethically fraught dimension. AI systems that assist in hiring, promotions, or performance evaluations may amplify existing societal and organizational biases if not designed with fairness in mind. Historical datasets used to train these algorithms often carry embedded gender, racial, or socioeconomic prejudices, which may be unintentionally replicated at scale (O'Neil, 2016). For instance, Amazon's now-discontinued hiring tool that penalized resumes containing the word "women's" exemplifies how biased data can result in discriminatory outcomes (Dastin, 2018). The opacity of such systems-the so-called "black-box" problem—further complicates accountability and prevents employees from challenging unfair decisions (Wachter et al., 2017). The psychological consequences of pervasive digital surveillance are equally serious. Continuous monitoring has been linked to increased levels of anxiety, stress, burnout, and feelings of alienation in employees (Mateescu & Nguyen, 2019). The phenomenon of anticipatory compliance, where employees alter their behavior out of fear of being watched-even outside working hours-can result in chronic stress and decreased job satisfaction. Over time, this leads to a degradation of psychological safety, which is crucial for open communication, collaboration, and risk-taking in innovative workplaces (Edmondson, 1999).

Informed consent in the digital workplace is another ethical grey area. The hierarchical structure of employer-employee relationships creates a power imbalance, whereby consent is often not truly voluntary. Employees may feel compelled to accept intrusive monitoring policies in fear of losing their jobs or being penalized (Moore, 2022). Moreover, organizations may bury surveillance clauses deep within complex privacy policies, leaving workers unaware of the full scope and impact of monitoring practices. This lack of clarity and meaningful choice undermines the very concept of ethical consent.

A further concern is the secondary use of employee data, where information gathered for productivity purposes is repurposed without employees' knowledge or consent. For example, data originally collected to improve workflow efficiency may be used in disciplinary hearings or shared with third-party vendors. This violates principles of data minimization and purpose limitation, and more importantly, erodes trust in employer-employee relationships (Bamberger & Mulligan, 2019). Unauthorized secondary use of data reflects a broader ethical failure in respecting the informational rights and expectations of workers.

The cumulative impact of these ethical risks demands a more human-centered approach to digital monitoring. Organizations must embrace monitoring frameworks that are proportional, transparent, and participatory, ensuring that surveillance is conducted with clear justification, minimal intrusion, and respect for individual rights. Embedding ethics-by-design principles into monitoring technologies-such as providing opt-in settings, explainable AI, and access controls-can help bridge the gap between technological capability and moral responsibility (Cavoukian, 2011). The ethical challenges posed by digital surveillance in the workplace are multi-dimensional, affecting not just legal compliance but the very fabric of workplace culture, fairness, and human dignity. As technology advances, organizations must proactively ensure that digital tools are aligned with values of trust, respect, and justice-est they create a future of work governed more by algorithms than by accountability.

CHALLENGES WITH CURRENT DATA PROTECTION LAWS

Despite considerable advancements in global data protection regimes, the effectiveness of privacy laws in the context of the digital workplace remains fundamentally limited. The transition toward data-intensive employment environments—powered by algorithmic management, biometric identification, and remote surveillance—has exposed major structural weaknesses in existing legal frameworks. These gaps are not just legal in nature but also deeply institutional, interpretive, and practical, calling for urgent reform.

One of the most persistent challenges is the ambiguity in key legal concepts. Privacy laws, particularly those derived from the European General Data Protection Regulation (GDPR), rely heavily on terms such as "legitimate interest," "necessity," and "proportionality." However, these concepts are highly context-dependent and lack precise boundaries, enabling organizations to justify broad surveillance measures under flexible interpretations (Voigt & Von dem Bussche, 2017). For instance, a company may claim that real-time monitoring of employees' screen activity is necessary for productivity, even though such practices may intrude into personal data or communication. This regulatory vagueness leaves too much discretion in the hands of employers, often at the expense of worker autonomy. Closely linked to this is the problem of informed consent, which is further complicated by power asymmetries inherent in employer–employee relationships. In theory, data protection laws emphasize the importance of voluntary, informed, and specific consent for data processing. In practice, however, consent in the workplace is often coerced, implicit, or formalistic-rendering it ethically and legally questionable (Moore, 2022). Many employees sign digital consent forms embedded in contracts or onboarding procedures without fully understanding the scope of surveillance or the implications of data processing. Because their livelihood depends on compliance, their "consent" lacks meaningful agency, reducing it to a procedural checkbox rather than a substantive right (Ajunwa, 2020).

Another major limitation lies in the weak enforcement of existing laws. Data protection authorities, particularly in under-resourced jurisdictions, often lack the capacity to conduct workplace audits or investigate compliance in small and medium-sized enterprises (Bennett & Raab, 2020). The enforcement gap is further exacerbated by the chilling effect on employees, who may hesitate to report intrusive practices for fear of retaliation or job loss. Whistleblower protections are often inadequate, and internal grievance mechanisms are either non-existent or ineffective. As a result, many violations go unreported and unaddressed, perpetuating systemic surveillance without oversight. Moreover, the speed of technological innovation far outpaces legal adaptation. Laws crafted years ago struggle to remain relevant in the face of emerging tools such as facial emotion recognition, AI-driven risk prediction, sentiment analysis, and wearable biometric trackers (Wright & Kreissl, 2020). These advanced systems operate in legal grey zones, exploiting loopholes or falling outside traditional categories of data regulation. The reactive nature of legislative reform-where laws respond after harm occurs-cannot adequately anticipate or mitigate risks introduced by new surveillance technologies. Another critical concern is the lack of algorithmic accountability.

While many organizations use machine learning and predictive models for HR-related decisions, few jurisdictions mandate algorithmic transparency or fairness audits. Consequently, employees affected by opaque systems have little recourse to challenge or understand the logic behind employment decisions such as termination, promotion, or performance scores (Wachter, Mittelstadt, & Floridi, 2017). Without mandated audits, bias detection, or explainability requirements, algorithmic systems may silently reinforce discrimination, all while remaining legally shielded.

Finally, cross-border data transfers present a significant compliance hurdle. In multinational corporations, employee data is often stored, processed, or analyzed across multiple jurisdictions, each with varying degrees of privacy protection. This fragmented global data landscape increases the risk of regulatory conflict, forum shopping, or data misuse, particularly when data moves between countries with weak oversight or inadequate enforcement (Greenleaf, 2018). Employees may find their data subject to foreign laws they are unaware of, further diluting their protections. Taken together, these structural, operational, and conceptual limitations illustrate the urgent need for tailored reforms in employee data protection law. As surveillance technologies become more intrusive, invisible, and embedded in daily workflows, legal systems must evolve from generic privacy safeguards to context-specific, employee-centered protections. Reform must not only address ambiguity and enforcement gaps but also embed principles of fairness, transparency, and worker participation into the design of digital workplace governance.

REFORMING DATA PROTECTION LAW FOR THE DIGITAL WORKPLACE

The imperative to reform data protection legislation stems from the increasing sophistication and pervasiveness of surveillance technologies in the digital workplace. As organizations integrate Artificial Intelligence (AI), biometric monitoring, cloud-based Human Resource Information Systems (HRIS), and productivity tracking software into daily operations, existing legal frameworks have proven inadequate in addressing the scope, depth, and ethical implications of such technologies. A forward-thinking, multi-dimensional reform is urgently needed-one that aligns legal safeguards with the evolving realities of algorithmic management and data-driven employment practices.

1. Defining Clear Boundaries of Acceptable Surveillance

The first step in reforming data protection law must be to legally define the boundaries of "reasonable" surveillance. Vague legal standards leave room for excessive or invasive practices, particularly when surveillance extends into personal spaces, such as an employee's home during remote work or personal devices used for hybrid roles. New legislation should clearly delineate permissible purposes for monitoring, strictly prohibit practices that lack a legitimate business rationale, and provide legal redress when boundaries are breached (Ajunwa, 2020). For example, webcam surveillance during remote meetings may be justifiable in some contexts but deeply intrusive in others-especially without a clear proportionality assessment.

2. Shifting from Consent to Employee Agency

Legal reform must also reconceptualize the role of consent in workplace data practices. Given the inherent power imbalance between employers and employees, consent often becomes coerced or symbolic. Therefore, legal structures should shift from mere consent models to agency-based rights, empowering employees through structural mechanisms. These include mandatory consultation rights, collective bargaining over surveillance technologies, and the right to object to intrusive monitoring practices. One promising legal tool is the introduction of Workplace Surveillance Impact Assessments (WSIAs), modeled after Data Protection Impact Assessments (DPIAs), but adapted for the unique conditions of employment settings (Custers, van der Hof, & Schermer, 2019). These would require employers to assess and justify the necessity and impact of surveillance technologies before deployment.

3. Promoting Algorithmic Transparency and Fairness

As algorithmic decision-making becomes embedded in recruitment, performance evaluation, and disciplinary actions, laws must demand greater transparency, accountability, and fairness. Employers should be mandated to disclose where and how AI systems are used in employment decisions and to explain outcomes in a comprehensible manner. This includes the logic, criteria, and data sets underpinning algorithmic models. Moreover, mandatory fairness audits must be conducted regularly to detect and mitigate algorithmic bias, especially in sensitive processes like hiring and promotion (Wachter, Mittelstadt, & Floridi, 2017). Importantly, automated decisions that materially affect employment outcomes must be subject to human oversight and appeal, ensuring that AI does not replace managerial responsibility or ethical judgment (European Commission, 2021).

4. Strengthening Data Minimization and Security Standards

Effective reform must include robust principles of data minimization and data security. This involves limiting the collection of employee data strictly to what is necessary for clearly defined purposes. Legal mandates should enforce shorter retention periods, purpose-specific use, strong encryption standards, and third-party vendor accountability-especially relevant for cloud-based HRIS solutions (Voigt & Von dem Bussche, 2017). These measures can significantly reduce the risks of data breaches, misuse, and unauthorized secondary use of employee information.

5. Embedding Employee Participation in Governance

To ensure democratic oversight, legal frameworks should promote direct employee involvement in surveillance-related decisions. This includes mandating works councils, privacy committees, or equivalent employee representative bodies to review and approve surveillance tools before implementation. In jurisdictions where formal worker representation does not exist, alternative mechanisms such as consultation platforms, ethics committees, or digital governance boards should be required to ensure transparency and legitimacy (Bamberger & Mulligan, 2019). Embedding participatory structures fosters trust, enhances accountability, and improves the legitimacy of monitoring systems.

6. Ensuring Stronger Enforcement and Remedies

Lastly, reforms must address the systemic lack of enforcement in current privacy regimes. Regulators need expanded budgets, technical capacity, and investigatory authority to proactively audit organizations and respond to employee complaints. Additionally, clear and accessible complaint procedures must be established so employees can report privacy violations without fear of retaliation. Penalties for non-compliance should be substantial enough to deter misconduct, especially among large multinational corporations that can otherwise absorb minor fines as operational costs. Ultimately, an effective legal framework must be visionary, adaptive, and rooted in human rights-designed not just to manage risks but to uphold the dignity and freedom of workers in the age of digital surveillance.

ORGANIZATIONAL GOVERNANCE AND BEST PRACTICES

Legal reforms are necessary; however, organizations must also take the role of ensuring they apply good governance practices that would ensure the ethical and responsible utilization of monitoring technologies. Good governance is initiated with open communication. The employees should know what data is gathered, the purpose of its gathering, the storage duration and the individuals who can access it (Bamberger and Mulligan, 2019). Companies ought to have internal accountability frameworks such as privacy committees, Data Protection Officers, and cross functional controls. Periodic auditing also enables the monitoring tools to be utilized in a proportionate and lawful manner.

Privacy-by-design principles can be used to design systems with privacy protection in mind. This will involve constraining data gathering, pseudonymization, and privacy settings that are controlled by the user (Cavoukian, 2011). Employees should also be involved in ethical governance. Consultative procedures Workshops, surveys, feedback committees enable workers to present concerns and take part in the monitoring of policies. Another necessary element is training. Managers, HR specialists, and employees have to be aware of risks to privacy, algorithmic bias, and responsible data management practices (Wright and Kreissl, 2020).

Finally, continuous improvement should be a priority at organizations. Policies must be updated on a regular basis, as changes in risks and expectations are expected to emerge with the advancement of technologies.

Organizations can develop trust and safeguard the dignity of employees by instilling ethical standards in the process of governance.

FUTURE OF WORKPLACE PRIVACY

Future of the workplace privacy will be informed by the new technologies, changing employee expectations and dynamic legal environments. The use of AI will infiltrate HR operations, and algorithmic transparency is one of the urgent priorities (O'Neil, 2016). Biometric surveillance can go farther to the cognitive or emotional sphere, and this creates new ethical and legal concerns. Working remotely will keep pushing the personal and professional boundaries. The future structures should be such that the domestic environments are not disclosed despite the efforts of the employers to be accountable (Moore, 2022).

There will be increased cybersecurity threats that will need advanced measures to secure important employee information. Cross-border compliance issues will be challenging to global organizations because various jurisdictions will use different privacy standards. Employees will require more agency, which will drive organizations to participatory governance, culturally. In specific, younger workers consider privacy as a basic right and demand transparency on the part of their employers (Ball, 2021).

Finally, the privacy of the future workplace will be determined by the application of technology that will not infringe on human dignity, fairness and autonomy. Human-centered paradigm is necessary to ethical digital transformation.

CONCLUSION AND DISCUSSION

The modern workplace is undergoing a profound transformation driven by the widespread adoption of Human Resource Information Systems (HRIS), algorithmic management, and AI-enhanced monitoring technologies. While these tools have undeniably improved operational efficiency, provided actionable workforce analytics, and enabled remote work capabilities, they have simultaneously introduced unprecedented challenges to employee privacy, autonomy, and well-being. This chapter has examined these tensions in depth, highlighting the structural, legal, and ethical deficits that characterize existing data protection frameworks in the employment context. One of the central arguments presented is that existing laws have not kept pace with the rapid evolution of surveillance technologies. Current regulations, including the General Data Protection Regulation (GDPR) and similar national statutes, remain constrained by vague definitions, weak enforcement, and outdated assumptions about power dynamics in the workplace. The pervasive use of biometric tools, predictive analytics, and opaque algorithmic systems further complicates the landscape, raising urgent concerns about informed consent, algorithmic bias, mental health, and cross-border data exploitation.

The ethical concerns are not peripheral-they are central to organizational legitimacy and employee well-being. Intrusive surveillance erodes autonomy, trust, and psychological safety, which are all foundational to a productive and innovative workplace. When employees are subjected to constant observation or automated judgment without transparency or recourse, the workplace risks devolving into a techno-authoritarian environment where compliance is prioritized over creativity, and fear overrides engagement. Addressing these concerns requires a holistic and humanistic approach to reform. Legal reform alone is insufficient. There must be a multi-layered response involving legislative redesign, ethical governance, algorithmic accountability, and participatory decision-making at the organizational level. The introduction of tools such as Workplace Surveillance Impact Assessments (WSIAs), stronger collective bargaining rights, algorithmic audits, and clearer boundaries around personal device monitoring are critical first steps. Additionally, embedding ethical values into the design of workplace technologies-through "privacy by design" and "ethics by design" frameworks-can serve as a proactive measure against future violations.

Ultimately, this chapter advocates for a paradigm shift: from a compliance-driven privacy model to one rooted in employee dignity, transparency, and shared responsibility. Privacy must not be treated as a regulatory hurdle, but as a strategic and moral imperative that reflects an organization's values and long-term commitment to its workforce. In this sense, privacy protection becomes more than a legal obligation-it becomes a tactical investment in building organizational trust, resilience, and sustainability in the digital age.

As we move forward, the central challenge is to reconcile technological innovation with fundamental human rights. Organizations, regulators, and technology developers must work collaboratively to design systems that empower rather than exploit, that inform rather than obscure, and that foster trust rather than suspicion. Only then can we build digital workplaces that are not only efficient but also fair, humane, and just.

REFERENCES

Ajunwa, I. (2020). *The quantified worker: Law and technology in the modern workplace*. Cambridge University Press.

Ball, K. (2021). *Surveillance, work and technology: New directions in workplace monitoring*. Routledge.

Bamberger, K. A., & Mulligan, D. K. (2019). *Privacy on the ground: Driving corporate behavior in the United States and Europe*. MIT Press.

Bennett, C. J., & Raab, C. D. (2020). *The governance of privacy: Policy instruments in the digital age* (3rd ed.). MIT Press.

Cavoukian, A. (2011). *Privacy by design: The 7 foundational principles*. Information and Privacy Commissioner of Ontario.

Choudhary, S., Yadav, M., & Srivastava, A. P. (2021). Cognitive Biases Among Millennial Indian Investors: Do Personality and Demographic Factors Matter? *FIIB Business Review*, *13*(1), 106–117. DOI: 10.1177/23197145211057343

Custers, B., van der Hof, S., & Schermer, B. (2019). *Privacy, data protection and cybersecurity in Europe*. Springer.

Dabrowski, W. (2019). Applying PIPEDA in the workplace. *Canadian Labour & Employment Law*, *23*(2), 145–167.

Davis, G. (2020). Digital workplaces and organizational transformation. *Journal of Management Innovation*, *14*(3), 45–62.

Deci, E. L., & Ryan, R. M. (2000). The "what" and "why" of goal pursuit: Human needs and self-determination. *Psychological Inquiry*, *11*(4), 227–268.

Kumar, M., Dagar, M., Yadav, M., Choudhury, T., & Luu, T. M. N. (2025). Navigating the future: Challenges and opportunities in intelligent RPA implementation. In *Intelligent Robotic Process Automation: Development, Vulnerability and Applications* (pp. 393–420). IGI Global. https://doi.org/DOI: 10.4018/979-8-3693-4365-4.ch015

Kumar, M., Nain, N., Dagar, M., Luu, T. M. N., & Kaur, K. (2025). Redefining work and outsourcing in the AI era: Challenges and opportunities. In *Global Work Arrangements and Outsourcing in the Age of AI*. IGI Global., DOI: 10.4018/979-8-3373-1270-5.ch021

Kumar, M., & Yadav, R., Sushma, & Yadav, M. (2025). Investigating the influence of digital and social media marketing on university brand equity: An in-depth literature review and bibliometric study. *Global Knowledge, Memory and Communication*, •••, 1–26. DOI: 10.1108/GKMC-07-2024-0426

Mateescu, A., & Nguyen, A. (2019). *Algorithmic management in the workplace*. Data & Society Research Institute.

Moore, P. V. (2022). *Employee surveillance and the new workplace*. Polity Press.

Nguyen, T. B., Kumar, M., Sahoo, D. K., Nain, N., Yadav, M., & Dadhich, V. (2025). Mapping the landscape of women entrepreneurs in micro and small enterprises: Trends, themes, and insights through systematic review and text mining. *F1000Research, 14*. https://doi.org/DOI: 10.12688/f1000research.163030.1

O'Neil, C. (2016). *Weapons of math destruction: How big data increases inequality and threatens democracy*. Crown.

Schwartz, P. (1999). Privacy and democracy in cyberspace. *Vanderbilt Law Review, 52*(6), 1601–1647.

Stone, D., Deadrick, D., Lukaszewski, K., & Johnson, R. (2015). The influence of technology on the future of human resource management. *Human Resource Management Review, 25*(2), 216–231.

Trivedi, S., Singh, A., Yadav, M., Kumar, A., & Srivastava, P. (2023). Intention to Use Social Media in Online and Blended Learning: Potential Predictors and Mediation of Collectivism. IEEE Transactions on Engineering Management, PP, 1–14. https://doi.org/DOI: 10.1109/TEM.2023.3257422

Voigt, P., & Von dem Bussche, A. (2017). *The EU General Data Protection Regulation (GDPR): A practical guide*. Springer.

Wang, J. (2021). Datafication and the future of digital work. *Information Systems Journal, 31*(4), 637–660.

Wright, D., & Kreissl, R. (2020). *Surveillance in Europe: A critical overview*. Routledge.

Yadav, M., Kumar, M., Alyousef, M. I., Dagar, M., Dewasiri, N. J., & Amoozegar, A. (2025). Mapping Research Trends on Gender Diversity, Work Stress, and Job Satisfaction in Higher Education: A Bibliometric Analysis. *International Journal of Learning. Teaching and Educational Research, 24*(8), 444–472. DOI: 10.26803/ijlter.24.8.19

Yadav, M., & Rangnekar, S. (2016). Role Clarity and Organizational Citizenship Behaviour: Does Tenure Matter? A Study on Indian Power Sector. *Global Business Review*, *17*(3, suppl), 207S–224S. DOI: 10.1177/0972150916631216

Chapter 4
The Legal Challenges and Opportunities of Using AI in HR Functions

Mohit Yadav
https://orcid.org/0000-0002-9341-2527
JGBS, O.P. Jindal Global University, India

Narayanage Jayantha Dewasiri
https://orcid.org/0000-0002-5908-8890
Faculty of Management Studies, Sabaragamuwa University of Sri Lanka, Sri Lanka & Qasim Ibrahim School of Business, Villa College, Maldives

Perfecto G. Aquino
Duy Tan University, Vietnam

ABSTRACT

Artificial Intelligence (AI) is rapidly transforming Human Resource Management (HRM), offering enhanced efficiencies and innovative approaches in recruitment, performance management, and various HR functions. This chapter explores the integration of AI in HRM, examining the potential benefits, legal challenges, and ethical considerations associated with its use. Key opportunities include improved recruitment processes, data-driven performance evaluations, and personalized employee experiences. However, challenges such as compliance with data protection laws, addressing algorithmic bias, and maintaining transparency are critical. The chapter provides a comprehensive overview of best practices for legal compliance and risk mitigation, and discusses future directions for AI in HRM, including advancements

DOI: 10.4018/979-8-3693-5390-5.ch004

in technology, evolving regulations, and ethical frameworks. Organizations must navigate these complexities to harness AI's potential while ensuring responsible and equitable use.

INTRODUCTION

This section introduces the reader to Artificial Intelligence and its potential in revolutionizing business sectors. Human Resource Management has not been left behind, and AI forms part of most of its processes. Such an integration has presented unparalleled opportunities for improving efficiency, accuracy, and strategic decisions within the system of human resource management. From streamlining recruitment and selection processes to optimizing performance management and employee engagement, AI has the potential to revolutionize how organizations manage their most valuable asset-human capital (Arslan et al., 2022). Like any other powerful tool, there exist certain difficulties in AI- HRM use, mainly on legal issues. Acquaintance with these challenges and related opportunities is important for HR professionals, lawyers, and leadership in every organization. First, applications of AI in HRM are manifold. AI algorithms in recruitment favor the automation of sourcing and screening applicants by reducing the time and cost it conventionally takes to do these things. AI is used to sift through a lot of data in finding the best candidates, using predefined criteria that reduce human biases, which may inflate hiring decisions (Basu et al., 2023). AI-driven performance management tools have been deployed to make more objective employee performance appraisals, leverage analytics to predict future performance, and identify the gaps in development. Beyond recruitment and performance management, AI has been extended in other HR functions: compensation management, employee training and development, and employee relations, introducing personalized experiences with individual employee needs in mind (Budhwar et al., 2022).

These advantages notwithstanding, AI use in HRM raises several serious legal issues. One of the major concerns is that of anti-discrimination legislation. While AI has a great potential to reduce biases, sometimes it is susceptible to perpetuating them through algorithms that are taught on biased data or through decision-making criteria representative of the existing biases within society. These may lead to a plethora of legal problems relating to discriminatory hiring or biases in performance appraisals. Another critical issue with AI in HRM pertains to data privacy. AI systems often process huge amounts of personal data, which needs to be handled in conformity with data protection laws, such as the General Data Protection Regulation of the European Union and the California Consumer Privacy Act of the United States. An organization would have to balance such legitimate requirements with concern for the privacy rights of employees (Chowdhury et al., 2023).

Another key legal complication arises from interpretive transparency into the algorithms used by AI. Most AI systems are a variety of "black box" in which there is poor insight into the thought processes leading to the derivation of a particular decision. Lack of transparency can result in various different legal issues if AI-driven decisions are questioned by employees or some regulating authority. An organization should be in a position to make an AI algorithm more interpretable and ensure that the decisions it takes are well explained in a form that is clear and understandable. In addition, AI surveillance of employees-such as observing productivity or behavior-raises a bevy of ethical and legal concerns about employee consent and autonomy (Hmoud, 2021).

In the light of these challenges, it is critical that organizations adopt best practices so that AI is used in an ethical and legally appropriate way in carrying out HRM. This will involve policies that ensure fairness and transparency, training of HR professionals on the legal implications of AI, and the establishment of strong data protection measures. By proactive handling of these issues, organizations can be well-placed to maximize benefits from AI in HRM with minimal risks on legal aspects (Kaushal et al., 2023).

This therefore means that as much as AI provides enormous opportunities for HRM to change the game, it also can pose similarly complicated legal challenges with which one must deal with caution. The integration of AI in HRM can be done successfully by following a balanced approach: in ways that maximize benefits provided through AI, while considering compliance with legal and ethical standards at the same time. Hence, this chapter goes deep into the challenges and opportunities so as to afford insight into and guide HR professionals and legal practitioners on how to navigate the ever-evolving landscape of AI in HRM (Lawler & Elliot, 1993).

ARTIFICIAL INTELLIGENCE IN RECRUITMENT

Artificial intelligence has brought remarkable changes in the way organizations attract, screen, and select candidates. By being able to bring down costs, and build more efficiency, AI applications will provide a number of benefits when it comes to recruitment. At the same time, it raises special legal challenges that organizations need to address with care to avoid falling foul of the law on anti-discrimination and data protection. This section will discuss the many applications of AI in recruitment, the associated legal challenges, and also the opportunities accruing to improve the process of recruitment (Malik et al., 2020).

Application of AI in Recruitment

AI has been integrated into every step of the recruitment process to make it systematic and data-driven. One of the important areas of application of AI in sourcing and screening candidates could be: AI-powered tools analyze volumes of data on resumes, social media profiles, and other online data for spotting candidates matching some job requirements. These tools can sift out unqualified applicants in no time and rank the rest of the candidates in order of suitability for the position, hence saving human recruiters a lot of time and effort (Sabil et al., 2023).

AI also extends the candidate experience through chatbots and other automated systems of communication. The AI-driven platforms can also interactively engage the candidates in real time by responding to their queries, updating them on the status of their candidature, and even scheduling interviews. This will enhance not only the candidate experience but also make the communication consistent and timely (Singh & Chouhan, 2023).

AI in Recruitment - Another important use of AI in recruitment is in the assessment of candidates. AI can carry out video interviews whereby, through algorithms, facial expressions, tone of voice, and word expressions are analyzed to evaluate the competencies of candidates, their emotional intelligence, and cultural fit. Besides, AI-based skills assessment can be introduced through simulations, gamified assessments, or coding challenges. These enable organizations to attain a more objective understanding of candidates' capabilities with less reliance on subjective judgment (Sipahi & Artantaş, 2022).

Legal Challenges

The use of AI in recruitment, as much as all the advantages can be seen, definitely presents some legal challenges with which an organization has to grapple. First and foremost, there is the issue of adherence to anti-discrimination laws (Strohmeier & Piazza, 2015). Even as AI can reduce human biases, it can inadvertently also reinforce them if the algorithms get trained on biased data. This would include, for example, when biases appear in historic hiring data-preferences toward certain demographic groups are reflected in this kind of data, which the AI system could pick up and enforce, therefore affecting discriminatory outcomes. Development of AI systems that perpetuate discrimination thus can lead to legal liabilities under anti-discrimination laws as placed by Title VII of the Civil Rights Act in the United States or the Equality Act in the United Kingdom.

Another more complicated aspect of legality is transparency and explainability in AI-driven decisions for recruitment. Most AI algorithms are "black box systems" that do not provide any clarity on how they actually came to a particular decision.

This section may prove to be tricky, especially when a candidate queries the process adopted while making a certain decision; therefore, this is an important requirement that an organization engages in explainable AI, where they can give clear, understandable reasons for hiring or rejecting a candidate.

Another major legal concern in AI-driven recruitment relates to data privacy. Indeed, AI-automated systems sometimes need substantial chunks of personal data: a resume, information from social media profiles, video recordings. All of these must be processed in observance of data protection laws, including such laws as the GDPR within the European Union or CCPA in the United States. Organizations should take strong measures to protect candidate data securely, store it safely, and process it, also informing candidates on how the data shall be used.

OPPORTUNITIES

Despite these challenges, AI-driven recruitment offers some opportunities for organizations to leverage this technology for better recruitment. One such opportunity greatly exists in the potential of reaching a fine level of diversity and inclusion. AI would be able to help organizations uncover a more comprehensive pool of candidates because it narrows the biases that occur during the screening and assessment stages of the recruitment process. AI-powered tools analyze the job description and include recommendations to make them more inclusive to further support diversity initiatives.

AI is also expected to make the recruitment process far more efficient by automating those time-consuming steps in the process, like manually scanning resumes and sending messages to candidates. Consequently, this frees up recruiters for more valuable tasks, such as building relationships with the top candidates and making strategic hiring decisions. Automation will, therefore, be able to reduce hiring times and costs and improve the quality of hire.

It could also be that AI provides such inputs that allow organizations to make more informed decisions while hiring. AI analyzes data from disparate sources and it surfaces patterns and trends that may go unnoticed by a human recruiter. This will make data-driven predictions more accurate on candidate success or improve candidate-job-role fit.

In all, AI has the potential to make recruitment a truly effective, data-driven, and inclusive process. At the same time, however, organizations must be sensitive to the legal complications arising from the use of AI in recruitment, particularly with respect to anti-discrimination legislation, transparency, and data privacy. If these complications could be overcome and the opportunities offered by AI seized, their recruitment would become better and improve along with better hiring outcomes.

AI IN PERFORMANCE MANAGEMENT

AI plays an increasingly critical role in performance management with tools and techniques that promise objectivity, efficiency, and predictability in employee performance appraisals. Performance management, over the years, has been the most challenging areas of human resource management; usually challenged on grounds of subjectivity and probable biases, being time-consuming for managers and employees alike. Therefore, AI can possibly help solve many of the problems by providing data-driven insights, automating routine activities, and enabling more personalized and continuous performance appraisals. On the other hand, the use of AI in performance management also raises several critical legal and ethical issues that organizations need to sort through with caution. The use of AI in performance management opens up a Pandora's box of legal issues, yet at the same time, it is an unprecedented opportunity to transform the very way organizations appraise and develop their talent pool. This section will cover applications of AI in performance management, the associated legal challenges, and opportunities for changing the way organizations assess and develop their workforce.

Applications of AI in Performance Management

AI can be potentially applied in different ways regarding performance management-from the setting of goals for performance, evaluation of outcomes of such performance, to providing feedback. Some of the most important applications are at performance appraisal, where AI algorithms analyze huge amounts of data on employee performance appraisals. For example, AI systems will analyze data from different sources such as productivity metrics, customer feedback, and peer reviews to create an all-round view about the performance of an employee. Aggregating and analyzing these data points, AI makes sure that human biases stay at bay, hence making assessments not only objective but also fair.

Another important feature of AI is that it enables continuous performance monitoring and feedback, thereby breaking with the mold of having annual reviews. With such AI-powered tools, the manager gets to have real-time insight into employee performance, thereby providing ample scope for timely and constructive feedback. These types of feedback loops help employees learn and grow at a much quicker pace but have the additional benefit of fostering an atmosphere of constant growth and learning. AI can also forecast patterns in performance data and enable organizations to proactively respond to issues, such as falling productivity or disengagement with their work, before they escalate into major problems.

Another critical use of AI in performance management is predictive analytics. AI can analyze historic performance data to predict future performance outcomes, enabling organizations to identify high-potential employees and those likely to underperform. These predictions enable HR managers to create more specific development programs, succession planning, and improvement plans that make sure the workforce receives support in those areas where it needs support. AI can also enable personalized performance management by providing tailored development needs and areas of improvement for every individual employee, along with recommending specific development activities or career tracks.

Legal Challenges

While AI has significant benefits for performance management, there are also a number of legal challenges arising from the use of AI that organizations will need to consider carefully. The first and foremost of these is potential bias in AI algorithms. While AI has the capability to reduce human biases in performance reviews, it also introduces new biases if the data on which the algorithms are trained is biased in and of itself. If historical performance data reflects systemic biases based on gender, race, or other protected characteristics, then the AI system using such data will perpetuate the biases in the evaluations it makes. This could also lead to legal liabilities from anti-discrimination laws, as discriminatory performance appraisals might affect decisions on promotion, salaries, and even termination of employees.

Another legal challenge develops around employee privacy and monitoring. Most AI performance monitoring applications naturally include the collection and analysis of employee activity, output, and communication in large amounts. This level of monitoring has raised many concerns about employee privacy, since most employees may not actually be aware of the extent or purpose of data gathering. Any use of AI by an organization for performance management has to be within the limits of the law on protection of data, such as the GDPR within the European Union, which calls for transparency and actual consent for processing. Furthermore, each organization has to make a grave moral judgment in regard to the use of AI for monitoring and evaluating employees-a balancing act between needs for knowledge related to employee performance and the autonomy/privacy of the employees.

Explainability of the AI performance reviews is another critical legal concern. Most of the AI systems are considered "black boxes" because the procedures of decision-making are complex or invisible to human insight. This lack of transparency is particularly problematic in the context of performance management, since it may create problems when AI-driven decisions are challenged on their merits, both by employees and even regulators. In other words, organizations have a duty to ensure AI algorithms used in performance management are interpretable, and they would be able to give clear explanations for the decisions they make. This is particularly the case for countries where employees can challenge appraisal decisions, or when regulatory bodies require organizations to prove the validity of their appraisal methods.

Opportunities

Despite these legal complications, AI affords many opportunities to enhance performance management practices. The most prominent opportunity relates to the possibility of achieving a more objective and equitable performance management system. AI operates with data-driven insights and doesn't apply subjective judgment, so this could reduce the impact of personal biases in performance evaluation. Such fairness applied will create better outcomes for all employees, including those from underrepresented groups, and it will help the organization build a more diverse and inclusive workforce.

AI also offers opportunities to enhance efficiency and effectiveness in processes related to performance management. With AI automating the routine tasks for data collection and analysis, HR professionals and managers can invest more time in strategic activities, coaching, and development. For sure, this will mean a way of enabling them to hold more meaningful and productive performance discussions now that as managers, they have access to real-time data and insights that inform their feedback. Also, continuous feedback that AI could enable would bring employees in line with organizational goals and enable them to make immediate changes in performance to create better overall performance outcomes.

Another opportunity to be made is around the personalization of performance management. AI has the ability to look at individual data from employees and find exactly where strengths are and weaknesses lie. Organizations can use this information to create development programs and career paths that best fit the employee at hand. This will lead to higher employee engagement and satisfaction, knowing their development is taken as an issue of importance by the organization. Also, with AI, organizations can spot high-potential employees with ease and help them develop further, so that they can handle leadership positions with ease.

In a nutshell, AI has the potential to actually revolutionize performance management by making it more data-driven, objective, and personalized. But the organizations will have to very carefully consider the legal challenges associated with its use, particularly those related to bias, privacy, and transparency. By actively working to address these challenges and leveraging the opportunities afforded by AI, an organization can build a much more effective and equitable performance management system-one that supports the growth and development of its workforce.

AI IN OTHER HUMAN RESOURCE MANAGEMENT FUNCTIONS

Artificial Intelligence is not only changing the face of recruitment and performance management, but it is highly influencing other HRM functions. In fact, adoption areas for AI in human resource management extend to include compensation and benefits management, employee training and development, and employee relations and engagement. The ability of AI to process large volumes of data, automate routine tasks, and provide valuable insights enables each of these functions to improve decision-making and overall HRM strategy. Yet all of these specific areas introduce very particular legal and ethical challenges with the integration of AI, raising substantial issues in terms of the ability of the organization to fully realize the benefits of AI while maintaining compliance with the law. This section examines some of the applications of AI within these HRM functions, the legal challenges they raise, and the opportunities they create for transforming HRM practices.

Compensation and Benefits Management

AI can help in effectively and efficiently managing compensation and benefits, which is a very critical HRM function directly linked with employee satisfaction and retention. AI-powered tools can analyze market data, organizational budgets, and employee performance metrics to help HR professionals come up with competitive compensation packages that are at par with industry standards and in line with organizational objectives. Example: AI automates the benchmarking of salaries and benefits to make sure competitiveness is not inequitable within the organization. AI can enable dynamic compensation for an organization by automatically adjusting based on real-time data to provide rapid responses to changes within the market or organizational priorities.

Another application of AI in the space is benefits management. AI can also help tailor benefits packages by analyzing employee preference, demographic, and usage patterns. For instance, AI may recommend a health and wellness program or retirement plan for a certain employee, considering age, lifestyle, and career stage. This level of personalization enhances satisfaction and engagement among employees, as benefits become more in line with their individual needs and preferences.

However, there are several legal complications that arise with the use of AI in managing compensation and benefits. Perhaps the most critical issue is related to the possibility that AI-driven compensation decisions are prejudicial. If the data the AI algorithms are trained on depicts historical pay differentials based on gender, race, or other characteristics that have protection from discrimination, then the AI system might further these biases by yielding inequitable pay practices. This exposes organizations to litigation on grounds of equal pay laws and anti-discrimination laws.

Secondly, there is no room for compromise with regard to transparency in AI-driven compensation decisions. It is most probable that employees and regulators may ask incisive questions when there are discrepancies in the manner in which decisions on compensation have been arrived at. The organizations will be bound to guarantee that their AI systems are not only non-discriminatory but also capable of furnishing understandable justifications for their decisions.

Employee Training and Development

AI is now going to further change the way employees are trained and developed, creating more customized and adaptive learning experiences than ever before. Traditional training programs adopt a one-size-fits-all approach that does not meet the diversified needs of employees who may be at varying levels of skill or different phases in their professional careers. AI tackles this challenge by considering unique employee data on past performance, learning preferences, and career goals to create personalized pathways in training. AI-powered learning platforms can recommend courses, resources, and activities that are identified to be aligned with specific employee development needs.

Even better, AI makes just-in-time learning a reality by providing employees with the right information or training at the exact time they need it. For instance, AI-powered platforms can offer employees relevant content when they engage in some new task or face any other challenge. In that way, they can understand through context. It not only makes the training highly relevant but also supports continuous learning and skill development-very much required in today's fast-changing work environment.

Legal Issues with AI in Training and Development: Data privacy and consent are the legal challenges associated with AI in training and development. Several AI mechanisms that are used for training require high levels of data on the employees themselves so that learning is more personalized. This would mean that organizations have to make sure that the collection, storage, and usage of this data are within the purview of regulations such as the GDPR or CCPA. Equally important, employees should understand how their information is to be used and that consent shall be sought where necessary. Besides, the trend raises ethical implications of allowing AI to decide career paths. While AI can make concrete recommendations, employers must ensure that the employees still take responsibility in making their choices concerning learning and development.

Employee Relations and Engagement

The importance of AI in employee relations and engagement, thus, helps the organization to know and respond to the needs and concerns of employees. Some of the most important usages of AI in this field involve sentiment analysis, whereby the AI tools analyze employee communications such as emails, survey responses, and social media posts as a way to measure the overall employee sentiment and predict problems. This will help the HR teams take necessary actions proactively, so that issues do not get out of hand, and hence improve satisfaction and reduce turnover.

AI might also catalyze employee engagement via more personalized and meaningful interactions between employees and HR. For example, AI-powered chatbots can handle routine inquiries to HR, provide employees with immediate answers to their questions, and even offer them personalized recommendations on benefits or training, or career opportunities. Such a tool would afford efficiency in the delivery of the services and make sure that it came at a time relevant for the employee.

Application of AI in employee relations and engagement, however, poses grave legal and ethical challenges. One of the major concerns is that AI will invade the privacy of employees. Like other forms of monitoring using AI, sentiment analysis may be perceived to be intrusive by employees, especially when they are less than fully aware of the extent to which their communications are being analyzed. The organizations should provide transparent data with respect to AI usage in these areas and take care of the privacy rights of employees, including informed consent wherever necessary, along with measures for sensitive employee data protection.

Another legal challenge is to ensure that the AI-driven engagement tools are deployed in such a manner that it generates, rather than undermines, trust between the employee and the organization. If employees feel the methods are invasive or too controlling, the AI tool will break the trust, which is doubtless counterproductive to ensure good engagement and morale. Organizations have to consider acutely the ethical implications of engaging AI in employee relations and engagements and try using such tools to enhance rather than detract from the experience of the employee.

Opportunities

The integration of AI into these HRM functions offers enormous opportunities for organizations to enhance their HR practices and improve employee outcomes. In compensation and benefits management, AI offers the potential to create more competitive and equitable compensation packages, improving employee retention and satisfaction. In training and development, AI can provide personalized learning experiences that support continuous skill development and career growth. Similarly, AI in employee relations and engagement helps an organization better understand

and deliver on the needs of employees, building a far more positive, supportive environment in the workplace.

By capitalizing on AI, the organization can also have more meaningful insights into the workforce, thus making quite reasonable decisions and strategy formulation. For example, AI would help in highlighting the trend and patterns of data relating to employees, such as what makes them perform very well or leave the company. These insights then become the basis of HR strategies and initiatives for better outcomes on both sides.

This means that with the huge opportunities for various enhancements in HRM functions, AI presents unique legal and ethical challenges that raise serious concerns. Organizations have to make sure their uses of AI are non-discriminatory, transparent, and respectful of the rights of employees. By overcoming these challenges and grasping the opportunities that come out of AI, organizations are able to shape appropriate, efficient, and employee-oriented human resource practices to ensure organizational success.

Ethical Issues

The use of AI in human resource management is a matter of growing relevance, and for which ethical consideration will always be required. Different advantages exist with the use of AI, such as increased efficiency, better decision-making, and potentially lower bias in decision-making. However, it also raises very important ethical issues that should be addressed by organizations. The concerns involve issues on fairness, transparency, privacy, accountability, and the impact of AI on the human element of HRM. In this section, we look at the ethical issues that arise in integrating AI into HRM, majorly in areas relating to recruitment and performance management, among other HR functions. We will also discuss strategies that organizations can adapt to navigate these ethical challenges to ensure the responsible and ethical use of AI (Wang, 2023).

FAIRNESS AND BIAS

One of the grimmest ethical issues of AI in HRM pertains to bias and unfair treatment. Usually, the use of an AI system is meant to diminish biases from a human element; however, such systems actually can carry on and increase current biases if not treated with care. AI algorithms are learning from data, and if that data reflects one or another biased practice-gender, racial, or age discrimination-the AI system may reflect the very same biases in decisions (Singh & Chouhan, 2023). For example, an AI system trained on biased historical data of hiring people from certain demographic groups might continue to show preference for candidates from those groups, thus indulging in discriminatory hiring practices (Khair et al., 2020).

Thus, the ethical issue in this regard is not only related to whether or not such practices are within legal boundaries but also encompasses the justice and equity elements through AI-driven human resource management. Organizations must be sure that their AI systems are trained by diverse representative data sets and also audited regularly to identify and mitigate biases. In addition, a range of teams need to be involved in the development and implementation of the AI systems so that various perspectives go into their creation and potential biases are resolved early in the process (Malik et al., 2020).

TRANSPARENCY AND EXPLAINABILITY

Yet another important ethical aspect is transparency and explainability with respect to AI systems as used in human resource management. Most AI algorithms, in particular those using machine learning, can often behave like a "black box" in which the process of decision-making is hardly intelligible to human beings. Such a lack of transparency may be problematic for HRM, considering the potentials for wide-ranging impacts on the career paths of individuals through hiring, promotion, or terminations (Kaushal et al., 2023). Therefore, employees and candidates might feel that they are being exposed to untransparent, potentially unfair decision-making processes and, therefore, cannot trust the organization.

Due to this ethical issue, organizations should make their AI systems explainable; the decisions of AI need to be transparent and understandable by the ones affected. Employees should be entitled with the right to know the behind-the-scenes mechanics of the decision-making process driven by AI and how those decisions will influence their current or future employment status or career development. The right to transparency not only covers technical transparency but also clarity on the use of AI in HR processes and what variables are used to make decisions (Sabil et al., 2023).

Privacy and Data Protection

Most of the AI applications in HRM involve collecting and analyzing vast volumes of personal information, thus creating serious ethical issues related to privacy and data protection. AI systems may analyze data from résumés and social media profiles, performance metrics, and even biometric data gathered from video interviews or workplace monitoring systems. This information may be able to yield gold for HRM, but collection and usage need to be treated with the utmost care in the protection of the privacy rights of employees (Singh & Chouhan, 2023).

Organizations have to ensure that their AI applications comply with relevant data protection laws: from the General Data Protection Regulation (GDPR) in the European Union to the California Consumer Privacy Act (CCPA) in the United States. This involves obtaining informed consent from employees and candidates prior to collecting their data, disclosing the purpose for which that data is used, and taking adequate security measures to avoid unauthorized access or hacking. In addition, organizations must weigh the ethics related to employing AI to monitor employees by balancing the need for data-driven insights with respect for employee autonomy and privacy (Wang, 2023).

Accountability and Responsibility

Accountability and responsibility issues, then, become increasingly relevant as AI systems make more and more HRM decisions independently. If there is a faulty or biased decision on the part of an AI system, who is held responsible-the developers of the algorithm, the HR professionals who implemented it, or the organization itself? These are questions showing the need for clear accountability structures when using AI in HRM.

The organization should ensure human oversight over the AI systems, particularly at those junctures of critical decisions related to hiring, performance appraisal, and disciplinary actions. AI must support human judgment rather than replace it. The identified role of AI is to provide data-driven insight in support of the human decision-maker. Where AI-driven decisions have potentially far-reaching implications for individuals, an appeal or review by human managers must be in place. By doing so, it ensures that workers shall have an opportunity to appeal in case they are treated unfairly by the AI system and that the organization remains liable for the actions of their AI tools (Budhwar et al., 2022).

IMPACT ON THE HUMAN ELEMENT OF HRM

The increasing role of AI in HRM is a cause for concern regarding its impact on the human element of human resources. Since HRM is essentially about managing people, building relationships, and fostering a positive organizational culture, there is a lurking fear that over-reliance on AI would eventually dehumanize HR processes where decisions are based on algorithms rather than human emphatic feelings or understanding (Malik et al., 2020).

For example, automated systems tasked with recruitment, performance evaluation, or employee engagement may replace valuable human contact between employees and HR professionals. This may promote a sense of alienation in the employees, who may feel they are being regarded merely as data rather than living, breathing individuals with their own unique experiences and needs.

In balancing this ethical issue, an organization should strive to have a balance in the place of AI and human interaction in HRM. AI should serve to complement and enhance the human aspects of HR. For instance, while AI is able to provide immense data and insight, it is very important not to eradicate the human element of HR in decision-making processes or interaction with employees personally. Organizations should also be committed to training HR professionals for effective collaboration with AI to ensure that these professionals make use of the tools of AI in a manner complementary, rather than corrosive, to the human part of HRM (Sabil et al., 2023).

Ethical AI Practices

Organizations will have to apply an identifiable set of ethical AI practices in negotiating the attendant ethical challenges that come with AI in HRM. These include:

1. Inclusive Development: Diverse teams shall be involved at the development and implementation stage of AI systems, so diverse viewpoints may be taken into consideration and any prospective biases come forward and be resolved.
2. Regular Audits: Regular audits of the AI systems should be conducted to find and eliminate biases, ensuring fairness, as well as compliance with legal and ethical standards.
3. Transparency: AI-driven decisions should be transparent and explainable, and the employees should be clearly communicated about AI's role in the HR processes.
4. Data Protection: Provide adequate protection through data protection mechanisms and regulatory requirements.
5. Human Oversight: Ensure continued human oversight over AI systems, especially at every point of critical decision-making, and provide an opportunity to appeal or review the AI-driven decisions.
6. Balance of Artificial Intelligence and Human Interaction: Aim for a proper balance in the application of AI with meaningful human interactions in the HRM process by ensuring that AI serves to support, not replace, the human aspect of HR.

Therefore, though AI offers significant benefits for HRM, it also raises severe ethical issues based on which organizations should take imperative action. The adoption of ethical AI practices within an organization can allow organizations to exploit the power of AI in strengthening HRM and ensure that the usage of AI is non-discriminatory, fair, and transparent with full respect for employee rights and dignity.

Regulatory Landscape

The integration of Artificial Intelligence into HRM presents a regulatory environment that is increasingly complex and dynamic, in which organizations find themselves. Considering the burgeoning AI-driven technologies in recruitment, performance management, and other areas falling under HR, there is an increasing need for regulatory frameworks that address unique legal and ethical challenges presented by such technologies (Gupta, 2024). The landscape of AI regulation in the realm of HRM stretches widely, from data protection and anti-discrimination to accountability, transparency, and observance of current labor laws, among others. This section examines the general regulatory landscape, significant legislation that impacts AI in HRM, emerging trends in AI regulation, and implications for organizations as they move toward the implementation of AI in their organizational HR practices (Malik et al., 2020).

DATA PROTECTION AND PRIVACY REGULATIONS

The most pertinent regulatory issues of AI in human resource management relate to data protection and privacy. In general, AI systems used for most human resource processes require immense volumes of personal data, such as sensitive information with respect to demographic details, work performance metrics, and even biometric data. Such information is gathered, stored, and processed under strict data protection regulations, which also vary from one jurisdiction to another (Mohammed, 2020).

The General Data Protection Regulation (GDPR), enacted by the European Union, is one of the broadest-reaching laws on data protection that influence AI in human resource management. The GDPR has imposed rigid obligations on organizations with respect to the collection and processing of personal data. It requires explicit consent from the individual whose data needs to be collected, information must be clearly given regarding the purpose of data use, and any storage has to be secure. Equally, GDPR allows access to one's data upon request, correction, or even deletion-the "right to be forgotten." (GDPR, 2016).

In this respect, AI in HRM within the ambit of GDPR demands that organizations institute a system to ensure transparency in the processing of information by AI systems regarding employees and candidates. In particular, it calls for explanations to be given for each AI-driven decision that has a significant consequence on a person's life, say hiring or termination. Moreover, organizations should put in place strict security controls against data breach and frequently review the use of AI systems with a view to ensuring that data minimization and purpose limitation in the principles under GDPR are observed.

The California Consumer Privacy Act, applicable to businesses operating in California, will also have great implications for AI in HRM. Similar to the GDPR, the CCPA grants rights of transparency, allowing an individual to know what personal information is collected, whom it is shared with, and for what purpose. The CCPA also provides rights to opt out from the sale of one's personal information and rights to erasure. Organisations using AI in HRM will need to be transparent regarding data processing and provide individual mechanisms to exercise privacy rights under CCPA compliance (Harding et al., 2019).

Beyond the GDPR and CCPA, other nations are also crafting or updating their data protection laws in response to issues raised by AI. For example, Canada's *Personal Information Protection and Electronic Documents Act (PIPEDA)* and Brazil's *Lei Geral de Proteção de Dados (LGPD)* also impose manifold requirements with respect to collecting, processing, and securing personal information relevant to AI driven HRM practices.

Anti-Discrimination and Equal Opportunity Laws

AI plays a part in human resource management that coincides with anti-discrimination and equal opportunity laws, especially in the recruitment process and performance management. This is put in place to avoid partiality in favor of ensuring that all people have equal opportunities regarding jobs, whether it be for their race, gender, age, disability, or other protected grounds (Hasnas, 2002).

For instance, the US Government prohibits employment discrimination, under Title VII of the Civil Rights Act, against race, color, religion, sex, and national origin. *The Americans with Disabilities Act (ADA)* and *the Age Discrimination in Employment Act (ADEA)* further prohibit discrimination based on a person's disability and age, respectively. The *Equal Employment Opportunity Commission (EEOC)* enforces these laws and issues guidance on how they apply to AI-driven HR practices.

Organizations using AI in human resource management must adhere to anti-discrimination legislation. If not carefully curated and monitored, AI systems may perpetuate biases either from the past data or from the algorithm itself. This could be something like an AI-powered recruitment tool, trained on biased data that may affect certain groups of demography at a disadvantage. The only way to minimize this risk is by undertaking regular audits, which would help such organizations detect and rectify all biases within their AI systems. They should also use different representative training data and take into consideration the expected effects of AI-driven decisions on protected groups.

The European Equal Treatment Framework Directive 2000/78/EC prohibits discrimination in employment based on religion or belief, disability, age, or sexual orientation. The directive does apply to AI-driven HRM practices; hence, organizations are supposed to ensure their AI systems do not lead to discriminatory outcomes. The regulators in the EU have highlighted the need for equity and transparency in AI; there is still a debate on whether specific regulations of AI are required regarding discrimination and bias (Malik & Rai, 2022).

EMERGING AI-SPECIFIC REGULATIONS

New legislation specific to AI will continue to emerge. As AI continues to develop, there is a growing consensus that regulations uniquely tailored to AI are necessary given the peculiar challenges and risks posed by this technology. A number of jurisdictions are currently developing or bringing into force legislation which specifically covers AI, and these have considerable ramifications for its use in HRM (Schuett et al., 2024).

The latest frontrunner in AI regulation is the European Union with the proposed *Artificial Intelligence Act.* The bill would create a general regulatory framework for AI by categorizing different AI systems according to the level of risk involved and thereby imposing specific requirements. High-risk AI systems, including those applied in employment, such as recruitment and performance management tools, will be subjected to stricter regulations. These may cover transparency, human oversight, and management of risks. It also aims at preventing discrimination, making the AI system non-discriminatory and fair. In the United States, the debate on the regulation of AI is hot, and a proper balance is sought between innovation and the need for safeguards against the risks from AI (Clarke, 2019). No comprehensive federal regulation of AI has been done so far, but several state initiatives and sector-specific guidelines are developing. For example, in *New York City, Local Law 144* of 2021 regulates the use of AI to make hiring and promotion decisions. It requires employers to conduct annual bias audits and to notify candidates if AI is used in making decisions about their candidacy. the *National Institute of Standards and Technology (NIST)* has published a voluntary *AI Risk Management Framework* that guides the development and use of AI at the national level in ways that are fair, transparent, and accountable.

Other countries, such as Canada and Australia, are likewise working toward AI-specific regulations with the intention of ensuring systems using AI are utilized in a responsible and ethical manner. Most of these regulations make provisions for data protection, transparency, prohibition on bias, and discrimination.

Compliance and Accountability

The complexity of the regulatory landscape with regard to AI in HRM calls for proactive steps by organizations to ensure that compliance applies with regard to applicable laws and regulations. This will entail the establishment of robust governance frameworks to take on ethical and legal challenges of AI. Organisations should outline clear lines of accountability with regard to artificial intelligence systems, ensuring that human oversight of activities is assured and AI-driven decisions could be reviewed and challenged (Sabil et al., 2023).

Organizations will also be required to keep themselves updated on the emerging regulatory developments in AI and develop practices that conform to the same. This could mean routine auditing of AI systems, reviewing policies on data protection, and training HR professionals on the ethical-legal dimensions of AI.

Besides, organizations should implement the use of best practices on ethical AI use in human resources management. This will involve institution guidelines on AI ethics, impact assessments, and consultations with stakeholders, including employees, in ways that make certain that AI use is consistent with organizational values and the rights of employees (Chowdhury et al., 2023).

Global Considerations

With multinational organizations, the regulatory complexity for AI in HRM further increases because of the variation in stringency across different jurisdictions. In this respect, organizations will have to address the challenge of multiple regulatory frameworks, commanding their own rules on data protection, anti-discrimination, and AI governance. This will require coordinated AI governance, taking local regulations into consideration while maintaining a consistent global approach (Malik et al., 2020).

Not all regulations stop at the border, and organizations should be aware that multinational organizations may be in violation, for example, of the GDPR even when processing data from EU citizens outside of the EU. Much as the CCPA has implications for organizations conducting business with California residents even if those organizations are based outside of California.

These challenges can be managed by organizations through the development of region-specific policies for AI and the use of flexibility in the design of AI systems to suit different regulatory requirements. This may be done through consultations with local legal and compliance experts who will be able to review and understand the constant changes in the regulatory environment and update AI practices accordingly (Hmoud, 2021).

The regulatory landscape around AI is very dynamic, and it has enormous implications for organizations willing to apply AI in their HR practices. Maintaining data protection laws, anti-discrimination legislation, and any other AI-specific frameworks put forward by various countries will be key to encouraging responsible adoption of AI within HRM. It thus requires organizations to be proactive in treading through this complex landscape by putting in place robust governance frameworks, periodic audits, and keeping themselves updated on regulatory developments. In that manner, it would allow them to leverage the full potential of AI in HRM while reducing legal risks and maintaining ethical standards (Lawler & Elliot, 1993).

BEST PRACTICES FOR LEGAL COMPLIANCE AND RISK MITIGATION

While more and more organizations are adopting the use of AI for HRM, it indeed remains important that legality is ensured and risks mitigated to avoid legal, ethical, and reputational problems. Application areas of AI in HRM range from recruitment and performance management to other HR functions that must be aligned with existing legal frameworks while considering emerging regulations. This section will discuss best practices that organizations can institute to ensure they are in not only the letter but the spirit of the relevant laws, which also sometimes provide a risk-mitigating framework on the use of AI in HRM (Chowdhury et al., 2023).

Perform Impact Assessments Extensively

The impact assessments, legal and ethical implications, and operational consequences need to be taken into consideration by organizations before the actual implementation of AI systems in managing human resources. Impact assessment in AI involves assessment on intended use of the AI system, risks that come with it, and compliance with regulatory requirements.

Legal Impact Assessment: In addition, an organization should assess compliance of an AI system with applicable law, including data protection regulations, anti-discrimination laws, and employment laws. Such a process should ensure that legal risks be identified and an AI system be designed from its inception to meet legal standards.

Ethical Impact Assessment: Beyond the legal compliances, organizations need to assess the ethical implications of AI use in HRM. These relate to examining potential biases, discrimination, and violation of privacy, with specific attention to making sure that the working of AI is non-discriminatory and fair.

Operational Impact Assessment: There is a need to understand how the AI system will integrate into prevailing HR processes. Every organization should determine whether this AI tool will complement and enhance or disrupt prevailing practices and whether employees and HR professionals are ready to work with AI.

These assessments help the organization to identify, well in advance, some of the legal and ethical pitfalls that may occur at an early stage of the implementation process and make necessary adjustments either to the AI system or in its deployment strategy (Singh & Chouhan, 2023).

Implement Transparent and Explainable AI

Transparency and explainability are desirable features that would make AI systems in HRM function within the rule of law and be trusted by employees. Explainable AI is defined as a class of AI systems designed to enable a clear and understandable explanation of their decision-making processes.

- **Model Explainability:** There should be interpretability within the AI models in the organization. This means that HR professionals and employees can understand how the AI system arrives at a certain decision, such as why this candidate was chosen or why this employee was given this appraisal rating. This is not only important for building trust but also for many regulatory requirements, such as the General Data Protection Regulation, which calls for explanations of automated decisions (Sipahi & Artantaş, 2022).
- **Communication:** Other than technical transparency, an organization should learn to communicate accurately with its employees and candidates regarding the role AI plays in HRM. That is to say, proper provision by management for information regarding the use of AI concerning decision-making, the type of data collected, and how these will be used needs to be made. Clear communication can alleviate apprehension and create a better perception of the new AI-driven processes of human resource management (Kaushal et al., 2023).
- **Auditability:** AI systems are auditable; the organization is able to track and replay the decisions made by AI systems. This therefore enhances the capability to investigate and resolve problems arising as bias or errors that might arise in decision-making. Regular auditing of AI systems can be an assurance of their continued compliance with legal and ethical standards.

Regularly Monitor and Audit of AI Systems

Continuous monitoring and auditing are quite necessary in making the AI systems keep up their compliance with the legal requirements and ethical standards over time. Indeed, the AI systems can actually evolve, while they process more data over time, leading to some changes in their behavior and outputs. Auditing regularly facilitates the detection and correction of unintended consequences that might occur due to the emergence of bias or a drift in performance.

Bias Audits: Bias audits should be periodically performed by organizations to ensure AI systems do not result in disadvantage for any group based on protected characteristics such as race, gender, and age. Bias audits are reviews of outputs from AI-driven decisions that aim to find and mitigate discriminating patterns whenever they exist (Kaushal et al., 2023).

Performance Audits: These test whether the AI system continues to return accurate and unbiased results over time. This, in fact, constitutes testing accuracy, consistency, and fairness of the AI system in making decisions of an HR nature.

Compliancy Audits: Regular audits for compliancy will keep the AI system current with emerging changes to legislation and regulation. The audits must be driven by independent Legal that have deep knowledge in AI and data protection laws to ensure the company's AI practices meet all requirements (Sipahi & Artantaş, 2022).

Foster a Culture of Responsible AI Use

The building of an organizational culture of responsibility in the use of AI is, therefore, a question of legal compliance and mitigation of risks. This means informing and training employees, and even more so HR professionals, on ethical and legal issues regarding AI in human resource management.

Employee Training: Organizations should periodically train HR professionals and other stakeholders in responsible use of AI. It should encompass training on identification and addressing possible biases, understanding obligations pertaining to protection of data, and interpreting AI-driven decisions.

Ethics committees and AI Governance: An ethics committee or AI governance board can help with the guidance of the responsible use of AI in the organization. They might oversee the development, implementation, and ongoing use of AI systems to make sure that it aligns with organizational values and complies with legal and ethical standards (Sabil et al., 2023).

Employee Involvement: The creation of a forum for discussion on the use of AI in HRM would be another conduit toward assurance from employees that the AI system will not violate their rights in any form. The organization should therefore accord the employees channels of expressing concerns or giving feedback concerning AI-driven HR functions.

Collaborate with Legal and Compliance Experts

With the somewhat complex regulatory landscape of AI in HRM, organizations should be working closely with legal and compliance experts throughout the full life of an AI system. For example, a legal expert can advise on how to manage the regulatory environment to ensure that the AI system meets the relevant code of laws and regulations right from the design phase through its deployment and beyond (Singh & Chouhan, 2023).

Legal Consultation: It is at this development phase that an AI system should involve legal experts to foresee potential legal risks. Such experts will advise on data protection, anti-discrimination laws, and other regulatory requirements that have to be observed while designing AI-driven HR processes.

Ongoing Legal Support: In the context of constantly developing regulations, ongoing legal support is necessary to maintain an organization operating within the bounds of the law in respect of AI. This might include updating the AI systems with changes in the law, or it could be in terms of modifying the processes of HR in dealing with new challenges arising due to regulations.

Third-Party Audits and Certifications: Where applicable, third-party audits or certifications may assist in validating the organization's AI practices. Third-party audits would further assure the stakeholders that the AI system is operating within the rule of law and other ethical standards.

Establish a Risk Management Framework

Without an appropriate risk management framework, it would be a structured way for organizations to identify, assess, and mitigate risks arising due to AI applications in HRM. The framework should encompass the whole lifecycle of AI: development and implementation up to ongoing use and monitoring (Tewari & Pant, 2020).

- **The identified risks:** Any risk management framework should ensure the identification of the potential risks posed by AI in HRM. This is to include, but not be limited to, legal risk related to breaching data protection legislation and the ethical risk, including bias and violation of privacy.
- **Risk Assessment:** After identifying such risks, an organization is under obligation to assess the impact and likelihood of such occurrences. This includes the severity assessment of each risk, prioritizing those that would have greater consequences for the organization and employees.

- **Risk Mitigation Strategies**: In relation to the above, an organization should devise strategies on how to mitigate these risks after assessing them. These could be strategies touching on deeper levels of safeguards on data protection, detection of bias, and mechanisms for human oversight.

Risk Monitoring: It means the implementation of continuous monitoring with respect to AI systems in order for the identified risks to be managed accordingly, and the new ones to be considered on time. Organizations should regularly go through a risk management framework, updating it in view of the evolution of the AI system, the evolution of the regulatory environment, or changes in the organizational context (Vrontis et al., 2023).

Adopt Privacy by Design and Default

Privacy by design and by default consist of a series of principles an organization should be embedding in their AI systems right from the very beginning. The whole approach in this method is to make privacy integral to the design and operations of the AI system, rather than an afterthought (Singh & Chouhan, 2023).

- **Data Minimization:** Organizations should adopt data minimization; organizations should collect only data that is strictly necessary for the operation of the AI system. This greatly reduces the effects in case of violation of privacy and, together with other measures, may help comply with data protection regulations such as the GDPR.
- **Consent:** This is the very first fundamental step-informed consent from employees and candidates. It means clear information should be provided on what data will be collected, for what purpose, and what are the rights of individuals regarding their data.
- **Anonymization and Pseudonymization:** Whenever possible, an organization should adopt anonymization or pseudonymization techniques to mask the identity of a person in data processed through AI systems. This reduces many privacy breaches and ensures data security to a great extent (Wheeler & Buckley, 2021).

LEVERAGE AI ETHICS FRAMEWORKS AND GUIDELINES

Ethics frameworks and guidelines on AI can be particularly useful to guide organizations in the responsible and ethically correct use of their AI systems for HRM. Many government bodies, industry associations, and academic institutions have been involved in developing these frameworks for use as best practices or guiding principles in the said ethics application of AI.

- **Adopt Industry Standards:** Organizations can adapt the use of industry standards related to AI ethics. These may include **IEEE Global Initiative on Ethics of Autonomous and Intelligent Systems** or the **OECD AI Principles,** that provide some standard in the foundations for responsible use of AI to help guide organizations in developing ethical AI practices.
- **Internal AI Ethics Guideline:** Apart from adopting external frameworks, organizations may also design internal AI ethics guidelines that best suit the context and needs of their situations. In this regard, the guidelines must state the organizational commitment towards ethical use of AI along with clear directives as to how HR professionals and other stakeholders shall act (Sabil et al., 2023).

The legal compliance and mitigation of risks in using AI in the HRM process are best ensured through a proactive multi-faceted approach. Such impact assessments, if done on a broad basis, together with the implementation of transparent and explainable AI, frequent auditing of AI systems, instilling a culture of responsible AI use, collaboration with legal experts, development of a risk management framework, application of privacy by design, and use of AI ethics frameworks will enable organizations to stay ahead of the regulatory curve (Kaushal et al., 2023). It helps the organization avoid legal risks but also contributes to building trust among employees, candidates, and other stakeholders in AI-driven HR processes (Wheeler & Buckley, 2021).

FUTURE DIRECTIONS

As AI continues to evolve, with further integration into Human Resource Management, the future promises to be a landscape of both opportunities and challenges. The future trajectory of AI in HRM will be shaped by the interplay between technological changes, new and evolving legal frameworks, and shifting organizational imperatives (Chowdhury et al., 2023). In this section we consider some of the possible future directions for AI in HRM by looking ahead to expected advances in AI technologies, legal and ethical issues that will be raised, and how organizations can work to position themselves for success in this dynamic environment.

Advances in AI Technologies

The future of AI in HRM will be marked by huge steps forward in AI technologies, including ML, NLP, and predictive analytics. These will result in even more sophisticated and precise AI systems that can address very complex HR tasks with greater precision and efficiency.

- **AI-driven talent management** involves systems that will, in the future, make talent management more personalized, precise, and actionable through insight into employee performance, career development, and retention strategies. Advanced tools leveraging AI may review reams of data to tease out patterns and trends that shape strategic human resources decisions, like identifying who may be a flight risk or illuminating those who hold high leadership potential (Basu et al., 2023).
- **Improved Employee Experience:** AI contribution to employee experience will grow further. Future AI systems are likely to provide more intuitive and personalized interfaces, such as AI virtual assistants, which in the future may possibly provide real-time support for employee inquiries, or AI-owered learning and development platforms, tailored according to individual needs. Such systems will create a more interactive and responsive HR environment, hence improving employee satisfaction and productivity (Strohmeier & Piazza, 2015).
- **AI for diversity and inclusion** can have an increased scope in the near future for organizations to make these concepts effective. Such advanced AI tools may assist in locating and reducing unconscious bias in recruitment, performance evaluation, and promotion. AI evaluates language patterns, behavioral data, and other signals to build fair and more inclusive workplaces and help HR professionals in such a process (Sabil et al., 2023).

Shifting Legal Landscapes

While AI is becoming imbibed within most HRM practices, legal landscapes also continue to evolve with new challenges and work out how AI in HR can conform to the emerging sets of regulations. A few trends are foreseen to influence the future legal frameworks that will be circumventing AI in HRM (Singh & Chouhan, 2023).

- **AI-Specific Legislation**: One such thing to watch in the future will be government AI-specific legislation in many parts of the world. These AI-specific laws may intend to address some of the unique challenges brought about by AI technologies, such as issues related to transparency, accountability, and non-discrimination in AI-driven decision-making processes. For example, such regulations can require that AI systems be explainable, that AI algorithms be well-documented, and the AI decisions be free of bias and non-discriminatory (Sipahi & Artantaş, 2022).

- **Data protection and privacy**: With the growing tendency of AI systems to rely on voluminous amounts of personal information, data protection and privacy laws will remain key to influencing AI use in HRM. Future regulations may enact more stringent thresholds on data collection, storage, and processing; based on explicit consent by employees and candidates. This will require organizations to keep pace with such changes through sound data protection and adherence to global standards of data privacy (Lawler & Elliot, 1993).
- **International Harmonization of AI Regulations:** The global nature of AI technology will also heighten the probability of harmonization in respect of AI regulations across jurisdictions. Jointly, international organizations and respective regulatory bodies will move towards harmonization by developing standardized guidelines and best practices for AI in HRM. The end result of such harmonization is that organizations can operate with ease across countries with consistent compliance concerning AI-related laws (Malik et al., 2020).

Ethical Considerations and Responsible Use of AI

The ethical implications of AI in HRM will continue to be one of the points of discussion and development. The increasingly sophisticated abilities of AI systems will require more comprehensive organizational approaches to ensuring ethical use of AI (Budhwar et al., 2022).

- **Ethical AI frameworks:** In the time to come, more articulated ethical frameworks related to AI and specific to industry can be developed. Those frameworks will address algorithmic biases, lack of bias, transparency, and their responsible use of employees' data. Organizations may have to commit their practices in AI accordingly with these frameworks to show faith in the ethical use of AI for trustworthiness among employees and stakeholders (Chowdhury et al., 2023).
- **AI Accountability Mechanisms:** The greater the autonomy of AI systems, the greater will be the need for accountability mechanisms that ensure AI-driven decisions are justifiable and susceptible to review. Indeed, in the near future, AI systems are expected to embed in accountability features such as automated auditing tools and decision logs, enabling an organization to track and review AI decisions (Hmoud, 2021). These mechanisms will be of para-

mount importance in addressing questions related to AI's impact on employee rights and ensuring that AI-driven HR processes are realized with fairness and transparency.

- **Employee Empowerment and Participation:** The future may see a shift toward greater employee empowerment and participation in AI-driven human resources processes. Policies and tools may develop in organizations that empower employees to exercise greater control over how their work lives are impacted by AI. These rights might include provisions to review and contest AI-driven decisions or rights to consent on the usage of one's personal data within the system. This will go a long way in building trust and ensuring, even as limits on AI use are developed, one will not hamper respect for employee autonomy and agency (Kaushal et al., 2023).

PREPARING ORGANIZATIONS FOR THE FUTURE OF AI IN HRM

To this end, organizations must ensure that they lead the way in managing the future of AI in HRM through proactive strategies that could hopefully prepare them for all emerging trends and challenges. In fact, a number of areas will be fundamental to ensuring that organizations remain competitive in an increasingly changing landscape (Tambe et al., 2019).

- **Continuous Learning and Adaptation:** In the light of continued changes in the AI ecosystem, both in terms of technologies and regulations, an organization would have to commit itself to continuous learning and adaptation. This will be in respect of keeping abreast of fresh developments in the area of AI, continued training of its HR people, and periodic refreshing of its AI systems with fresh capacities that would meet emerging legal and ethical standards. An organization culturally attuned to continuous learning would therefore be better placed to achieve the potential value from AI by mitigating its risks (Tewari & Pant, 2020).
- **AI Governance through Collaboration:** Effective governance of AI will pervade throughout an organization, from the HR department to the legal departments, and IT and data management. An organization may incorporate cross-functional AI governance committees or working groups overseeing the development, implementation, and monitoring of AI systems in HRM. This could help in collaborative efforts toward ensuring that AI systems are utilised responsibly and as intended within the values and goals of the organization (Vrontis et al., 2023).

- **Strategic Partnerships and Ecosystem Engagement:** In the future, AI in HRM will probably be developed with increasing active participation of external partners such as vendors of AI systems, academic institutions, and regulatory bodies. The organizations will benefit by entering into strategic partnerships which guarantee the latest availability of state-of-the-art AI technologies, research insights, and guidance on regulatory issues. Engagement with the wider AI ecosystem helps an organization to keep up to date with AI innovation and emerging standards (Wheeler & Buckley, 2021).
- **Human-Centered AI Design:** With the continuous change that AI is bringing into how HRM operates, investments by organizations into human-centered AI design principles will increase. The lurking sentiment here is to design such AI systems that enhance human judgment and decision-making rather than replacing them. Future AI systems in HRM should support HR professionals with informed, empathetic, and fair decisions rather than leaning wholly on a wholly automated process. A human-centered design of AI can help organizations have more ethical, transparent, and organizationally value-oriented AI-driven HR processes (Arslan et al., 2022).

The future of AI in HRM is bright and has a lot of potential for changing how organizations manage human resources. Along with the advancement of AI technologies, organizations will also have to deal with the complex and continuously changing landscape of legal, ethical, and operational challenges. From being abreast of the latest in technology to newer legislation and best practices for using ethical AI, an organization will, therefore, be able to extract optimum value from AI on its journey of innovation and enhancing HR outcomes (Basu et al., 2023). Going forward, a delicate balance between leveraging AI's potential with due consideration of legal principles, ethics, and needs of employees would be the key. Clearly, organizations that will succeed at this will be well-placed to lead the future of HRM in this, the age of AI (Budhwar et al., 2022).

CONCLUSION

With Artificial Intelligence now fully integrated into human resource management, it brings very transformative potential, thus enabling significant enhancement in all human resource processes, starting from recruitment and performance management to the broader HR functions. This integration, however, is not without complex legal, ethical, and operational challenges that organizations have to address if they are to realize the full benefits of AI while safeguarding their employees' rights and appeals, and maintaining regulatory standards.

AI applied to HRM has the potential to optimize many functions of HR. In recruitment, AI may further facilitate the process of hiring, enhance candidate matching, and reduce biases, thus making the hiring process more efficient and equitable. On performance management, AI enables data-driven insight, objective evaluations, and continuous feedback, thereby enhancing employee development and organizational performance. Moreover, the role of AI in other HR functions, including employee engagement and learning, ushers in avenues for more personalized and responsive HR experiences that will drive higher levels of employee satisfaction and productivity.

Despite all these benefits, the deployment of AI into the realm of HRM is not without challenges. Legal compliance is of utmost importance because the AI systems should be aligned with the prevailing data protection regulations, anti-discrimination laws, and employment standards. If the regulatory environment happens to be evolving, it requires organizations to commit themselves to being informed of any new legal requirements and that these types of AI systems are developed and used in a way which will comply with such requirements. The failure on an organization's part to comply with legal requirements will lead to significant penalties and reputational damage.

Ethical considerations are also a basis on which AI shall be deployed responsibly within HRM. There are issues related to algorithmic bias, transparency, and data privacy that have to be addressed in order not to create unwarranted adverse impacts. Organizations should implement such practices that make the AI systems operate in a nondiscriminatory and transparent fashion, and ensure that employee data is dealt with according to the highest standards of privacy and security. Setting up ethical AI frameworks, auditing on a continuous basis, and embedding a culture of responsible usage of AI is some of the key steps toward mitigating ethical risks and fostering trust among employees and stakeholders.

The future of AI in HRM is set to take shape from continuous changes in technology matched by continuous changes in the legal framework that governs the application of technology. New emergent AI technologies will accord a hitherto unparalleled degree of sophistication and accuracy to HR solutions, while the new regulations will tackle the challenges thrown up by AI. Organizations preparing for these changes must adopt proactive strategies that ensure continuous learning, collaborative AI governance, and human-centered AI design. Agility and responsiveness will help organizations capitalize on AI's potential for improving HR practices without losing sight of compliance and ethical integrity.

In sum, AI integration in HRM is an opportunity for innovation and improvement in organizational HR processes. Such integration, however, needs to be pursued and addressed with caution in view of the attendant legal, ethical, and operational challenges. Hence, organizations that can enable these challenges and apply best practices have much to gain from the capabilities of AI but also contribute to a fairer and more responsible use of technologies within a workplace. The journey of AI-enhanced HRM is continuous adaptation and adherence to standards of ethics; hence, those who are in this journey stand at a better chance to take the lead in this future of HR.

REFERENCES

Arslan, A., Cooper, C., Khan, Z., Golgeci, I., & Ali, I. (2022). Artificial intelligence and human workers interaction at team level: A conceptual assessment of the challenges and potential HRM strategies. *International Journal of Manpower*, *43*(1), 75–88.

Basu, S., Majumdar, B., Mukherjee, K., Munjal, S., & Palaksha, C. (2023). Artificial intelligence–HRM interactions and outcomes: A systematic review and causal configurational explanation. *Human Resource Management Review*, *33*(1), 100893.

Budhwar, P., Malik, A., De Silva, M. T., & Thevisuthan, P. (2022). Artificial intelligence–challenges and opportunities for international HRM: A review and research agenda. *International Journal of Human Resource Management*, *33*(6), 1065–1097.

Chowdhury, S., Dey, P., Joel-Edgar, S., Bhattacharya, S., Rodriguez-Espindola, O., Abadie, A., & Truong, L. (2023). Unlocking the value of artificial intelligence in human resource management through AI capability framework. *Human Resource Management Review*, *33*(1), 100899.

Clarke, R. (2019). Regulatory alternatives for AI. *Computer Law & Security Review*, *35*(4), 398–409.

GDPR, G. D. P. R. (2016). General data protection regulation. *Regulation (EU) 2016/679 of the European Parliament and of the Council of 27 April 2016 on the protection of natural persons with regard to the processing of personal data and on the free movement of such data, and repealing Directive 95/46/EC.*

Gupta, R. (2024). Impact of Artificial Intelligence (AI) on Human Resource Management (HRM). *International Journal For Multidisciplinary Research, doi, 10.*

Harding, E. L., Vanto, J. J., Clark, R., Hannah Ji, L., & Ainsworth, S. C. (2019). Understanding the scope and impact of the california consumer privacy act of 2018. *Journal of Data Protection & Privacy*, *2*(3), 234–253.

Hasnas, J. (2002). Equal opportunity, affirmative action, and the anti-discrimination principle: The philosophical basis for the legal prohibition of discrimination. *Fordham Law Review*, *71*, 423.

Hmoud, B. (2021). The adoption of artificial intelligence in human resource management and the role of human resources. [). Wydawnictwo Naukowe Akademii WSB.]. *Forum Scientiae Oeconomia*, *9*(1), 105–118.

Kaushal, N., Kaurav, R. P. S., Sivathanu, B., & Kaushik, N. (2023). Artificial intelligence and HRM: Identifying future research Agenda using systematic literature review and bibliometric analysis. *Management Review Quarterly*, *73*(2), 455–493.

Khair, M. A., Mahadasa, R., Tuli, F. A., & Ande, J. R. P. K. (2020). Beyond Human Judgment: Exploring the Impact of Artificial Intelligence on HR Decision-Making Efficiency and Fairness. *Global Disclosure of Economics and Business*, *9*(2), 163–176.

Lawler, J. J., & Elliot, R. (1993, June). Artificial intelligence in HRM: an experimental study of an expert system. In *Proceedings of the 1993 conference on Computer personnel research* (pp. 473-480).

Malik, A., & Rai, G. C. (2022). Need Of Laws For Anti-Discrimination And Equal Opportunity. *Cosmos: An International Journal of Art and Higher Education*, *11*(2), 61–66.

Malik, A., Srikanth, N. R., & Budhwar, P. (2020). Digitisation, artificial intelligence (AI) and HRM. *Human resource management: Strategic and international perspectives, 88*, 103.

Malik, A., Srikanth, N. R., & Budhwar, P. (2020). Digitisation, artificial intelligence (AI) and HRM. *Human resource management: Strategic and international perspectives, 88*, 103.

Mohammed, M. A. (2020). Ethical Implications of AI Adoption in HRM: Balancing Automation with Human Values. *NEXG AI Review of America*, *1*(1), 1–15.

Sabil, S., Bangkara, B. A., Mogea, T., Niswan, E., & Timotius, E. (2023). Identification of HRM Improvement Strategy Using Artificial Intelligence in Modern Economic Development. *International Journal of Professional Business Review: Int. J. Prof. Bus. Rev.*, *8*(6), 10.

Schuett, J., Anderljung, M., Carlier, A., Koessler, L., & Garfinkel, B. (2024). From principles to rules: A regulatory approach for frontier AI. *arXiv preprint arXiv:2407.07300*.

Singh, A., & Chouhan, T. (2023). Artificial intelligence in HRM: role of emotional–social intelligence and future work skill. In *The Adoption and Effect of Artificial Intelligence on Human Resources Management, Part A* (pp. 175-196). Emerald Publishing Limited.

Sipahi, E., & Artantaş, E. (2022). Artificial intelligence in HRM. *Handbook of Research on Innovative Management Using AI in Industry 5.0*, 1-18.

Strohmeier, S., & Piazza, F. (2015). Artificial intelligence techniques in human resource management—a conceptual exploration. *Intelligent Techniques in Engineering Management: Theory and Applications*, 149-172.

Tambe, P., Cappelli, P., & Yakubovich, V. (2019). Artificial intelligence in human resources management: Challenges and a path forward. *California Management Review*, *61*(4), 15–42.

Tewari, I., & Pant, M. (2020, December). Artificial intelligence reshaping human resource management: A review. In *2020 IEEE international conference on advent trends in multidisciplinary research and innovation (ICATMRI)* (pp. 1-4). IEEE.

Vrontis, D., Christofi, M., Pereira, V., Tarba, S., Makrides, A., & Trichina, E. (2023). Artificial intelligence, robotics, advanced technologies and human resource management: a systematic review. *Artificial intelligence and international HRM*, 172-201.

Wang, Q. (2023). The Impact of AI on Organizational Employees: A Literature Review. *Journal of Education. Humanities and Social Sciences*, *19*, 45–53.

Wheeler, A. R., & Buckley, M. R. (2021). The current state of HRM with automation, artificial intelligence, and machine learning. In *HR without People?* (pp. 45–67). Emerald Publishing Limited.

Chapter 5
Impact of Globalization in HRM Reforms

Shivani Dhand
https://orcid.org/0000-0002-4809-1365
Mittal School of Business, India

Jeayaram Subramanian
JGBS, O.P. Jindal Global University, India

Damith Gangodawilage
https://orcid.org/0000-0001-7968-6284
Qasim Ibrahim School of Business, Villa College, Maldives

Thi Minh Ngoc Luu
https://orcid.org/0000-0002-5972-7752
International School, Vietnam National University, Hanoi, Vietnam

ABSTRACT

This chapter examines the impact of globalization on Human Resource Management (HRM) reforms, highlighting the challenges and opportunities organizations face in a rapidly changing global landscape. It explores key areas such as global talent management, diversity and inclusion, labor laws, HR technology, training and development, compensation, and ethical considerations. As organizations expand internationally, they must navigate cultural differences, regulatory compliance, and the integration of advanced technologies to optimize their HR practices. The chapter also discusses future trends, emphasizing the importance of employee well-being, corporate social responsibility, and agile HR strategies. By understanding these dynamics, HR professionals can develop effective strategies to foster inclusive and adaptable work environments that thrive in a globalized economy.

DOI: 10.4018/979-8-3693-5390-5.ch005

INTRODUCTION

Globalization has dramatically transformed the nature of business, changing a local market into an interconnected network across the world. These changes and their implications on HRM have transformed the very direction in which organizations must adapt their strategies for managing this more diverse, mobile, and technologically advanced workforce . (Al Ariss et al., 2014). Companies, therefore, cannot remain confined within the borders of nations; they have to operate within a world of people, cultures, and legal systems across borders and continents. As a result, HRM had to become more strategically focused-from its erstwhile administrative role-so as to gain global competitiveness and operational efficiency (Budhwar & Debrah, 2013).

In a nutshell, globalization of markets is creating a rationale for reforms in HRM; the organizations are seeking to converge practices while remaining sensitive to local differences. Recruitment, talent management, compensation, and employee development are no longer an issue of one geographical context. Companies have to think about attracting talent from a global pool, manage teams across cultures, and ensure compliance with labor laws and regulations across various jurisdictions. These challenges require adaptable HRM approaches that are in tandem with the strategic global goals of an organization (Cascio & Boudreau, 2016).

Furthermore, globalization had brought out the necessity for diversity and inclusion at work. Increasingly multinational, a workforce more necessitates the need to ensure environments where cultural differences are respected, yet this can still ensure cohesion and collaboration. This shifted the HRM policy from just being an efficiency agenda and rather to a 'supportive and inclusive workplace culture'. In this respect, the roles that are played by the HR professionals now are far more than cultural sensitivity, but also involve international labour law expertise, as well as international leadership development, highlighting HRM as the process of integration into globalization (Collings & Mellahi, 2009).

This chapter discusses the impact of globalization on HRM reforms, particularly how the developments in globalization have modified the human capital management of organizations. Specifically, this chapter delves into talent acquisition and employee development, compensation strategies, and labor relations, which shall be provided further with an examination to discern the transformations globalization has made to these key HRM functions and the future of it (DeNisi & Murphy, 2017).

HISTORICAL BACKGROUND OF HRM AND GLOBALIZATION

Human Resource Management (HRM) Before Globalization

During the pre-globalization period, the HRM functioned mainly in a national context. It was dominated by narrow and administrative functions such as payroll, employee relations, and adherence to the labour laws of the region. During this stage, HRM was viewed as a back office support function that cared little about the strategy of an organization. Companies were largely geographically bound, and the sourcing of human resources and management were strictly anchored on local talent pools. The scope of HR policies and practices was strictly confined within the domestic labor markets, cultural norms, and national employment legislations, and thus international factors played negligible roles. The emphasis was on internal efficiencies rather than global scale external competitiveness (Dowling et al., 2017).

Since the firms mainly served their local or national markets, the workforce was typically uniform and not much diversity was required to be appreciated or accommodated through cultural and diversity training. The training and development programs were primarily compliance and technical skill enhancements appropriate to the local industry situation. Performance management and compensation also fitted national norms since they resembled local economic sentiments and labor market dynamics. This era of HRM was reactive in nature, looking to address the short-term operational concerns rather than holding a foresight perspective about a broad, long-term impact from changing global markets (Farndale et al., 2010).

The Emergence of Globalization and Its Initial Influence on HRM

The last decades of the 20th century marked the beginning of a new age for HRM and was a resultant of these forces that engineered the globalization movement. As the means of communication and transportation improved, with technology bringing in its wake to the means of expansion and making it easier for business organizations to be transborder, the MNCs started to appear. Thus it led to a complete change in HR practices as this global expansion of companies required more dynamic as well as strategic management of human resources. HRM thus evolved from the traditional administrative role into an integral organizational strategy, since business organizations required an international vision for survival in international markets (Friedman, 2014).

At this stage, the companies faced issues with managing the dispersed and diverse workforce. The onset of globalization ushered new complexities for the HR professionals, including talent from different countries, understanding multiple legal frameworks and workers with differences in culture. Organizations that now operated across wider territories beyond their native lands needed a balance between the required standardization of HR policies and tailoring that was required to meet the demands of the locality. This period also witnessed the beginning of HRM changing from a purely efficiency orientation to innovation, leadership, and cross-cultural competencies (Ghemawat, 2016).

Key Milestones in HRM Reforms Driven by Globalization

Globalization spurred the acceleration of HRM reforms in the latter half of the 20th century and the early years of the 21st century. A few important events converged to form the human capital of present-day management. The most crucial reform initiated global talent management strategies. As business expansion worldwide rose, so did the knowledge that talent acquisition had to draw from a global pool. It led to the setting up of global recruitment practice and expatriate programs. Companies began sending employees across borders, and multinational companies increased the demand for stronger expat and repatriation procedures, as support is required for successful adaptation to other cultures and work environments (Hofstede et al., 2010).

The growing salience of diversity and inclusion in working practices was another hallmark-the growing heterogeneity of workforces at each level, brought about by globalization. HRM policies increasingly started to reflect the necessity of developing cultural sensitivity and incorporating diverse perspectives into the organizational fabric of the company. On the contrary, a force driving the international practices of human resource is harmonization of the labor law and emergence of international standards of labor highly advocated for by bodies like International Labour Organization, ILO. The reforms were done to strike equality and justice at workplace irrespective of borders and ensured uniformity in labor standards around the world without demurring the legal framework of a place (International Labour Organization, 2020).

Technological advancements also mattered a great deal in this regard: the development of digital tools and Human Resource Information Systems (HRIS) made it easier and faster for multinational enterprises to control their international employees while aggregating the data and harmonizing all HR processes from various countries. This technological development helped the HR departments become more data-driven by analyzing analytics for talent management, performance evaluation, and employee engagement strategies across international boundaries (Jackson & Ruderman, 2018).

The historical context of HRM and globalization depicts a transformation from an administratively localized function to a strategic global discipline. Globalization has challenged the sphere of HRM, compelling it to expand skills and competencies to new challenges and opportunities to transform the way the organization manages its workforce and positions HR at the head of global business success (Janssens & Steyaert, 2019).

GLOBAL TALENT MANAGEMENT

Globalization has expanded the horizon of talent management so greatly that organizations are forced to take the most strategic and international approach toward selection, development, and actual retention of employees. Since companies operate across various countries, it is impossible for them to survive in such a competitive global economy without bringing in the best talent from around the world. This has resulted in global talent management, a very important element of Human Resource Management that incorporates finding, developing, and retaining high potentials that emerge through boundaries. Organizations have to operate in complex labor markets, legal systems, and cultural contexts to ensure they can attract and retain the best global talents (Kaufman, 2014).

Attracting and Retaining Global Talent

Global talent recruitments represent their unique share of challenges and opportunities for HR professionals. The biggest challenge, perhaps, is to win the global competition for the best talent in the world. This is an increasingly nomadic world as skilled professionals can work anywhere-and for any organization around the world-compelling organizations to differentiate themselves as employers of choice. This competition has sent the companies scrambling to come up with various creative strategies to attract the top talent across the globe, including competitive compensation packages, flexible working arrangements, and strong employer branding that is culturally resonant (Kshetri, 2018).

This requires a workplace with diversity and inclusion, and people get valued, respected, and engaged. For this purpose, today, employee engagement surveys, mentorship programmes, and leadership development initiatives have become critical for loyalty building and reducing turnover of global employees (Meyer, 2017).

Global Recruitment, Selection, and Onboarding

To do international recruiting, HR has to adjust its strategy according to the needs of a local market and maintain a uniform global framework for talent acquisition. International recruiting is all about knowing the subtleties of various labor markets-that is, the availability of talent in one country and local employment laws, cultural norms and expectations in another. Most firms have adapted the centralize with localize hiring model between the centralized strategy and localized operationalization for such issues. For example, though the international recruitments may follow only one policy, locally, the organization teams that are part of an HR department may be allowed to come up with their own recruitment policies tailored to meet specific requirements of their local environment (Noe et al., 2021).

In selection, it is also at this point where talent choice becomes crucial. Organizations have to evaluate these candidates in relation to skills and experience which can be acquired, but also as to whether they will fit a particular culture and change into a global work setup. Cross-cultural competence and language skills plus the ability to work in diverse teams have become the cornerstones of success for global assignments. Most organizations have incorporated rigorous selection processes, including assessment centers and behavioral interviewing, to ensure that individuals are globally prepared to support international operations (Parry & Tyson, 2019).

In addition to the above, onboarding global recruits is yet another challenge. Global firms need to design their onboarding program in such a way that while it would mitigate regional cultural and operational differences, it should work towards a unified organizational culture. Cross cultural training, relocating support, and the integration of expatriate employees in new conditions would be part of it. Effective onboarding programs ensure newly recruited employees, whoever is local or international, is supported and aligned with the missions and values of the organization right from day one (Punnett, 2018).

Cross-Border Talent Mobility and Expatriation Challenges

Employee mobility is one of the vital aspects of global talent management, with particular emphasis on expatriation programs. Expatriation involves the temporary or permanent transfer of an employee to another country either due to significant reasons such as filling critical roles, supervising local teams, or gaining international experience. Even though expatriate assignments have immense benefits in the form of professional development and inter-regional knowledge transfer, they pose massive challenges for the organization as well as the expatriate employee (Robbins & Judge, 2020).

The support that should originate from the HR department, for example, in the form of relocation help, cultural training, and language training, may not resolve the problems he or she is likely to encounter relating to getting along with the new culture. This essentially increases the risks of assignment failure or preterm return. To minimize these risks, companies have begun to be more concerned with preassignment evaluation, cultural training, and continuous support during the process of expatriation (Schuler et al., 2011).

In addition to expatriation, HR practitioners are now more concerned with in-patriation-assigning employees from foreign subsidiaries to the headquarters as a substitute for filling assignments in order to benefit from gaining experience and reinforcing the relationship between the home and host offices. Both expatriation and inpatriation management are a double-edged sword for the HR teams: having to deal with the pragmatic concerns and emotional issues regarding cross-border mobility while keeping workers feeling appreciated and cared for in their global assignments (Stahl et al., 2012).

Developing and Retaining Global Leaders

The increased demand for leaders who can manage across borders is manifold as companies continue to expand globally. It is high time that developing international leaders with negotiating and managing skill complexity cross global markets became very essential for talent management worldwide. Such people are adept at managing divergent teams, are culturally sensitive, and lead by a mindset of globalization. To meet this demand, organizations have created comprehensive leadership development programs through international assignment, cross-cultural training, and mentoring (Stone et al., 2015).

Companies that invest in leadership development and give career-enabling opportunities are able to hang onto their best talent. It is equally a part of succession planning, whereby organizations prepare to have leaders for critical positions as the company expands into new markets (Ulrich et al., 2012).

It would require the HR professionals to develop new strategies for talent attraction and development and for retaining a global workforce; challenges of cross-border recruitment, selection, and mobility need to be placed at the forefront. By making a diverse workforce feel valued and included, companies can enhance their global competitiveness and develop a leadership pipeline that can thrive in an interconnected world (Al Ariss et al., 2014).

Diversity and Inclusion in a Globalized Workforce

As the geographical boundaries continue to break down due to globalization, organizations are increasingly working in multicultural environments; therefore, D&I forms an integral part of an organization's HRM strategy. In this regard, D&I has transformed globalization into a new mechanism where companies must deal with employees from different countries who come with their cultural norms and expectations. Embracing diversity and fostering inclusion are going to be ways companies will succeed in the present global market because of the enhancement of innovation, employee engagement, and organizational performance (Brewster et al., 2016).

The Importance of Diversity in a Globalized Workforce

There are various benefits to organizations as a result of diversity when working with a globalized workforce. A diverse group of people provides a wider perspective and a diverse pool of ideas as well as methodological inputs while trying to solve a problem that would make an organization come across and offer its services to other clients coming from diverse backgrounds. It is even more important because the expansion of businesses into another region also demands knowledge of local customs and preferences for a competitive advantage (Budhwar & Debrah, 2013).

In addition to that, diverse teams generate innovation since they challenge traditional thinking. Through work on a project, individuals who have different experiences and points of view are more likely to develop original solutions and foster innovation. Researchers have found that that diverse teams outperform homogeneous teams in decisions and in related innovation tasks. Hence, one can say that diversity is not just a moral requirement but also an organizational prerogative for corporations working globally (Cascio & Boudreau, 2016).

Diversity alone does not suffice; therefore, it needs to be mixed up with inclusion. Inclusion is that where every employee of the organization from diverse backgrounds is valued, and he or she gets equal opportunities and resources. On the other hand, if diversity is not blended with inclusion, then it would eventually result in the inhibition of organizational performance through being disengaged, conflicted and misunderstand by employees. That's why making an inclusive work culture is as important as to achieve diversity (Collings & Mellahi, 2009).

THE ROLE OF HR IN PROMOTING INCLUSION

In a globalized workforce, there is a lot that HR can do to champion inclusion for the employees. Design policies and practices that make every employee valued, respected, and included begins at the base with recruitment and hiring practices that recruit diverse candidates. The HR department may need to ensure that job postings are inclusive as inadvertent exclusion through job posting should not be done. Now, recruitment strategies have to tap into wider sources of talent, including non-traditional channels and outreach to underrepresented groups (DeNisi & Murphy, 2017).

Once diverse talent is brought into the organization, HR professionals need to empower the organization to be hospitable to everyone and to help them succeed in their workplace. Training programs with cultural awareness and sensitivity need to be developed and implemented to equip employees with the requisite skill to navigate cross-cultural interaction successfully. Cultural competency training is important for global-level corporations because it helps employees appreciate the difference in communication styles and social and work practices between cultures (Dowling et al., 2017).

Equally, the HR departments should ensure policies that aim at creating fair opportunities for every member in the organizations. This means processes to achieve promotion and allowances plus development to be clearly spelt out and transparent. There should also be no systemic barriers that would mean groups of workers are unable to advance. Exploration of mentorship initiatives, employee resource groups, and leadership training may further enhance the development of an underrepresented employee as they may receive equitable growth opportunity and promotion opportunities to that of their peers (Farndale et al., 2010).

Addressing Cultural Differences and Cross-Cultural Management

One of the major challenges in managing diversity as part of the globalized workforce is dealing with the impact of cultural difference. The modern-day worker comes from different cultural backgrounds, which may reflect contrasting styles of communication, ethics, and attitude towards authority. For instance, direct communication and assertiveness will be appreciated the most in some cultures. Conversely, indirect communication and subordination to the authorities would be highly appreciated in other cultures. Such an outcome may sometimes lead to misunderstandings and conflicts if not managed well (Friedman, 2014).

HR professionals play an important role in managing across cultures. Hence, they empower the managers and employees to work really effectively across cultures by providing cultural awareness training that will make an employee aware of and respect the differences in numerous cultures. HR makes it possible for managers to have resources for managing diverse teams. HR can promote such practices as cross-cultural mentorship and team-building activities that foster collaboration and understanding among employees from varying backgrounds (Ghemawat, 2016).

Besides, the HR departments should develop an inclusive culture where the employees feel comfortable in presenting their cultural identity. An organization can encourage its employees to share their cultural traditions and values and share with one another their different viewpoints. Corporations can celebrate cultural diversity through activities such as international days, cultural exchange programs, or diversity and inclusion weeks meant to show the various cultures that comprise their workforce (Hofstede et al., 2010).

The Business Case for Inclusion in a Global Workforce

Besides the imperative moral argument, there is a powerful business case for creating an inclusive workforce in a global context. Furthermore, workplaces that are inclusive also attract the best talent because candidates make diversity and inclusion concerns even more central to their decisions of which work environment to join (International Labour Organization, 2020).

Having inclusion at work in a global team can help overcome cultural boundaries and promote effective collaboration, making companies better able to take full advantage of their diverse workforce to drive performance and competitive advantage in global markets. (Jackson & Ruderman, 2018).

Overcoming Barriers to Inclusion

Even though the benefits of diversity and inclusion are clear, a number of hurdles surface ahead of the organization that needs to be crossed in order to have an inclusive workplace. The first hurdle is the unconscious bias. Often described as being blind to many things, unconscious bias can trigger discriminatory behavior in an individual despite him not intending it. The role of the HR department would be to establish programs to raise awareness of unconscious bias and strategies on how to overcome such unconscious biases while recruiting or promoting staff or in communicating daily with others (Janssens & Steyaert, 2019).

Targeted mentorship schemes or leadership training could also address the issue by targeting high-potential employees with diverse backgrounds. Hiring and promotion practices should have equity and transparency (Kaufman, 2014).

Finally, distances of place and culture create an extreme difficulty in cultivating a homogeneous, integrated culture across global organizations. The HR departments will have to develop this by creating open communication channels for the regions to be mutually cooperative with collaboration among the members and a common purpose and value system (Kshetri, 2018).

More importantly, human resource plays a critical role in ensuring that diversity is not only achieved but also an inclusive environment where all employees can be valued and have a chance to contribute to its success. For the effective utilization of global workforce, organizations must address cultural differences, provide inclusive policies, and overcome barriers (Meyer, 2017).

IMPACT OF GLOBALIZATION ON LABOR LAWS AND EMPLOYMENT POLICIES

Globalization has changed labor laws and employment policies globally, and therefore, has offered organizations and laborers some advantages and disadvantages. As corporations operate across boundaries, national labor rules, employment legislations, and international norms form a maze to move through. Generally speaking, the effects of globalization on labor legislation and employment policies manifest in three crucial aspects: the convergence or harmonization of regulations, the emergence of international labor standards, and the flexibility with workers' rights (Noe et al., 2021).

Harmonization of Labor Laws and Employment Standards

This complexity has called for a drive toward harmonizing the labor legislations to present more standardized employment practices, especially within the trade blocs, such as the European Union (EU), North American Free Trade Agreement (NAFTA), and the Association of Southeast Asian Nations (ASEAN) (Parry & Tyson, 2019).

The directives also set minimum standards that are to be integrated in each country, and thus produces much greater uniformity of labor protections across Europe. This harmonization is beneficial both to employers and employees, reduces compliance costs for businesses that operate in several countries, yet it enables the various countries to ensure that each worker's basic rights and protections are preserved (Punnett, 2018)

The Role of International Organizations in Shaping Labor Policies

International organizations include, among others, the International Labour Organization (ILO), the World Trade Organization (WTO), and the United Nations (UN). Such organisations have shaped labor laws in a globalized world. Such standards are expected to ensure a leveled playing ground of workers around the globe, which would do away with practices such as forced labor and child labor, all the while attempting to promote fair treatment of employees across kinds of industries (Schuler et al., 2011).

Labor provisions also form part of trade agreements and oblige signatory countries to adhere to certain labor standards, which hence gives a rise in global norms in a local legal framework (Stahl et al., 2012). That has led to a double-edged sword: to raise labor standards protecting workers in a globalized world, and then to enforce them in different national contexts (Stone et al., 2015).

Employment Flexibility vs. Workers' Rights

Globalization has also influenced labor laws through creating increased demands for labor flexibility. Since companies compete in a very dynamic and competitive global marketplace, they sometimes require greater flexibility in hiring, in terms of when it is safe to hire; in firing, in terms of when it is safe to let go; and in managing the workforce. This has led to various non-traditional forms of employment, such as temporary contracts, part-time work, or freelance and gig work. Flexible forms of employment will thus enable companies to adapt quite rapidly to fluctuations in the market and manage labor costs better, especially in sectors such as technology, logistics, and services (Ulrich et al., 2012), job stability or rights to collective bargaining are two such benefits. In fact, globalization has sometimes led to labour market deregulation so that companies can bypass traditional labor laws designed to protect full-time workers more easily (Al Ariss et al., 2014).For example, the European Union has the "Directive on Transparent and Predictable Working Conditions," which is intended to protect job security for gig and temporary workers through providing the right of access to fundamental rights, such as paid leave and protection against unfair dismissal (Brewster et al., 2016).

Improved labour market competitiveness is attained but now concerns arise as to the vulnerability of workers, especially in sectors where exploitation would most probably occur, like agriculture and manufacturing (Budhwar & Debrah, 2013).

The Gig Economy and New Employment Models

Globalization is an important driver of the gig economy as profoundly affecting labor laws and employment policies throughout the world. In general, this type of work is defined as a labor market characterized by the predominance of short-term contracts or freelance work as opposed to permanent job positions. Gig workers-the majority being independent contractors-dont qualify for employee benefits such as health care coverage, retirement plans, or paid leave, sparking controversies over some reforms asked by some experts on labor laws (Cascio & Boudreau, 2016).

With labor reforms that redefine employment relations, various countries are now moving to correct the balance posed by a growing gig economy. For example, in the UK and the United States, courts have ruled that some gig workers should be reclassified as employees, hence allowing access to labor protections and even other accompanying benefits. Other countries are working toward new legal categories of providing a minimum level of rights to gig workers without being fully categorized as employees (Collings & Mellahi, 2009).

As the sector continues to develop, governments will need to adjust labor laws to care for workers in this new sector but to keep it flexible because that is what makes gig work attractive to both workers and employers (DeNisi & Murphy, 2017).

Labor Law Compliance in Global Supply Chains

Globalization has, for the first time, focused attention on labor law compliance in global supply chains. In any scenario where companies outsource most of their production to countries that are offering low-cost enterprise, it is a serious cause for concern that labor rights have been abused in the factories of the suppliers. There are however several areas where complaint erupts as regards poor working conditions, remunerations and worker safeguards that create stronger demands for accountability and transparency among global supply chains (Dowling et al., 2017).

To address these concerns, many companies have welcomed codes of conduct and CSR initiatives that bind them to ethical labor practices in supply chains. Generally, such codes oblige suppliers to adhere to minimum labor standards, including wages, hours of work, health and safety, and child labor. Some companies also practice periodic auditing of suppliers for such compliance (Farndale et al., 2010). The UK Modern Slavery Act and the French Duty of Vigilance Law are among such legislation that is aimed at ensuring accountability for labor rights violations in company's supply chains (Friedman, 2014).

In some instances, this violation does not reach reports when there are documented agreements formalized by the respective companies in respect to ethical practices. Thus, globalization has necessitated a call for more awareness concerning the demands for the adoption of more enforceable and effective international frameworks and partnerships that should facilitate the protection of workers (Ghemawat, 2016).

Moreover, supply chain globalizations also resulted in labor rights violations in different outsourced productions. With globalization, more expedited by new technologies, governments, organizations, and other stakeholders must work together in formulating labor policies that will integrate economic competition with workers' rights to have a just and fair global workforce (Hofstede et al., 2010).

Digital Transformation of HRM

Globalization has caused the process of digital transformation in HR functions to become rapid, and therefore, it is an absolute necessity for organizations to integrate technology in the effective management of their dispersed workforce. Centralized solutions will include HR technology platforms, which are better known as Human Resource Information Systems (HRIS) and Human Capital Management (HCM) systems. They provide assistance with employee data, payroll, benefits, and compliance across multiple countries. Some of the systems even provide live access to your employees' information across global workforce trends, cross-border compliance management, and consistency in HR practices (Jackson & Ruderman, 2018).

For MNCs, this digital transition has turned out to be very necessary for standardizing their practices with respect to HR functions across various locations in the world. With cloud-based HR platforms, firms ensured that hiring, compensation, and performance evaluation policies are being followed uniformly across locations so that the firm would not be opaqueness and in adherence to the law in every location while driving the corporate culture of the organization to unify the regions involved. (Janssens & Steyaert, 2019)

Talent Acquisition and Artificial Intelligence

The biggest changes brought about by HR technology in terms of globalization are possibly by ensuring talent acquisition transforms through the use of artificial intelligence, machine learning, and many more. These digital platforms enabled companies to tap wider global pools of talent, reaching the very best candidates in the world. AI-driven recruitment tools transformed how organizations source, screen, and select talent since such tools automatically execute tasks like resume screening, candidate matching, and initial interview scheduling (Kshetri, 2018).

AI algorithms can scan numerous resumes in less than a few seconds. This implies that, easily, it will pick the resumes of those applicants who fall under the specific criteria for the job. The hours a company might spend scrutinizing resumes manually might drop by far as such systems will scan through social media profiles, online portfolios, and professional networks to seek out someone's skills and fit in an organization. Another way AI tools are used to facilitate hiring is during initial video interviews. Using NLP, AI software assesses candidates' communication skills and their responses to streamline recruitment procedures (Meyer, 2017).

In the international setting, AI-based solutions help bridge geographical distance in acquiring talent. Because offshoring is an increasingly significant phenomenon in today's world due to globalization, organizations can connect with talent from remote regions or locations without worrying about distances. Although it expands the pool of available talent to the optimum mix of diverse talent in organizations, it promotes more in-house diversity that helps dissolve typical climaxes often confined to homogeneous groups based on personal background, habits, behavior, and rationalization (Noe et al., 2021).

But on the flip side of making use of AI for recruitment are the issues of bias and fairness. Efficiency improvements are a sure bet on the agenda list of AI, but the algorithms may unwittingly propagate biases that exist within old data or even in the design of the system built. As companies go global with AI-based HR technologies, they must also ensure that the incorporated products have inclusive, unbiased data, which are audited from time to time to avoid discriminatory practices (Parry & Tyson, 2019).

Data-Driven Decision Making and Predictive Analytics

Globalization has not only heightened the diversification but also the complexity of managing a workforce geographically distant from the company. Decisions must be driven by data; and, in the contemporary business environment, HR technology, especially big data analytics, is capable of giving the HR manager so much insight about the behavior, performance, or engagement of the employees of an organization across different regions. More specifically, predictive analytics gives an organization sufficient information to predict workforce trends so that it can take proactive decisions about the high turnover rate, skills gaps, or declining productivity in any region (Punnett, 2018).

For example, a predictive analytics solution can process volumes of historical data to reveal its HR teams patterns on the attrition rate by identifying the functionalities with a high risk of losing employees. Similarly, analytics tools can assist organizations identify skill shortages in specific places and may adjust their talent development and training programs accordingly. This capability has strong significance in a globalized environment where workforce trends and skills demands vary highly across different markets (Robbins & Judge, 2020).

With this avenue of data analytics, it then becomes possible to assess the effectiveness of a company's global HR strategy. Based on analysis of employee engagement, job satisfaction, and performance data, companies can assess what sort of impact their policies have in particular regions and accordingly make changes so that they align with local cultural as well as organizational demands. This data-driven approach then helps HR teams align their practices with market-specific demands while keeping overall operations in sync with corporate objectives (Schuler et al., 2011).

Improving the Employee Experience through Remote Work During globalization of business operations and HR technology, the focus has been increasingly on improving the employee experience in the fields related to remote work. As more businesses engage in hybrid and remote work models, HR technologies will take center stage to drive engagement, communication, and employees' well-being across borders. Digital platforms created for employee engagement, such as collaboration tools, learning management systems (LMS), and virtual wellness programs, make it possible for organizations to host an entire working environment for employees spread all over (Stahl et al., 2012).

All these platforms enable employees to collaborate in real time, access resources for professional development, and participate in company-wide initiatives despite their geographic location. For instance, just through Slack, Microsoft Teams, and Zoom, people can communicate and collaborate across time zones, which makes it easier for global teams to work together. Moreover, LMS provides the ability to gain access to training and development opportunities that are vital for the growth of a global workforce (Stone et al., 2015).

Indeed, HR technology enables businesses to monitor and care for the well-being of their employees through virtual wellness programs and digital health platforms. Companies will know the employee's work-life balance, mental health, and ultimate job satisfaction status. Therefore, remote workers are taken care of and part of the organization. Such tools help businesses design an excellent employee experience, encouraging more engagement and productivity, even when working in a distributed setting (Ulrich et al., 2012).

Employee Experience and Remote Work

A compliance management system across a globalized workforce is indeed quite trying because the organization has to comply with different laws of labor, tax, and employment standards in different regions. HR technology can simplify compliance by giving real-time access to updates in the legal arena, automating payroll and benefits administration, and ensuring the alignment of employment practices with regional requirements. Most of the HR platforms have integrated compliance features that would enable an organization to navigate the different complexities of labor laws across different regions with reduced risks of non-compliance (Al Ariss et al., 2014).

For example, global HR platforms can update tax rates, minimum wage requirements, and social security contributions automatically based on the location of the employee. Such systems also help manage visas, work permits, and other legal documentation needed for international hires. Organizations will thus minimize risks from legal penalties as well as ensure compliance with local regulations (Brewster et al., 2016).

More importantly, technology can help organizations deal with data privacy and security risks - one of the most salient concerns in this increasingly globalized workforce. Organizations can be expected to follow laws and regulations about their employees' data, especially now that the General Data Protection Regulation (GDPR) by the European Union has recently been enforced. HR software equipped with strong encryption and privacy features help an organization keep sensitive information about their employees confidential, thus reducing the danger of data breaches or legal cases (Budhwar & Debrah, 2013).

HR technology has been so transformative for organizations regarding their global workforce in this globalization era. It's all the way from AI-driven recruitment and predictive analytics to cloud-based HR systems and employee engagement platforms- all of which help businesses simplify HR processes, make more informed decisions, and improve work experience across borders. As globalization continues to fuel the growth of multinational operations, HR technology will increasingly have to play a very significant role in helping organizations grapple with the intricacies of global compliance, workforce management, and talent development to remain competitive in the global marketplace (Cascio & Boudreau, 2016).

Training and Development in a Global Context

In an economy characterized by globalization, the role of training and development has acquired a new importance in the organizational operational philosophy as it expands to operate through borders and expand its workforce. This requirement for a diverse, highly skilled and adaptable workforce becomes essential for maintaining a competitive edge in the global markets, as are training and development programs for employees. The uniqueness of the challenges also demands improvement in the technical and soft skills of employees, with due consideration to the challenges arising from cultural differences and varied regulatory environments as well as the ever-accelerating pace of technological change (Collings & Mellahi, 2009).

CROSS-CULTURAL TRAINING AND GLOBAL COMPETENCY DEVELOPMENT

Thus, the essence of training and development lies in preparing employees to work effectively within a global system. With the globalization of business, various aspects of business have been developed differently in different regions. As such, employees often work along with colleagues, clients, and partners belonging to different cultures. It demands more than technical skills; instead, it demands cultural competencies that allow people to navigate the many cultural differences bearing implications on styles of communication, ways of work practices, and organizational expectations (DeNisi & Murphy, 2017)

Cross-cultural training programs would become a valuable means of promoting competency globally in the workforce. These training programs are focused on making the employees aware of the cultural practices, values, and codes of conduct of various regions. Cultural awareness reduces the chances of miscommunication, improved teamwork, and ends up with better relationship with your foreign stakeholders (Dowling et al., 2017).

Leadership skills also make up competency development worldwide. Global teams managers and leaders need a range of competencies that enable them to manage diverse workforce, cross-cultural conflicts, and foster the inclusive work environment. Cultural intelligence is also provided in the leadership development programs such as with traits like emotional intelligence and adaptive communication skills can cater adequately to the team and improve performance in a business landscape that has increased global involvement (Farndale et al., 2010).

Technology-Driven Learning and Development

Introduction of digital technologies in learning and development has made it easier, scalable, and adaptive to the requirements of a global labor force. E-learning platforms, virtual classroom, and learning management systems now make it easier for organizations to deliver their training programs across borders. Companies can ensure that standardized training programs are provided to employees across the globe using these digital tools; thus, each member of the team will have access to similar resources for learning (Friedman, 2014).

In addition, the internet-based training may be formatted according to the specific needs of each employee based on region. For instance, features such as language translation and localized content can be included in the training modules so that the content can remain more local, which can allow training to be relevant and effective. In this manner, it will enable employees to receive technical and professional training, besides learning how to apply those skills within their specific local context (Ghemawat, 2016).

Other virtual training methods provide malleability, and they allow employees to learn at their own pace and according to their personal time. This is very helpful in a global environment, where employees may be based over more than one time zone. Thus, there is incessant updating of skills through learning resources because employees update their knowledge with continuous changes in technology and industry trends to keep up with the competencies in a dynamically changing global marketplace (Hofstede et al., 2010).

Lifelong Learning and Global Workforce Development

Lifelong learning becomes an integral component of the workforce development in an increasingly interconnected and dynamic global economy. Organization's need to continuously develop skill due to rapid technological changes and shifting market pressure has increased following globalization. Employees are no longer just required to learn current specific job skills but also how to learn continuously, accordingly assuming new roles, mastering new technologies, and adapting new processes (International Labour Organization, 2020).

Many organizations are embracing lifelong learning as an effective way to prepare their workforce for the future. This means making available ongoing access to training through on-the-job learning, multiple sources of learning, and the possibilities of career advancement. Organizations are also now focusing on the need to upskill and reskill their workforce for new roles within the organization brought about by automation, AI, and other job disruptions (Jackson & Ruderman, 2018).

Global companies are using training packages that can focus on both hard skills as well as soft skills; those that will be required to prepare employees for the future of work. Technical training refers to digital literacy, data analytics, and cybersecurity, among others. Organizations today have become highly technology dependent. However, at the same time there is an upsurge in soft skills such as adaptability, critical thinking, and collaboration while working in a different environment, especially in a global scenario where diverse groups have to work together to solve intricate problems (Janssens & Steyaert, 2019).

Aligning Global Training with Local Regulations and Needs

Global training and development programs need to harmonize with the legal, cultural, and economic conditions of the regions in which they are being implemented. One of the significant challenges that multinational companies face is how they can ensure that their global training programs align with the labor laws and regulations of the countries under which they operate. Some regions are very particular about employee certification requirements, while others have rules on safety training or industry-specific compliance standards. To stay in compliance with regulatory requirements, organizations will need to be flexible in accommodating their training programs globally according to the local requirements while maintaining them as uniform around the world (Kaufman, 2014).

Differences in the economy and education between regions also impact the effectiveness of global training. A great deal in the emerging markets is diverse in terms of education levels, degrees attained, and technology access, making it impossible for them to participate fully in the standardized training programs that are designed for global companies. Companies are now turning to a hybrid approach, combining global best practice with localized solutions. This could involve providing basic training to the workforce in less technologically oriented areas or mentorship programs designed to close gaps in technical knowledge (Kshetri, 2018).

Training at a global level, yet aligned to local needs, means that employees across all regions are complying not only with the local regulations but are empowered with such skills and knowledge as would allow them to meaningfully contribute to the organization. It fosters more open and fair learning for all employees, who are not restricted to their locational settings and are able to develop and grow professionally (Meyer, 2017).

Measuring the Effectiveness of Global Training Programs

With organizations continuing to invest in global training and development, measuring these programs is essential to determine whether value is indeed being gained from them. Others could include engagement, retention rates, development of skills, or performance improvement. In fact, getting feedback from employees from different regions helps an organization pinpoint area where its training programs need to be modified to suit the needs and/or cultural differences of the locals (Noe et al., 2021).

More and more companies operating in this global scenario use data analytics to monitor the results of their training programs. Advanced analytics tools make it possible for HR teams to evaluate the outcomes of training with respect to demographics, regions, and job roles. This data can be used to fine-tune training strategies and identify areas of skill gaps, contributing to development initiatives that align with global business needs and regional needs (Parry & Tyson, 2019).

Training and development across the globe became an imperative component for an organization in the new business world. Cross-cultural competency, technological expertise, and continuous learning appeared to be more relevant and sharper than ever; thus, their solutions required integrated flexible trainings. It will prepare their people for changing dynamics in a rapidly shifting global marketplace by applying digital technologies, tailoring training to local needs, and setting a culture of continuous learning. Thus, they will also enhance engagement, productivity, and competitiveness worldwide (Punnett, 2018).

COMPENSATION, BENEFITS, AND PERFORMANCE MANAGEMENT IN A GLOBAL CONTEXT

In a globalized work environment, pay, benefit, and performance-related practices are becoming more complex. In this regard, while developing and implementing plans in an environment of multiple countries, organizations must create compensation packages and performance management systems that are responsive to the diverse legal frameworks, economic conditions, and cultural expectations in each region. This calls for a balance between the consistency of global policies and the specific requirements of locales, so that the employees may be paid appropriately and motivated enough to thrive and maintain competitiveness in the relevant regions (Robbins & Judge, 2020).

Global Compensation Structures

Perhaps the key challenge to global human resource management is to work out the compensation structure based on regional conditions of local markets, with some equity for the whole organization. Compensation costs can differ dramatically from one country to another because of differences in standards for cost of living, inflation rates, tax systems, and labor laws. Consequently, the compensation of employees needs to be adjusted to suit the local conditions so as not to be at a disadvantage in the labor market (Schuler et al., 2011).

Most companies tend to adopt a hybrid framework, in which there is an implication of a framework across the globe at a different level locally. The compensation framework developed globally tends to provide the dos and don'ts of compensation through reference to pay equity and transparency at the organization-wide level. It also includes local modifications in terms of flexibility and scope to consider differences in various regions, say giving a base salary by topping up based on regional cost of living or reconfiguring bonus structures to fit labor expectations at the local level (Stahl et al., 2012).

Strategies in compensation globally also have to take cognizance of the differential views of pay across cultures. As had been discussed before, in some areas, the base salary could be central to the compensation package while in others, it is the benefits, allowances, and even non-monetary benefits such as extra leave days or opportunities for training that command most value. Understanding such regional preferences will only increase the incentive of compensation packages that will make employees feel good about their jobs (Stone et al., 2015).

Benefits and Global Mobility

Organizations need to think of employee benefits the same way when they are global, including health insurance, retirement plans, and well-being programs. That is, benefits packages within multinational organizations have to be compliant with local rules and have to satisfy the expectations of different people working in various regions. For example, some countries could demand compulsory health cover or retirement pay, which would shape the benefits, while others could demand fewer costs to leave the workplace or a better work-life balance (Ulrich et al., 2012).

Global mobility is also another demanding aspect of managing benefits with expats and employees in international assignments. For this, support and housing allowances, among other expatriate benefits such as relocation support to smoothen the transition of people from one country to another, have to be in place for all employees moving around the world. Tax equalization and social security benefits need to be managed so as not to create differences in "take-home pay" due to different tax systems between the home country and the host country (Al Ariss et al., 2014).

Competitive benefits draw and retain talent and are critical in the international market. The more affluent benefits packages and more clearly defined specific needs and expectations of a given region will enable organizations to better improve employee satisfaction and engagement. Moreover, benefits, including professional development, flexible working conditions, and family-friendly policies, can be significant partners in improving the employee value proposition for the globally dispersed workforce (Brewster et al., 2016).

Performance Management and Cultural Differences

Another area significantly affected by globalization is performance management. As managing performance in a multinational organization necessitates systems adaptable to the diverse cultural values, norms, and expectations from one country to another, this complexity is added to performance management since what is considered "high performance" in one country is something quite different in another country due to dissimilar work practices, communication styles, and even cultural attitudes toward leadership and feedback (Budhwar & Debrah, 2013).

In countries that emphasize individualism, performance management might be more concerned with the achievements and merit-based incentives of the individual. In contrast, performance appraisals in more collectivist cultures might place greater emphasis on teamwork, collaboration, and group success. This is knowledge that can enable designing suitable performance management systems that are fair and effective across regions (Cascio & Boudreau, 2016).

To address the differences, many international companies eliminate the annual performance review and make use of the continuous feedback models with great flexibility. Continuous performance management allows the managers and the employees to continuously discuss issues concerning such matters as goals and progress levels, as well as needs for further development, in acceptance by all cultures. It translates to more frequent recognition of achievements and an accelerated discovery of training needs and areas requiring support, so leading to a more agile and responsive workforce (Collings & Mellahi, 2009).

The global performance management system must be aligned with the global business objectives while catering to regional differences in the goals and performance metrics. For example, standards on customer service can be a global objective, but the specific performance goal for employees would vary based on the nature of the customer base, competitive scenario, and market conditions (DeNisi & Murphy, 2017).

Incentive Programs and Global Motivation

Incentive programs have been the cornerstone for driving performance and motivating employees within global organizations. The designing of incentive programs would face a challenge, as the cultural drivers of motivation differ dramatically from one culture to another. In some regions, reward of choice may be bonuses or commissions, whereas in other regions, recognition, career advancement opportunities, or extra vacation days may yield far more motivation (Dowling et al., 2017).

Organizations are increasingly adopting customizable incentive programs which allow the employees to choose from a variety of reward options. A system known as flexible or cafeteria-style benefits is sometimes adopted. Such a system provides choice, and if the employees have the right to make the choice in the incentive they want to receive for the internalization, it increases their motivation and satisfaction level. It could be additional paid leave to an employee in Europe but cash bonus and an opportunity to develop professional skills, for example, for the same fellow in Asia (Farndale et al., 2010).

In addition to the aspects of employee motivation and satisfaction, global incentive plans should not neglect local tax implications and legal constraints. For instance, in some countries, the bonus, stock option, or other types of financial incentive are strictly regulated; organizations must thus handle these issues delicately and be cautious not to contravene those laws. Conversely, variations in tax treatment over regions may also impact the attractiveness of certain types of incentives (Friedman, 2014).

Managing Pay Equity and Fairness Globally

Ensuring pay equity and fairness across global operations is one of the critical challenges faced by HR leaders in multinational organizations. Globalization has created much more need for transparency and consistency in compensation and performance management since employees in different regions compare what they are paid and the benefits against colleagues worldwide. Discrepancies in compensation between regions can become an issue of dissatisfaction, disengagement, and even a cause for legal disputes if considered unfair (Ghemawat, 2016).

Organisations are investing in global pay equity audits and compensation benchmarking to try to address concerns over pay equity. This entails examining the pay structures of a firm by regions, jobs, and demographics for disparities in compensation. Organisations can, therefore promote increased trust and engagement on the side of their employees (Hofstede et al., 2010).

An observable impact of globalization exists on compensation, benefits, and performance management and, therefore, calls for flexibility, sensitivity towards the culture, and relevance towards local approaches being adopted. In a global marketplace, the best compensation approach always seeks to find a balance between globalization and localization such that employees across the globe are treated fairly and motivated to work with all the energy required. Performance management systems should also be flexible, promote a culture of continuous feedback, respect cultural differences, and align with the business goals of the region. With investments in seamless, fair, and culturally sensitive compensation and performance management practices, an organization is better poised to attract and retain talented employees toward sustained success in a globalized economy (International Labour Organization, 2020).

ETHICAL CONSIDERATIONS AND SOCIAL RESPONSIBILITY IN A GLOBALIZED HRM FRAMEWORK

Ethical and CSR issues developed particularly within the human resource management framework under globalization. Global integration of economies and labor markets exert pressure on organizations to be highly proactive in a socially sensitive manner; it requires a more socially responsible attitude. Business is conducted and operated across different countries; the norms of ethics, labor practices, and social expectations vary. It is also just to treat businesses equitably, and the modes of doing so come in the form of sustainable business practices (Jackson & Ruderman, 2018).

Ethical Recruitment and Employment Practices

One critical ethical issue of global HRM is fair recruitment and employment practices by the firm in its different regions. Firms could operate in countries whose worker legal protections differ, and in some areas, local law sanctions practices which are regarded as unethical or illegal by other measures in the world. This sets up a moral obligation on the part of multinational corporations to establish and enforce the ethical standards of recruitment, which are usually more than just apparent compliance with local laws (Al Ariss, Cascio, & Paauwe, 2014,Janssens & Steyaert, 2019).

For instance, merit must accompany candidate hiring because organizations should not be racially biased, gender biased, ethnically biased, or bias with the economic status. International firms have to take initiatives to respect the dignity of labor by refraining from hiring juvenile laborers, wages lesser than the market wage, and not employ labor under compulsion. This ethical dimension applies to the value chain whereby businesses must show ethical compliance at the local levels as well as at its suppliers as well as contractors (Kaufman, 2014).

Ethical recruitment also includes transparent employment contracts, well-defined job expectations, and observance of International Labor Standards, as embedded in the International Labour Organization. As the world becomes highly interdependent, global organizations are accountable not only to local governments but also to international stakeholders, consumers, and advocacy groups demanding this ethical business practice (Brewster, Sparrow, Vernon, & Houldsworth, 2016,Kshetri, 2018).

Fair Compensation and Labor Equity

Globalization made people realize that firms around the world paid labor in different regions very differently. Where such global differences exist within the same firm, and cannot be explained by the payee's countries' cost of living or local labor markets, ethical concerns exist. Payment equity by region is a compliance issue and an ethical issue as well (Budhwar & Debrah (2013) & Meyer, 2017).

All employees, irrespective of the countries where they work, should be ensured fair wages and benefits (Cascio & Boudreau, 2016). It encompasses granting sufficient health benefits, retirement plans, among other benefits in compensation with a standard which is well enough to meet or surpass the minimum legal standards in every local place where they are working. Moreover, businesses should strive not only to meet the minimum legal requirements but also ensure that there is a system of justice and equity prevalent across their entire companies worldwide (Noe et al., 2021).

More than wage considerations, ethical matters also involve working conditions. All companies operating globally must ensure to provide workers in developing countries with a safe and healthy working environment (Collings & Mellahi, 2009). This includes adequate protection against the dangers of the workplace; reasonable working hours; and respect for workers' rights to organize and join labor unions, where appropriate (Parry & Tyson, 2019).

Human Rights and Labor Standards

As the markets of organizations are expanded globally, they are confronted with inconsistencies in human rights and labor standards among countries. In some areas, the inadequacy of regulations and laws regarding labor leads to an increase in working under hazardous conditions, minimal wages, and lack of job security. The company is exempted from such laws by local legislations, hence there is a moral responsibility adopted and practiced by companies that are multinational (DeNisi & Murphy, 2017, Punnett, 2018).

Respect for human rights is viewed as a part of responsible business conduct. Organizations should not have conducted any form of operations, let alone providing supply chains, around the world that are involved in the acts of human rights violation or forced labor, child labor, and human trafficking. In this regard, indirect employee labor under subcontractors or third-party vendors may be more prone to labour exploitation (Robbins & Judge, 2020).

Apart from being compliant with international labor standards, it is also hoped that multinational organizations support the societies within which they operate positively. This includes diversity and inclusion, equal opportunities for all employees, and active promotion of gender equity and engagement in support of marginalized groups. In so doing, organizations will be able to create a more equitable and just workplace that speaks well of their dedication to human rights and social justice (Schuler et al., 2011).

Corporate Social Responsibility (CSR) in HRM

Corporate social responsibility is perhaps the most critical addition to the global strategies of HRM. Employee-based CSR activity will have significant impacts on the company's reputation, talent retention, and eventual success. Role of HR departments in CSR activities will be critical in international context while being aligned with labor ethics, sustainable development, and community engagement (Stahl et al., 2012).

One of the biggest CSR dimensions in the human resource management arena is environmental sustainability. International companies are now being compelled to minimise their carbon footprint, decrease waste, and adhere to sustainability processes when conducting every aspect of business, including ensuring that company HR policy and procedures related to business travel, office energy consumption, or telecommuting are sustainability-compatible with the overall goal of the corporation. Another is that it can foster an environmental awareness culture by offering trainings in sustainability and calling for employee participation in the promotion of environmental conscious actions (Stone et al., 2015).

CSR also demands support for the community in which the organizations operate. Multinationals could contribute to the employment areas; however, it is expected that they give back meaningfully through investments in community development, education, health, and other community projects. HR can support and promote corporate volunteering among employees while contributing toward positive activities that are for the well-being of the local communities (Ulrich et al., 2012).

Apart from that, CSR in HRM operates through diversity and inclusion at the workplace, equal opportunities to all the employees, and social justice initiatives. Corporations that have openness and fair representation of their population globally are complying with ethical practices while at the same time improving the work environment. It is more innovative as well as collaborated (Al Ariss et al., 2014).

Addressing Ethical Dilemmas in Global HRM

Navigation of global ethical dilemmas while going about HRM requires a very careful balance between respect for local culture and universal ethical considerations. Where such a clash occurs between cultural norms of a given country and the ethics of some global organizations, it can be quite challenging. For example, some regions have cultures that seem to tolerate gender-based discrimination or other inequalities that would not even be tolerated in other parts of the world (Brewster et al., 2016).

In such scenarios, HR professionals must consider decisions that enhance and promote human rights and ethical principles while at the same time being sensitive to practices and customs of the locality. These may either include working together with local stakeholders to gradually adjust towards international ethical standards or make the difficult call to withdraw operations from locations where unacceptable practices cannot be changed (Budhwar & Debrah, 2013).

Global companies will serve as role-play models in promoting and practicing ethics that bring about a new paradigm shift in the region in which they operate. Through implementing a culture of integrity, openness, and social responsibility within multinational companies support a contribution to positive social change while remaining competitive within the global market (Cascio & Boudreau, 2016).

Ethics and social responsibility are integral for the success and sustainability of HRM practices in an increasingly globalized world. Therefore, globalization presents diverse complex ethical issues from adequate remuneration and labor equity to human rights promotion and sustainable development. This helps an organization strengthen its global workforce that is comprehensive and socially responsible in achieving business results with added values to society through embedding ethical principles and CSR into HR strategies (Collings & Mellahi, 2009).

CHALLENGES AND FUTURE TRENDS IN GLOBAL HRM

Groomed continuously by the rapid evolution of technology, changing workforce demographics, and increasing expectations from society, the landscape of Human Resource Management continues to evolve in a globalised context. While globalization indeed brings the organization many opportunities in utilising diverse talent and expansion, it is fraught with great challenges that global HR professionals are today expected to address. This section identifies the key challenges facing global HRM and highlights future trends shaping the field (DeNisi & Murphy, 2017).

Challenges in Global HRM

1. Cultural Diversity and Integration

Cultural diversity in the workforce is probably the most substantial challenge to HRM in an international context. Global companies operating from a variety of countries should be aware of the cultural differences between individuals, which affect each person's behavior, communication styles, and expectations at work. Misunderstandings through cultural differences can cause conflicts, lower morale, and eventually reduce productivity levels among employees. Culturally sensitive training programs and supportive policies must be formulated by HR professionals for effective handling of teams with diversity (Dowling et al., 2017).

2. Compliances with Legislations and Labor Standards

It's rather confusing for a global organization to navigate the web of labor laws and regulations of a country. Compliance with local laws, international labor standards, and ethical business practices are crucial, but vary considerably from one region to another. The role of an HR professional is to keep themselves updated with changes in regulations and work with their respective organizations so that all legal requirements are met but, at the same time, adhere to ethical standards. Non-compliance may lead to legal damages, reputational damage, and even financial losses (Farndale et al., 2010).

3. Talent acquisition and retention

The HR departments have to continuously work on attracting and retaining the top talents in any global market. With the increase in competition for skilled employees, organizations also need to reclassify themselves to differentiate themselves from others in order to attract good talent. To retain such talents in these rapidly changing environments of the world, compensation packages, career development opportunities, and a positive working culture would be required. The new recruitment strategies for human resources professionals also require the department to evolve with a centric employee-centric environment to enhance engagement and loyalty (Friedman, 2014).

4. Technological Integration and Adaptation

Technology advancement and integration can also become a problem and an opportunity for global HRM. Technological integration may reduce clerical work within the HRM space and motivate employees toward effective engagement. It may, however, be forcing the organization to shift gear and adopt new tools and platforms. It requires the training and support of HR professionals and employees in the implementation of applicant tracking systems, performance management software, and learning management systems. On the other hand, balance must be struck by organizations between the gain of technology and human bonding and connection at the workplace.(Arendt, H., 1958). (Ghemawat, 2016)

5. Cross-Border Mobility and Distributed Work

Remote work, coupled with global mobility, has shifted the concept which organizations have regarding talent mobility. Flex work allowed the organization to tap a bigger pool of talents, but the ease in communication, collaboration, and engagement among employees are also being challenged. HR specialists must strive to incorporate remote teams and make the employees feel as engaged as those on-site and in an environment they can identify with. The other challenge in international assignments relates to visas and moving, which has to be carefully planned (Hofstede et al., 2010).

Future Trends in Global HRM

1. Employee Well-Being and Mental Health

With a rising awareness about how mental health factors relate to total well-being, the attention of organizations has taken the form of incorporating employee wellness into HRM strategies. In such global contexts, HRM will focus on enabling supportive environments for managing mental health issues and integrating work-life balance systems and access to wellness resources. Flexibility in work arrangements, mental health days, and employee assistance programs, among other initiatives to attract and retain talent, will define such an environment (International Labour Organization, 2020).

2. Artificial Intelligence and Data Analytics Integration

Integration of AI and data analytics in HRM: The future of workforce management - The integration of AI and data analytics in HRM is going to transform the way organisations deal with their workforce. An AI-based system might make the recruitment process easier, talent management better, and performance or other needs of the organisation regarding the employees stronger. HR professionals would have to make effective use of data analytics for sound judgments regarding employees and point out trends or improve general HR efficiency. But these technologies also bring forth ethical questions about data privacy and bias toward individuals and groups of people (Jackson & Ruderman, 2018).

3. Diversity, Equity, and Inclusion (DEI)

The call on a global diversity, equity, and inclusion is gaining grounds, and organizations are increasingly and more expected to demonstrate their commitment to the principles. It is such a scenario that future trends in global HRM will be worth emphasizing: diversity leadership, equitable hiring, and an inclusive culture of the workplace. Organizations that find significant and relevant expressions of DEI will get good reputations and encourage innovation, thereby increasing employee satisfaction. HR practitioners would be rather important in implementing the DEI initiatives and evaluating the effectiveness of these initiatives on organizational performance (Janssens & Steyaert, 2019).

4. Sustainability and CSR

As climate change and social responsibility continue to increasingly feature in the news, organizations will be driven by the need to demonstrate their commitment to sustainability and CSR. Sustainability practices must feature within the framework of future HRM strategies, therefore, including telecommuting to decrease carbon footprint, supporting diversity initiatives, and community service projects where employees' participate and engage. HR professionals will be responsible for ensuring that what organizations say they believe in is adapted toward sustainability goals and corporate culture responsibility.

5. Agile HR Practices

In this dynamic global environment, agility in HR practices will be needed to immediately respond to the needs of the market by organizations. Agile HRM is about embracing the lines of flexibility, collaboration, and responsiveness in HR processes that allow such organisations to shift course and innovate as conditions allow. Such a trend will require HR professionals to adopt new workforce planning approaches, overhaul the performance management, and beef up employee engagement efforts so that an HR culture of continuous improvement and adaptability is developed. (Kshetri, 2018). It will happen when HR professionals can make a difference and create an inclusive, ethical workplace that positively impacts the bottom line. (Meyer, 2017)

CONCLUSION

Globalization has had an immense impact in changing the HRM of the organizations in relation to the way they focus on their strategies in dealing with their workforce. Global business expansion often presents unique challenges and opportunities with a need to better understand those related to cultural diversity, regulation, and ethics. This chapter, therefore, examines the various dimensions of globalization of HRM, which include international talent management, diversity and inclusion, labor laws and regulations, technological change, training and development, compensation, and ethical responsibilities. (Noe et al., 2021)

With interconnectivity across the world, managing diverse teams calls for cultural sensitivity and inclusiveness. Organizations can create a well-inclusive work place culture embracing various perspectives for better engagement, creativity, and performance. Over and above this, over global labor laws and ethical standards, companies are to set up frameworks that exercise fairness and guard the rights of the employees working in all regions. (Parry & Tyson, 2019)

This incorporation of technology into the practice of HR works out to determine both challenges and opportunities for the organizations. Through AI and data analytics, HR professionals would be able to make informed decisions on recruitment, performance management, and employee engagement. They, however have to be cautious about the implications of data usage and need to focus more on the privacy of employees. (Punnett, 2018)This shift toward sustainability and social responsibility should improve the organizational reputation and support the creation of a more equitable and just workplace. (Robbins & Judge, 2020)

In a nutshell, the problems and trends unveiled in this chapter focus on the imperative role of HRM in dealing with the intricacies of globalization. Organizations embracing diversity, ethical practices, and innovative approaches are well positioned to develop resilient and adaptable workforces for performance in the global mainstream. As human resource professionals continue to adapt their strategies in line with the changing world, they will play a significant role in constructing a future in which organizations can prosper while fulfilling their ethical responsibilities and contributing positively to society. (Schuler et al., 2011)

REFERENCES

Al Ariss, A., Cascio, W. F., & Paauwe, J. (2014). Talent management: Current theories and future research directions. Journal of World Business, 49(2), 173–179. (Stahl et al., 2012)

Brewster, C., Sparrow, P., Vernon, G., & Houldsworth, E. (2016). International human resource management (4th ed.). Kogan Page. (Stone et al., 2015)

Budhwar, P., & Debrah, Y. (Eds.). (2013). Human resource management in developing countries. Routledge. (Ulrich et al., 2012)

Cascio, W. F., & Boudreau, J. W. (2016). The search for global competence: From international HR to talent management. SHRM Foundation. (Al Ariss et al., 2014)

Collings, D. G., & Mellahi, K. (2009). Strategic talent management: A review and research agenda. Human Resource Management Review, 19(4), 304–313. (Brewster et al., 2016)

DeNisi, A. S., & Murphy, K. R. (2017). Performance appraisal and performance management: 100 years of progress? Journal of Applied Psychology, 102(3), 421–433. (Budhwar & Debrah, 2013)

Dowling, P. J., Festing, M., & Engle, A. (2017). International human resource management (7th ed.). Cengage Learning. (Cascio & Boudreau, 2016)

Farndale, E., Scullion, H., & Sparrow, P. (2010). The role of the corporate HR function in global talent management. Journal of World Business, 45(2), 161–168. (Collings & Mellahi, 2009)

Friedman, T. L. (2014). The world is flat: A brief history of the twenty-first century (3rd ed.). Picador. (DeNisi & Murphy, 2017)

Ghemawat, P. (2016). The laws of globalization and business applications. Cambridge University Press. (Dowling et al., 2017)

Hofstede, G., Hofstede, G. J., & Minkov, M. (2010). Cultures and organizations: Software of the mind (3rd ed.). McGraw-Hill. (Farndale et al., 2010)

International Labour Organization. (2020). Global employment trends. ILO Publications. (Friedman, 2014)

Jackson, S. E., & Ruderman, M. (Eds.). (2018). Diversity in work teams: Research paradigms for a changing workplace. American Psychological Association. (Ghemawat, 2016)

Janssens, M., & Steyaert, C. (2019). A practice-based view of diversity management. Academy of Management Annals, 13(1), 1–49. (Hofstede et al., 2010)

Kshetri, N. (2018). The emerging role of big data in key development issues: Opportunities, challenges, and concerns. Big Data for Development, 1(1), 1–20. (Jackson & Ruderman, 2018)

Meyer, K. E. (2017). International business and management in emerging economies. Journal of International Business Studies, 48(1), 1–17. (Janssens & Steyaert, 2019)

Noe, R. A., Hollenbeck, J. R., Gerhart, B., & Wright, P. M. (2021). Human resource management: Gaining a competitive advantage (12th ed.). McGraw-Hill. (Kaufman, 2014)

Parry, E., & Tyson, S. (2019). An introduction to HRM in the public sector. Taylor & Francis. (Kshetri, 2018)

Punnett, B. J. (2018). International perspectives on organizational behavior and human resource management. Routledge. (Meyer, 2017)

Schuler, R. S., Jackson, S. E., & Tarique, I. (2011). Global talent management and global talent challenges: Strategic opportunities for IHRM. Journal of World Business, 46(4), 506–516. (Parry & Tyson, 2019)

Stahl, G. K., Björkman, I., & Morris, S. (2012). Handbook of research in international human resource management. Edward Elgar. (Punnett, 2018)

Stone, D. L., Deadrick, D. L., Lukaszewski, K. M., & Johnson, R. (2015). The influence of technology on the future of human resource management. Human Resource Management Review, 25(2), 216–231. (Robbins & Judge, 2020)

Ulrich, D., Younger, J., Brockbank, W., & Ulrich, M. (2012). HR from the outside in: Six competencies for the future of human resources. McGraw-Hill. (Schuler et al., 2011)

Chapter 6
Microaggressions, Power, and HRM Reform:
Rethinking Gendered Labor Rights in India

Sneha Kadyan
https://orcid.org/0000-0001-6745-4419
Jindal Global Business School, O.P Jindal Global University, India

Firdous Ahmad Malik
https://orcid.org/0000-0002-7815-0143
Department of Management, University of People, USA

ABSTRACT

Microaggressions, power, and Human Resource Management (HRM) reform require rethinking from a gendered labor rights perspective in India. The chapter is an endeavor in this direction as it examines the problems that everyday workplace interactions routinely experience that often maintain gender-based hierarchies, which legal reforms and mainstream HRM reforms find it difficult to resolve. This chapter focuses not on extreme cases of sexual harassment and workplace discrimination, but on microaggressions as potent and often used tools of power over workers and employees, especially women and marginalized groups that seize the everyday suffering and torment across office spaces, factory floors and within supply chains and beyond in sectors such as garments and textiles. This chapter provides a critique of the current HRM reform in India by grounding it in sociology and using microaggressions as a framework to examine daily gendered harms and the legal infrastructure that has been established to protect women in their workplace.

DOI: 10.4018/979-8-3693-5390-5.ch006

1. INTRODUCTION: WHY MICROAGGRESSIONS MATTER FOR HRM REFORM

The chapter argues that the formal legal reforms such as the Sexual Harassment of Women at Workplace (Prevention, Prohibition, and Redressal) Act (POSH, 2013; Jadhav & Kulkarni, 2020) and the recent labor code reforms, while have significant normative and administrative impacts, but they do not adequately manage to remedy more subtle and often everyday interpersonal and intersectional harm that are responsible for recreating gender inequalities in the factories, offices, and supply chains. This argument is positioned with insights from theories of microaggression and power, intersectionality, labor studies as well as relevant empirical studies from India from within the garment sector. The aim of the chapter is to highlight the functioning of microaggressions as a potent form of social control that is deeply pervasive and functions to discipline labor. It raises the need to re-envision HRM reforms and change institutional design to involve moving from compliance checklists and to spotlight the situated listening mechanisms and tools for redressal of worker issues, incorporate intersectional training and legally mandated third-party reporting on these issues.

This study is contextualized within the backdrop of the post-2013 legal landscape of the Sexual Harassment of Women at Workplace (Prevention, Prohibition and Redressal) Act and its subsequent POSH Rules (Kanskar & Pal, 2021). There are also the recent labor codes that have been consolidated to four codes by the Indian government to standardize employment and regulate it (Mishra & Dwivedi, 2024). Within these recent legal reforms and regulations that try to codify the employer's duties to prevent and redress harassment against women, recent scholarship laments that they are narrow in focus and individualized, with event-based violations mostly, leading to limited engagement with structural inequalities and persisting of non-sexual forms of everyday harm against women (Mishra & Dwivedi 2024; Chaudhary & Remesh, 2021; Chaigater, 2021). Another important point on the other side to note is that, recent scholarship (Hart, 2021; Ringblom, 2022; Oosterom et al., 2022) points to the fact that gendered atrocities at the workplace are often routine and relational that frequently go unnoticed. While cannot be explicitly identified as incidents of sexual harassment or criminal offence, they do tend to have a cumulative negative effect on women. The nature of this routine harm is referred to as microaggressions, described as verbal and nonverbal interpersonal exchanges in which a perpetrator causes harm to a target whether intended or unintended, emanating (Sue & Spanierman, 2020) in US-based race literature but now becoming a common framing for the understanding of the gendered and intersecting nature of workplace harm worldwide.

In this regard, a sociological analysis becomes paramount as legal mechanisms do not operate or exist in isolation. It has been found that law interacts with organizational norms, with managerial intentions and motivations, with labor market dynamics and even with social hierarchies of caste, class, religion etc.) (Pandey, & Spoorthi, 2023, Bapuji et al. 2024). This chapter, therefore, seeks the response to the fundamental question of: what is the role of microaggressions in gendered labor subordination at the workplace?

2. THEORETICAL FRAME: MICROAGGRESSIONS, POWER AND INTERSECTIONALITY

2.1 Microaggressions as a Sociological Object

Microaggressions considering the literal meaning of the term, minor offenses, from a sociological perspective are not merely minor. In fact, the significance of microaggression lies in their widespread everyday occurrence, acceptance, normalization, and cumulative effect. The impact is felt through subtle ways, such as degrading comments made indirectly at a minority group or exclusionary jokes that are based on stereotypes (Sue & Spanierman, 2020). When we apply this framework to gendered workplace interactions, we can see that it relates to situations and cases where there might be systematic disruptions, infantilizing comments about domestic care, assumptions about one's capabilities, or routine assignment of low-status tasks to women, these would all be considered examples of gendered microaggressions. When we use a socio-structural grounding approach to understand microaggressions, they point to interpersonal rudeness as often deep-seated power hierarchies that persist and continue to be supported by organizational culture, market dynamics and labor market segmentation. Feminist sociologists in fact, have been highlighting for long that the violence inflicted upon women at their place of work is actually a result of the organizational structures that facilitate oppression (Acker, 1990; Britton, 2017). Microaggressions, therefore, from this lens maybe minor but still especially important in their cumulative impact generated through gender and class.

Microaggression exemplifies Collins's (2000) framework of the "matrix of dominations", which illuminates the social divisions where institutional arrangements, symbolic meanings and interpersonal relations also crosscut each other. In another way then, microaggressions lie at the intersection of interpersonal connection but also, they have an institutional function, as they entrench and deepen hierarchies in HR systems, labor laws and socio-economic disparities. The Indian workplace is affected by caste, class, gender, and similar forms of social stratification which makes these microaggressions a reflection of structural power relations, and not just individual biases. Moreover, microaggressions can be applied to what can be called "slow violence" (Nixon, 2011), within which overt harassment or assault also may not have an impact, that microaggressions do. Microaggressions slowly exhaust the workers by embedding deep constant fear and internal conflicts within themselves to maintain self-esteem, which in the end leads to normalization and even acceptance of such discriminatory and unjust treatment that is meted out of them. In certain sectors, where manual work is often the prime mode of activity, such as in textiles, garments or logistic and services, we find that the manifestations of microaggressions could reflect in a supervisor publicly lamenting a female employee's performance at work and doubting her commitment to work because of gender bias or unobtrusively excluding her from training and promotion opportunities.

To add a further sociological insight, studies on "emotional labor" (Hochschild et. al., 1983) along with work on "aesthetic labor" (Warhurst, 2016) also suggest that organizations often are found to be very strong in controlling workers' feelings, looks and even behavior through a gendered lens. The female employees are often assumed to be "pleasant", "accommodating" and "non-confrontational", thereby making microaggressions an everyday feature of their loves. HR systems, in addition hardly ever give credit to female employees for being assertive and in fact, if they do, they are labelled as "not fitting", "not a good team player" and similar such opinions are expressed about women, reflecting what Castilla (2025), captured as the "paradox of meritocracy".

By combining labor law and HRM reforms, a sociological approach uncovers microaggressions in the margins of legal definition, that are not laid out in legal terms nor considered as transgressions by employees themselves but nonetheless, they occur daily. This is important to note as sexual harassment through microaggressions is a common form of gendered hostility against women in the workplace and the HRM reforms need to bridge this conceptual and legal gap.

Theoretical frameworks, therefore, enable us to view microaggressions not as peripheral problems from the sidelines, but as core issues in the process of workplace gender injustices and inequalities. Consequently, the sociology of HRM should redefine what violence means in a broader sense and should include the psychological, banal, and institutionalized harms that affect women's labor rights in India.

2.2 Power, Discipline, and the Labor Process

Another lens that is important to use and adopt for microaggressions is through the perspective of the labor process, wherein we may find that microaggressions may actually be an informal tool for controlling employee behavior and bring it in line with managerial demands of the organization, without explicit use of formal disciplinary measures. In addition, piece rate systems, and many forms of employment are not stable and when they are combined with microaggressions they create very strong types of surveillance and self-discipline where vulnerable groups may be in very precarious situations. The impact is further intensified as they work with gendered division of labor, humiliation, and dismissive remarks of higher authorities against for example women, which has a negative result on women's anyways lower bargaining power within patriarchal societies and workplaces.

2.3 Intersectionality and Positional Vulnerability

Microaggressions are intersectional as for example, an unmarried young female employee belonging to a lower caste, being a migrant, whose speaks a non-dominant dialect will experience microaggression in all of these ways, which would be different from another woman's experience higher on the caste or class hierarchy. The intensity of the first will be more. Therefore, intersectionality is so important to understand for generic HRM policies which may not cover caste, migration, class, religion, and other forms of stratification, thereby overlooking many potent patterns of creating disadvantage.

3. LEGAL FRAMEWORKS AND HRM REFORM IN INDIA: POSH, LABOR CODES, CSR AND BEYOND

3.1 POSH Act (2013): Positives and Persistent Problems

There is no denying to the fact that the POSH Act was a breakthrough in law to classify sexual harassment as a statutory workplace offence, that requires employing organization to mediate and intervene through the methods that have been laid down by this Act, such as the internal mechanisms, employer responsibilities and employer liability. However, even with such strong measures, implementation problems have persisted and plague legal and empirical critiques. One such problem is that smaller organizations are not mandated to have internal complaint committees or ICCs. They are required to be managed by the managers themselves and they have the final say over complaints. For obvious reasons, the stigma and the fear of persecution may prevent employees from making complaints. It highlights how not all organizations may have the resources or even the independence to make for fair and effective resolution of cases. Research points out that it is often the case that the implementation of the POSH act is often a paper exercise, with trainings and mock drills for employees for sure, but structural issues and institutional problems remain unchallenged (Malik, 2024; Oommen, 2023).

3.2 Recent Labor-Code Reforms: Promise, Politics, and Uncertainties

Through early 2020s and until the present times, India is invested in overhauling its entire labor regulations by consolidating it to 4 labor codes that comprise of wages, industrial relations, social security and occupational safety (More & Jadhav, 2023). The Indian government has stated that this move is contemporary and improves efficiency as the renewed codes with be user-friendly and even have a component of portability of benefits, thereby widening the access provided by social security measures and the clarity and ease of understanding of the rules, specifically for the general public including women.

However, the reforms have met with enormous resistance from unions and in general debates and discussions as the claim being made against them is that such revisions will allow employers to hire/fire employees easier and could end up weaking collective bargaining power of workers and putting women at risk (Chaudhary & Ramesh, 2021). Thus, while the revisions to the codes concerning occupational safety and protection to health can be used to combat workplace violence, but a complete safety and redressal of issues, especially for informal workers, is no guaranteed (Chigater, 2021).

3.3 Corporate Social Responsibility (CSR), Environmental, Social and Governance (ESG), and Global Buyer Pressure: Compliance or Care?

Organizations generally use Corporate Social Responsibility (CSR) claims along with ESG audits for forwarding compliance formalities to their suppliers. These include having codes of conduct, anti-harassment clauses and adopting checklists for different kinds of audits. However, it has been found that axiomatic audit driven compliances while could lead to stricter standards, it does not always lead to real change and may comprise of only symbolic adherence to the new changes in the way the organization is now structured (Jamali, 2010; Power, 2021). In such cases, where global supply chains, like that of garments, that deal with high pressure tactics, may end up with management aligned audits, very strict and tight delivery timelines, that have been linked to occupational health risks and a various form of gender-based violence (Brown, 2021). Evidence of such an impact if found in the Indian garments and textiles sectors, where the influence of buyers' purchasing practices, domestic procurement practices and inadequate HR norms intersect to create a channel of compounding daily risks for majority of women workers in these supply chains (Ghosh, 2021; Sapre, 2024).

When applying a sociological lens to the codes on wages, industrial relations, social security and occupational safety, health and working conditions code (OSH-WC), these reforms appear to be in stark conflict with the daily hardships of women and marginalized employees, much worse in the case of informalized, subcontracted, and global value chain from particular sectors, like garments and textiles. While these codes unify and consolidate old laws and enactments, they still do not capture the routinization of violence deeply embedded in organizational cultures, where women suffer consistently. For example, if you take the case of OSHWC code, while it gives emphasis to physical safety standards, it does not specifically address gender-sensitive workplace culture, psychological harms and stress or even every-day hostility towards women (Anjanappa, 2025). Such an approach then makes it challenging for microaggressions to be recognized as labor rights issues.

What is also noteworthy is that these revised labor codes not only reduce the area of state inspections but also augment self-certification mechanisms. This is problematic as research points to how they have led to the weakening of governance measures and oversight (Sundar, 2021). Considering the above issues, the POSH Act (2013) still is the most potent legal framework for addressing gendered harm at the workplace. However, our study reveals that a sociological perspective to it illuminates that implementation challenges remain. Internal complaint mechanism often does have a connection, the members may not also be adequately trained in dealing with gender sensitive issues or trauma informed pathways. In particular, female employees are often not aware of their rights in contracts and fear losing their jobs, if they choose to report their ordeal. The Act might we add also is limited in addressing caste based and other class mediated tensions that may not always be explicit and occur as microaggressions. As evidence suggests, Dalit, lower caste women continue to face discrimination at workplaces in India (Sharma & Geetha, 2021).

What is also challenging is the special circumstances in which organizations operate, wherein, HRM reforms in India are primarily based on ESG, CSR and similar mechanisms of global supply chain compliance that are easier for international buying agencies to audit for compliance such as attendance, wages, fire safety. These mechanisms and such an approach however, overlooks cultural aspects which often are the roots of the discrimination and harassment women experience at work, making it a paradox and described as "audit culture" problem by Power in 1997. It is emphasizing the documentation aspect but does not focus on actual transformation and resolution of these problems.

In the textile and garment sector, compliance audits are under scrutiny for what has been called, "the social auditing failures" (Anner, 2020), within which the factories are able to clear all audits and ensure compliance, but on the ground, reality speaks a different story where the workers continue to suffer from various forms of abuse, verbal, sexual and discrimination. Hence, when we focus on microaggressions we are trying to capture, quantify and objectively document the compliance reported. It is, therefore, imperative that the HRM changes be in line with supply chain standards of risk and lead to concrete reform rather than be a mere façade or performance.

The current climate in the EU and the Global North with the recent development of the EU Corporate Sustainability Due Diligence Directive and the Human Rights Due Diligence laws are expected to have an impact on Indian employers (Boni, 2023; Velluti, 2024). It will involve a closer scrutiny on workplace culture of Indian organizations, including a focus on gender rights. However, the laws execution in India will be subject to how the HRM interprets them and accepts them. However, what is assured is that without a due emphasis on sociological insights into power, culture and intersectionality, even the more advanced mandates and approaches may end up becoming inefficient in impact the community of women workers in India.

A final aspect that must be considered is related to developments in digital HRM. The latest adaptation of algorithmic monitoring, productivity tracking applications along with digital grievance mechanisms are leading to new digital vulnerabilities (Ajunwa, 2018). While digital mechanisms are effective in automated penalties, confidential reporting, in having productivity dashboards for monitoring and transparency of performance reviews, these are also leading to biases that reflect in microaggressions, referred to as "technological discrimination" by sociologists (Benjamin, 2019). Thus, while HRM reforms are seeing reform through global developments and modernization with digital infrastructure and similar developments, they still grossly fail in dealing with complexities of gendered harm. A sociological imagination and critical outlook is necessary for paving the way through the everyday forms of microaggressions for combatting violence against women and addressing it as labor rights problems, rather than being labeled as interpersonal conflicts.

4. EMPIRICAL LANDSCAPE: MICROAGGRESSIONS AND GENDERED VIOLENCE IN INDIAN WORKPLACES

The literature on microaggressions in Indian workplaces is scant but developing and report the impact of microaggressions on mental health, job satisfaction and retention among women workers and other marginalized communities (Bakshi, 2024; Purang et al, 2025). While there is scholarly work on the informal sector and garment factories that illuminates the more blatant forms of abuse and violence as well as economic coercion against women, they do acknowledge that subtle forms of everyday harassment and exploitation of women workers such as domestic workers, factory workers, informal workers, continue to exist through routine slighting, sexual connoted remarks and discrimination at work, which reduce the bargaining power of women in these settings and their access to resolution to these problems (Raman & Krishnan, 2021; Thakkar, 2024; Mezzadri, 2021).

4.1 Garment and Textile Sector: A Concentrated Site of Overlap

The garment and textile sector is crucial to take note of in this chapter as it employs a very number of women workers. Moreover, the organization of workforce is in a hierarchical manner and buyer driven, within which subcontracting is a usual practice (Khaled & Ansar, 2024). Such conditions create circumstances for both macro aggressions as well as microaggressions. Evidence from South Asia is rife with instances where supervisor's behavior has been under the radar for normalization and routinization of sexualized banter (Nahar, 2024). Even in India, garment factories have been caught the news for strategically silencing women for their fear of losing their jobs, using blackmailing strategies against them and even social ostracism, which are further intensified in the case of migrant and lower caste women workers (Tripathi, 2022; Chaudhary et al., 2024). Thus, sociological research should highlight both institutional reforms such as internal complaint mechanisms and audit regimes and even consciously and strategically target social practices that maintain inequality.

4.2 Microaggressions, Mental Health and Mobility

Microaggressions are associated with mental health issues such as anxiety, depression and impact occupational performance (Desai et al., 2023). They also lead to an unhealthy work culture, lack of satisfaction with job, higher leaves due to increased stress and low employee turnover. Women in Indian workplaces are often found to be showing such patterns due to routine nature of microaggressions at their workplaces that are further intensified due to formal precarity, such as fixed term contracts or inadequate social protection, which all together makes reporting such issues challenging for resolution (Bakshi, 2024).

Empirical insights from different workplaces from India inform us that microaggressions are widespread, in formal as well as informal sectors. The nature of these microaggressions is often determined by the industry, the social demographic profile of the workforce combined with the corporate culture of these organizations. When we pay attention to the garment industry, it is quite evident that supervisors regularly apply such microaggressive techniques to control labor. For example, female workers have reported name-calling such as being labelled as "slow", "careless" or even "unfit" for manufacturing jobs, reflecting a tendency to deny capabilities of women and justify the segregation of genders in certain occupations (Mezzadri, 2017). Such processes often reflect a softer coercion at work through which microaggressions eventually shape productivity and output by humiliation and shape rather than violence (Mishra et.al., 2023).

IT and corporate sector, also has these patterns, but they are less visible and are found to be in a more coded format. For instance, there might be exclusion from critical meetings, seeing leadership to be a masculine trait and similar assumption. Nathan et al. (2022) illuminate how digitalization also has not had a positive impact in eradicating these discriminating practices, even though it appears to be fairer, and merit based. though they seem to be based on merit.

In household domain, where women work in millions, is another example where microaggressions are tied to personal relationships of labor (Rani et.al., 2025). There have been instances where comments about mannerisms, a worker's cleanliness, and similar casteist/classist microaggressive expressions undermine the worker's dignity, rights, and worth as human beings. Such instances elucidate the existence and impact of symbolic violence (Buroway, 2019) that are made to appear normal or mundane but are extremely important to note as the HRM structures for regulation do not exist in such domains of work.

When we take the case of academia, healthcare sector or civil society organizations, women have expressed that microaggressions are strongly rooted in the social structuring of these organizations too (Salmon, 2024). Senior male colleagues frequently interrupt junior female colleagues. They may use ideas without acknowledgement and put their agency at risk, excluding them from important matters and areas for work, growth, and performance. Many of these types of exclusionary practices are referred to as "tokenism by Kanter (1977), where there is magnification of women as symbolic but devoid of any real decision-making power. Moreover, studies by Teltumbde (2010) and (Sengupta et al., 2021) argue that caste system is not dead and still holds relevance even today. There are caste-based differences that find their way into professional assessments and understanding of what counts as decency. Such insights deeply raise the call for a sociologically informed intersectional lens through which HRM reforms can be worked upon to resolve and tackle complex experiences of discrimination and prejudice at places of work.

5. THE SOCIAL LIFE OF HARM: GENDER, POWER, AND HRM REFORM IN CONTEMPORARY INDIA

As the above discussion illustrates, in most cases, HRM reforms are unable to fully deal with microaggressions. In this chapter, we classify three ways in which HRM reform can obscure reforms to these microaggressions.

In the first instance there can be commodification of compliance. Rather than being a tool of critical engagement of workplace culture, compliance becomes a paper process or a tick-box exercise that does not really lead to any actual transformation.

Secondly, there needs to be a renewed approach to understand assessment of HR units. Are we only assessing productivity turnover and similar business indicators? Such an approach may prevent grievances to be prioritized, protecting the employer and the image of the organization. It may lead to backend settlements of disputes, rather than structural reforms that pluck the root cause of the issue.

Thirdly, we find that there can be audit blind spots where ESG and buyer audit processes in terms of the bureaucratic paperwork on policy manuals or complaint committees and the visible outcomes, such as cases reported may find a mention. However, micro level insights and microaggressions in their subtle forms may escape notice, even though they have a compounding effect and lead to harm over a longer period.

The above three aspects then lead to a paradox where there is development and improvements in the formal mechanism to combat harassment, but the very mechanism may make it extremely challenging to see relational harm, consider their impact and look for potential solutions to them.

6. REFRAMING LABOR RIGHTS: FROM COMPLIANCE TO CARE

Our study advocates for a more relational, care-focused and intersectional approach to assess and remedy the impact of microaggressions. This chapter makes the following recommendations towards this end.

6.1 Principles for a Care Oriented HRM

Firstly, worker-centeredness should be the hallmark of such approaches as we need to give clear voice and agency to the marginalized individuals and groups, from women to migrant workers, to contract workers.

Secondly, this agency and voice should adopt an intersectional lens that considers the cross-cutting impact of caste, class, ethnicity, race, or gender.

Thirdly, there must be the assurance that grievance mechanisms are disconnected from line management and are representative of workers by having worker elected leaders for independence and legitimacy.

Fourthly, there must be a focus on proactive and consistent prevention through regular training sessions that are embedded in cultural change and practices through mentorship or peer learning interactive circles.

Finally, public data should be the approach to build transparency and accountability. Such data should anonymize complaints and outcomes and should be focused on legally enforceable schedule and resolution.

6.2 Institutional Designs and Practices

The chapter makes the following recommendations for institutional designs and practices.

First, there should be Worker-Elected Redress Councils (WRCs): Such councils should primarily include worker-elected representatives that is made up of different stakeholders from contract to migrant labor, even industry experts and civil society actors for different perspectives, and impartial approaches. Consideration should be made towards formal recognition and rapid response funds for contingencies and emergency support services.

Second, there should be provisions for reporting and remediation that are easy and accessible for everyday issues. For example, anonymous verbal reporting boxes or mobile based audio notes. There should be a strong stance on response and follow-ups, that are also documented.

Third, legal support should be provided for independent and third-party ombudspersons at the industry-cluster level for grievance redressal, when internal mechanisms fail to bring respite. They should also have considerable power such as interim protections till investigations are on.

Fourth, worker-centered audits must be mandated that involve participatory approaches such as confidential worker interviews for capturing organizational culture and relational indicators.

Fifth, training should also be more engaging with active dialogue rather than a one-way lecture. It should be based on the premise of reflective practices that facilitate dialogue, open and deep conversations.

7. LIMITATIONS AND DIRECTIONS FOR FUTURE SCHOLARSHIP

This chapter has provided considerable gaps in HRM reforms. It documents the pervasive nature of microaggressions in Indian workplaces. It would benefit to have more comparative insights on the extent of these microaggressions in different states of India and over a long-term period that actually capture the career outcomes as a consequence. Moreover, it would also benefit to focus these discussions on men and their experiences with gendered microaggressions at workplace. Finally, it will also be ideal to examine the interventions and measures that can reform and bring improvements in the outcomes generated by such deep-seated microaggressions.

8. CONCLUSION

Microaggressions are important as they impact the daily engine of workplace organization and dynamics. Minor dismissals, comments and disparagements taken together, consistently over long periods of time have a negative impact on women's ability to function, express and contribute at their workplaces. The new norms of HRM in India, such as the POSH framework, the new labor codes and developments in CSR and audit regimes, while enable organizations with legal mandates and mechanisms for dealing with workplace challenges, they are not sufficient. This chapter highlights a sociological focus on relational, intersectional, and power-laden everyday practices that are routinized and require to be in the spotlight. A stronger reform of HRM is raised by this chapter for an even stronger political will, allocation of resources and changes to organizational culture that are towards worker-centered governance. Without this shift and these profound changes, the legal reforms will only generate formal compliance and will not really resolve the everyday microaggressions women face at their workplaces, thereby continuing gendered labor inequality.

Hence, we raise a transformative call for HRM to deepen its reach and move beyond compliance and focus more on cultural transformation keeping in mind the local and regional socio-cultural contexts. The first step in this direction, is to acknowledge microgressions and see their impact on gendered labor rights, and not disregard them as minor issues between individuals.

A sociological approach to microaggressions can compel organizations to

Firstly, develop mechanism that enable reporting of anonymous pattern-based issues.

Second, require that HR professionals are trained in understanding intersectionality and the matrix of domination that can uncover caste, gender, class as well as regional dynamics.

Thirdly, any grievance audit that is undertaken must be done through third party to ensure that no power disparities impact this process.

Fourthly, employees should lead panels to evaluate the organizational culture and provide regular inputs for improvement.

Finally, psychosocial risk perspectives must be part of labor policies of organizations.

With respect to the garment and textile sector that was addressed in this chapter, it is important to emphasize that global supply chains should focus on relational accountability than just tick off compliance on paper. This would keep workers and marginalized communities at the center and would give them a voice and freedom to express themselves. However, such a change requires a holistic and integrated approach within which efforts from HR departments, trade unions, gender specialist, industry representative and civil society actors need to work together. HRM reforms should give attention to microaggression not as subtle but powerful influence over power in the lived experiences of marginalized women. Such reforms should undertake cultural diagnostics to measure how workers are impacted with dignity, respect, and inclusivity, and therefore go beyond physical safety and the issue of wages. This chapter emphasizes that situating microaggressions within sociological paradigm, it is possible to use an intersectional approach to workplace studies and focus on gendered labor practices.

REFERENCES

Acker, J. (1990). Hierarchies, jobs, bodies: A theory of gendered organizations. *Gender & Society*, *4*(2), 139–158.

Ajunwa, I. (2018). Algorithms at work: Productivity monitoring applications and wearable technology as the new data-centric research agenda for employment and labor law. *Louis ULJ*, *63*, 21.

Anjanappa, J. (2025). Balancing Growth and Safety: Occupational Health Risks, Policy Gaps, and Inclusive Frameworks in India's Renewable Energy Transition. *Policy Gaps, and Inclusive Frameworks in India's Renewable Energy Transition (May 07, 2025)*.

Anner, M. (2020). Squeezing workers' rights in global supply chains: Purchasing practices in the Bangladesh garment export sector in comparative perspective. *Review of International Political Economy*, *27*(2), 320–347.

Bakshi, P. (2024). Language, religion, and workplace discrimination: Intersectional microaggressions in India. *Asian Ethnicity*, *25*(2), 185–214.

Bapuji, H., Chrispal, S., Attri, P. S., Ertug, G., & Soundararajan, V. (2024). An integrative review of management research on caste: Broadening our horizons. *The Academy of Management Annals*, *18*(2), 506–549.

Benjamin, R. (2019). *Race After Technology: Abolitionist Tools for the New Jim Code* (1st ed.). Polity.

Boni, A. (2023). Towards mandatory human rights due diligence: the European Corporate Sustainability Due Diligence Directive.

Britton, D. M. (2017). Beyond the chilly climate: The salience of gender in women's academic careers. *Gender & Society*, *31*(1), 5–27.

Brown, G. D. (2021). Women garment workers face huge inequities in global supply chain factories made worse by COVID-19. *New Solutions*, *31*(2), 113–124. PMID: 33966528

Castilla, E. J. (2025). *The Meritocracy Paradox: Where Talent Management Strategies Go Wrong and How to Fix Them.* Columbia University Press.

Chaudhary, T., & Remesh, B. (2021). Changing scenario of Indian labour and new labour codes: A critical analysis. *Christ ULJ*, *10*, 1.

Chigater, S. (2021). Labour Law Reforms and Women's Work in India: Assessing the New Labour Codes From a Gender Lens. *Available at SSRN* 3947175.

Collins, P. H. (2000). Patricia Hill Collins. *Intersectionality and Matrix of Domination, 28.*

Desai, V., Conte, A. H., Nguyen, V. T., Shin, P., Sudol, N. T., Hobbs, J., & Qiu, C. (2023). Veiled harm: Impacts of microaggressions on psychological safety and physician burnout. *The Permanente Journal*, *27*(2), 169. PMID: 37292028

Ghosh, J. (Ed.). (2021). *Informal women workers in the Global South: Policies and practices for the formalisation of women's employment in developing economies.* Routledge.

Hart, C. G. (2021). Trajectory guarding: Managing unwanted, ambiguously sexual interactions at work. *American Sociological Review*, *86*(2), 256–278.

Hochschild, A., Irwin, N., & Ptashne, M. (1983). Repressor structure and the mechanism of positive control. *Cell*, *32*(2), 319–325. PMID: 6218886

Jadhav, S., & Kulkarni, S. (2020). Sexual Harassment of Women at Workplace in India: A Review of the POSH Act 2013. *Journal of Real Estate. Construction Manager*, *35*(4), 36–43.

Jamali, D. (2010). MNCs and international accountability standards through an institutional lens: Evidence of symbolic conformity or decoupling. *Journal of Business Ethics*, *95*(4), 617–640.

Kanskar, S., & Pal, D. (2021). Reconceptualizing Sexual Harassment: Extending the POSH Act, 2013. *Jus Corpus LJ*, *2*, 467.

Kanter, R. M. (1977). *Men and women of the corporation.*

Khaled, A. F. M., & Ansar, A. (2024). Bangladesh's ready-made garments sector rebound: Revisiting gendered labor precarity and dependency. *Asian Jorunal of Comparitive Politics*, *9*(2), 218–237.

Malik, D. (2024). *Sex-based Harassment in the World of Work: Examining Evolving Jurisprudence Under India's Posh Law.* Cambridge Scholars Publishing.

Mezzadri, A. (2017). *Sweatshop regimes in the Indian garment industry.* Cambridge University Press.

Mezzadri, A. (2021). Indias informal capitalism: social structures of accumulation, forms of exploitation and social reproduction in the Sweatshop Regime. In *Handbook on social structure of accumulation theory* (pp. 152–168). Edward Elgar Publishing.

Mishra, A., & Dwivedi, A. (2024). Labor laws in India: History, evolutions, and critical analysis. *Labor History*, *65*(5), 678–698.

Mishra, A., Joseph, R., Gangadhara, M., & Lobo, R. (2023). Body as machine: Health vulnerability of women garment factory workers in India. *SSM. Qualitative Research in Health*, *4*, 100301.

More, A. A., & Jadhav, S. (2023). Implications of the New Labour Codes in India: A Comprehensive Analysis. *Jus Corpus LJ*, *4*, 298.

Nahar, H. L. (2024). *Addressing the silence: A study on the underreporting of sexual violence among female garment workers in Bangladesh* (No. 64). GLU Working Paper.

Nathan, D., Kelkar, G., & Mehta, B. (2022). Platform economy, techno-nationalism, and gig workers in India. In *The Routledge Handbook of the Gig Economy* (pp. 374–391). Routledge.

Nixon, R. (2011). *Slow Violence and the Environmentalism of the Poor*. Harvard University Press.

Oommen, S.S. (2023). The cost of silence: Examining the long-term impact of sexual exploitation on women in the workplace. *Issue 2 Indian JL & Legal Rsch, 5*,1.

Oosterom, M., Huq, L., Namuggala, V., Nazneen, S., Nankindu, P., Sultan, M., ... & Azim, F. (2022). The gendered price of precarity: Voicing and challenging workplace sexual harassment.

Pandey, S. K., & Spoorthi, B. (2023). Understanding the Social Consequences of Legal Developments in India. *Journal of Survey in Fisheries Sciences*, *10*(1), 3095–3104.

Power, M. (1997). *The audit society: Rituals of verification*. OUP Oxford.

Power, M. (2021). Modelling the micro-foundations of the audit society: Organizations and the logic of the audit trail. *Academy of Management Review*, *46*(1), 6–32.

Purang, P., Dutta, A., & Biwalkar, S. (2025). You do not belong here: Experiences of microaggression among Indian women engineers. *Gender in Management*, *40*(7), 891–909.

Raman, A. V., & Krishnan, L. R. K. (2021). Invisible Scars: Female Ready-made Garment Workers' Gendered Exploitation. *Indian Journal of Industrial Relations*, *56*(4).

Rani, A., Raman, K. J., Antony, S., & Thirumoorthy, A., & B, C. (2025). Microaggression and Its Impact on Lower Caste Women with Psychiatric Disorders in India. *Violence and Gender*, *12*(1), 35–42.

Ringblom, L. (2022). “It is just a joke!” informal interaction and gendered processes underground. *NORA*, *30*(2), 94–107.

Salmon, U. (2024). “It’s wicked hard to fight covert racism”: The case of microaggressions in science research organizations. *Gender, Work and Organization*, *31*(3), 727–748.

Sapre, S. R. (2024). *Made in India: Contestation and Power Dynamics in Export-Oriented Garment Production in the Indian Context*. Michigan State University.

Sengupta, S., & Guchhait, S. K. (2021). Inequality in contemporary India: Does caste still matter? *Journal of Developing Societies*, *37*(1), 57–82.

Sharma, B., & Geetha, K. A. (2021). Casteing gender: Intersectional oppression of Dalit women. *Journal of International Women’s Studies*, *22*(10), 1–7.

Sue, D. W., & Spanierman, L. (2020). *Microaggressions in everyday life*. John Wiley & Sons.

Sundar, K. S. (2021). The shaky foundation of the labour law reforms. *The Hindu*.

Teltumbde, A. (2010). Globalization and caste. *Voice of Dalit*, *3*(2), 101–138.

Thakkar, S. (2024). Exploitation, harassment, and violence: Lived experiences of women paid domestic workers in India. *Journal of South Asian Development*, *19*(1), 44–60.

Tripathi, G. (2022). A comprehensive study on sexual harassment in india and its impact on women well being and social dynamics.

Velluti, S. (2024). Labour standards in global garment supply chains and the proposed EU corporate sustainability due diligence directive. *European Labour Law Journal*, *15*(4), 822–850.

Warhurst, C. (2016). From invisible work to invisible workers. *Invisible Labor: Hidden Work in the Contemporary World*, 214.

Chapter 7
Regulating the Private Sector:
Opportunities, Risks, and Transnational Governance Pathways for HRM Reform

Mohan Kumar
https://orcid.org/0000-0002-5171-0892
Faculty of Commerce and Management, SGT University, India

Nandan Kumar Jha
Center for Disctance and Online Education (Management), Galgotias University, Greater Noida, India

Ali Najeeb
https://orcid.org/0000-0003-4663-9347
Qasim Ibrahim School of Business, Villa College, Maldives

Himanshi Rajora
https://orcid.org/0000-0001-5686-3030
JGBS, O.P. Jindal Global University, Sonipat, India

ABSTRACT

The digitalization of modern workplaces has accelerated the adoption of Human Resource Information Systems (HRIS) and surveillance technologies, transforming organizational efficiency and control. While offering operational benefits, these tools pose critical threats to employee privacy, autonomy, and fairness. This chapter examines the ethical and legal challenges of digital monitoring, highlighting gaps in current data protection frameworks. It explores issues such as algorithmic bias,

DOI: 10.4018/979-8-3693-5390-5.ch007

consent under power asymmetry, psychological harm, and cross-border data risks. Arguing for comprehensive legal reform, the chapter advocates a human-centric model emphasizing proportionality, transparency, and participatory governance. Proposed solutions include Workplace Surveillance Impact Assessments, algorithmic audits, and employee involvement in monitoring decisions. By aligning legal innovation with ethical responsibility, the chapter offers pathways to balance technological advancement with fundamental employee rights

INTRODUCTION

The globalization of the world economy and the expansion of global production networks (GPNs) have profoundly transformed the labor landscape, positioning questions of working life and employee well-being at the core of global governance debates. This era is marked by a new phase of capitalist 'Landnahme,' wherein companies expand value production far beyond their traditional formal boundaries, increasingly integrating hitherto non-capitalist forms of work. Consequently, Human Resource Management (HRM), traditionally focused primarily on achieving economic organizational performance, has been compelled to redefine its mandate. This strategic reorientation has led to states prioritizing flexibility over protection to maintain economic competitiveness, driving the adoption of increasingly formalized models such as Sustainable HRM (SHRM), which conceptually incorporates principles like long-term organizational survival through resource regeneration and the comprehensive care of employees and the environment(Stankevičiute & Savanevičiene, 2018). Yet, the practical implementation of this philosophy often clashes with the economic imperatives driving these same global transformations.

Despite the rhetorical emphasis on human resource development and renewal inherent in models like SHRM, the dominant trend in labor practice remains the relocation of work to spheres outside the traditional protective framework of labor legislation, resulting in heightened precarity and a profound degradation of legal conditions. This crisis is acutely manifested across several critical domains, including segmented national labor markets and transnational global supply chains (GSCs). Nationally, states, driven by economic considerations, have utilized policy reforms that prioritize flexibility, creating dual labor markets saturated with easily terminable fixed-term and temporary contracts. This process effectively undermines protective rights associated with traditional employment status(Jalón Aymerich & Herce, 2020).

The emergent digital economy exacerbates these dynamics. Platforms operating under models like cloud-working and crowdsourcing utilize "regulatory arbitrage" to exploit ambiguities in existing legislation. By classifying workers as independent contractors, platforms circumvent mandatory compliance with fundamental safety and social security provisions. This continuous exposure to precarious employment, often lasting 12 or more months, is consistently linked to severe adverse health outcomes, notably increased symptoms of poor mental health and reduced self-rated general health (Kumar, Dagar, et al., 2025)(Pulford et al., 2022).

Furthermore, within transnational GSCs, reliance on voluntary Corporate Codes of Conduct (CoC) and external auditing has been exposed as often insufficient or ineffective in achieving long-term improvements in factory labor standards. Evidence suggests that auditing frequently operates less as a tool for genuine improvement and more as a filtering mechanism used primarily to identify and remove only the worst offending factories. This enforcement deficit stems from structural challenges related to transparency and accountability, exposing gaps across multiple governance functions, specifically concerning oversight, anticipation (foresight), continuous monitoring (hindsight), and organizational continuity (resight). This dual failure-the internal national deregulation and the external transnational enforcement deficiency-is predicated on the pervasive imbalance of power that favours capital mobility and corporate interests over the fundamental protection of workers (Liukkunen, 2020) (Nguyen et al., 2025).

This chapter seeks to systematically analyze the critical tension between the aspirational rise of social and sustainable HRM frameworks (which advocate for employee participation, fairness, and compliance beyond mere legal minimums) and the sustained practical erosion of labor rights driven by globalized and digitized employment models. We posit that this divergence stems from persistent failures in institutional adaptation, political prioritization, and enforcement mechanisms that allow the conversion of structural flexibility into widespread precarity.

Specifically, this research addresses the following core questions:

1. **RQ1:** How do shifting global economic priorities, particularly those related to capitalist *Landnahme* and digital transformation, necessitate and constrain proposed reforms in private-sector HRM models?
2. **RQ2:** What specific regulatory and institutional deficits permit the continued prevalence of precarious work models within global supply chains and platform economies, despite the high validity of international "decent work" norms?
3. **RQ3:** How do internal HRM formalization efforts conflict with the underlying structural inequalities of the labor relationships they attempt to govern, particularly in their failure to mitigate distributional problems of labor?

The scholarly significance of this chapter is threefold. First, it advances theoretical understanding by bridging the managerial perspective of strategic HRM/SHRM with critical analyses rooted in institutional political economy and transnational labor governance. Second, it offers a crucial framework for analytically evaluating the inherent limitations of relying on voluntary compliance mechanisms (such as CSR and auditing) in the face of structural economic pressures, contributing empirical context to the debate on the efficacy of corporate self-regulation. Finally, by detailing the functional connection between institutional deficits and the increasingly evident adverse social and health outcomes linked to labor precarity, this work provides a strong normative basis for arguing in favor of urgently reforming global regulatory and enforcement structures to ensure genuinely sustainable and equitable employment relations worldwide.

CONCEPTUAL FOUNDATIONS

The conceptual framework necessary for understanding contemporary global labor relations rests upon the dynamic interplay between modern Human Resource Management (HRM) practices, national labor regulation regimes, and the evolving landscape of international labor standards, all negotiated within the broader architecture of global labor governance. This intricate system attempts to reconcile the demands of economic competitiveness and market flexibility with the universal imperative of social justice and worker protection.

HRM Reform and the Sustainable Imperative

Historically, HRM research largely focused on achieving organizational economic performance, frequently viewing employees primarily as a means to an end. This perspective prioritized efficiency, often leading to the *consumption* rather than the *development* of human resources. Modern HRM reform, encapsulated by models such as Sustainable HRM (SHRM), challenges this narrow view. SHRM is seen as an extension of Strategic HRM (SHRM does not refute the aspects of Strategic HRM), but shifts the focus to long-term organizational survival and viability, which requires the regeneration, development, and renewal of the human resource base (Kumar et al., 2024; Kumar, Yadav, et al., 2025).

SHRM mandates a broader concept of success by acknowledging multiple bottom lines, explicitly recognizing economic, social, human, and environmental outcomes. Core characteristics defining SHRM include: establishing a long-term orientation, demonstrating care of employees, balancing the inevitable necessity of profitability, fostering flexibility, practicing fairness and equality, and maintaining compliance beyond labor regulations. This shift attempts to bring humanity back into HRM by prioritizing employee well-being as a necessity for long-term survival, especially given contemporary issues such as burnout, stress, and difficulties in balancing work and private life. Crucially, SHRM introduces the idea of anticipating the negative effects of business operations, often applying the framework of negative externality theory to address harm not just to employees, but also to their families and communities.

Labor Regulation and the Crisis of Flexibility

Traditional national labor law has historically served a foundational protective function, existing primarily to safeguard the weaker party-the employee-against the employer's superior contractual power. By sanctioning distinct rights, labor law explicitly seeks to compensate for inherent power imbalances, thereby situating employment relations more clearly within the public domain(Pérez & Canevaro, 2016).

However, in recent decades, states facing global economic competition have actively embraced regulatory strategies that prioritize flexibility over labor protection to maintain economic appeal. This drive toward deregulation often involves curtailing previous labor rights to make the labor market more flexible. In Spain, this process has been documented as a trajectory of liberalisation characterized first by dualism (creating temporary contracts at the margin of protected employment) and subsequently moving towards deregulation at the core (reducing severance costs and enabling unilateral employer changes) (Cárdenas, 2023). This systemic pursuit of flexibility often leads to precarious employment-a condition encompassing employment instability, low material rewards, limited opportunities for training, and an erosion of employee rights and protection. Persistent exposure to precarious employment (lasting 12 months or longer) is associated with adverse health outcomes, particularly symptoms of poor mental health and reduced self-rated general health. This situation highlights a profound conflict: the legal pursuit of market flexibility risks undermining the fundamental protective mandate of labor law, transferring risk and insecurity from employers to workers (Boes et al., 2017)(Yadav, Mittal, et al., 2024).

International Labor Standards and Global Labor Governance

The crisis of national regulation, exacerbated by globalization, necessitates governance mechanisms that operate beyond territorial state law. Global Labor Governance (GLG) is the conceptual system concerned with norm-setting for the social dimension of globalization. At its core is the International Labour Organization (ILO), whose founding purpose is rooted in the belief that world peace must be built upon social justice(Waas, 2021).

The ILO operationalizes GLG through International Labour Standards (ILS), centered on the vision of Decent Work. Decent Work consists of four strategic pillars: rights at work, employment creation, social protection, and social dialogue. Crucially, the concept of Decent Work affirms that traditional labor law mechanisms, focused solely on the employment contract, are insufficient to address the labor question universally. Instead, Decent Work explicitly extends protection and attention to all forms of work, including the informal economy and non-standard arrangements.

Distinguishing Hard Law and Soft Law

The ILS framework employs a mixed methodology of *hard* and *soft* law instruments:

Hard Law: ILO Conventions represent binding international treaties that acquire legal effect for member states only upon formal ratification. These include the fundamental labor rights or core labor standards (FLRs)-such as freedom of association and prohibition of forced/child labor.

Soft Law: ILO Recommendations provide guidance on policy, legislation, and practice but are not open to ratification, and thus carry persuasive but non-binding authority. Outside the ILO, soft law also includes Corporate Social Responsibility (CSR) Codes of Conduct and voluntary multi-stakeholder standards adopted unilaterally by companies or industry groups(Sanders et al., 2018).

GLG must navigate the tension between the legal force of Hard Law and the flexibility of Soft Law. While Hard Law guarantees foundational worker rights, its effectiveness often hinges on sufficient enforcement within domestic legal systems. Conversely, Soft Law mechanisms, particularly voluntary CSR standards, face criticism regarding their sufficiency, as auditing is often employed merely as a filter to remove the worst offenders rather than a tool to ensure long-term improvement, potentially serving corporate branding over worker welfare. The overarching challenge for GLG is that while the validity of norms (their institutional and discursive acceptance) may be high globally, their facticity (compliance and implementation) is often low, creating a "double diagnosis" of crisis. The struggle to achieve genuinely universal social justice requires coordinating public international legal efforts with the influence exerted by private market forces, ensuring that flexible employment models do not permit "regulatory escape" from fundamental labor protection.

THEORETICAL FRAMEWORK

The transformation of Human Resource Management (HRM) is a complex response to intertwined global economic pressures and evolving social demands, marked simultaneously by powerful calls for fundamental change and entrenched institutional resistance. Analyzing this phenomenon requires a multi-theoretical framework encompassing Institutional Theory, the Resource-Based View (RBV), Stakeholder Theory, Transnational Governance Theory (TGT), and Comparative

HRM. This analysis will explore how these perspectives reveal the critical drivers enabling HRM reform and the deep-seated barriers impeding genuine progress, often resulting in superficial compliance rather than systemic transformation.

Institutional and Comparative HRM Drivers and Barriers

Institutional Theory (IT) posits that organizational structures and practices are shaped by the regulatory, normative, and cognitive elements of their environment, driving isomorphism through coercive, mimetic, or normative pressures. A primary driver of HRM reform, particularly toward flexibility, stems from coercive state intervention aimed at improving national competitiveness and attracting foreign investment. For example, Indonesia's Job Creation Law exemplifies a national effort toward labor deregulation, streamlining permits and legalizing longer fixed-term contracts to boost the investment climate. This top-down imposition forces private organizations to adopt more flexible employment models, representing a coercive institutional driver for change. Similarly, many Latin American countries pursue pro-market policies aimed at reducing inefficiencies and stimulating Total Factor Productivity (TFP), reflecting a belief that less government intervention and greater economic freedom boost national productivity (Policies, 2023)(Yadav, Kumar, et al., 2024).

However, institutional forces often act as significant barriers. Comparative HRM literature shows that long-established regulatory frameworks, deeply embedded in a country's history, resist rapid transformation. In Spain, the labor market trajectory evolved from protected employment to a dualization phase (1984–1996) based on precarious temporary contracts at the margin, eventually leading to full deregulation at the core (1997–2019). This shows that rather than immediate change, institutional change often follows non-linear pathways, using stratification (dualism) as a strategy that later enables core deregulation. Furthermore, internal state capacity and regulatory structure act as profound barriers. In Uzbekistan, the judicial system's weakness in handling labor disputes is attributed to judges lacking specialized employment expertise, leading to ineffective procedural mechanisms. This systemic failure to enforce hard law prevents effective HRM compliance, reinforcing that theoretical legal frameworks alone are insufficient drivers of reform(Musakhonovich et al., 2024).

Resource-Based View and Strategic Imperatives

The Resource-Based View (RBV) drives HRM reform by defining human capital and unique organizational capabilities as sources of sustained competitive advantage.

From this perspective, implementing advanced HRM practices (such as integrating technology or enhancing specific employee skills) is a strategic necessity.

A key driver identified by RBV is the pursuit of innovation, particularly in capital-intensive sectors. Studies in China's manufacturing sector show that flexible employment positively contributes to enterprise innovation input and output. This relationship is successful because firms integrate superior Information Technology Capability (ITC), which acts as a moderator, enabling efficient resource allocation, communication, and knowledge capture across the enterprise. ITC helps mitigate the drawbacks of temporary employment by storing and internalizing the knowledge provided by external workers (You et al., 2023).

A significant barrier recognized by RBV is the risk inherent in investing in human capital. Multinational enterprises (MNEs) pay a wage premium to experienced employees largely to retain them and prevent the spillover of firm-specific knowledge to competitors, particularly in countries where intellectual property protection is weak. This defence mechanism against knowledge erosion drives up operational costs and highlights a core tension: MNEs must invest in human resources (training, experience) to exploit their Firm-Specific Advantages (FSAs), but simultaneously must defend those investments, leading to complex and often unequal wage distribution patterns. Furthermore, if public organizations adopt digital HRM tools (like Human Resources Information Systems or HRIS), their effectiveness is contingent upon employees possessing the necessary competence (ability) and motivation to utilize them. For instance, Indonesian public service workers experienced low innovation outcomes from HRIS adoption, suggesting that coercive technological implementation alone, without addressing underlying factors like ability and motivation, renders the technology merely complimentary, not compulsory (Satispi et al., 2023)(Yadav et al., 2025).

Transnational Governance and Stakeholder Dynamics

Transnational Governance Theory (TGT) analyzes the effectiveness of regulatory mechanisms that span national boundaries, such as Global Production Networks (GPNs) and international labor standards. Stakeholder Theory (ST) focuses on how firms manage the often-competing demands of different constituent groups (e.g., workers, consumers, NGOs, governments).

A core TGT barrier to genuine HRM reform is the persistent enforcement deficit and the ineffectiveness of voluntary compliance measures. Auditing systems deployed via Corporate Codes of Conduct (CoC) in global supply chains often fail to achieve long-term improvements in labor conditions. Audits tend to function primarily as a filtering mechanism to remove the worst offenders rather than as a tool for fundamental improvement. This weakness is exacerbated by strategic deception at the factory level, where workers and management collude to hide non-compliance from external auditors, often motivated by a temporary sense of reciprocal exchange where workers expect the management to address core demands (like wages or working hours) later(Hoang, 2019).

In the emerging gig economy, TGT identifies the problem of regulatory escape. Platforms evade existing labor protections by classifying workers as independent contractors and leveraging technological features-algorithmic management-to control the labor process, maximizing profit while shedding employer responsibilities for safety, pensions, and unemployment. TGT highlights the resulting regulatory gaps: a lack of oversight (knowledge gaps), hindsight (accident underreporting), resight (discontinuous improvement due to high turnover), and foresight (inability to prioritize emerging risks).

Conversely, external stakeholder pressure can act as a powerful driver for reform. Citizen and consumer activism, supported by the legitimacy of international norms, creates normative pressure on MNEs (ST). For instance, public opinion across major middle-income democracies (Brazil, India, Indonesia) shows surprisingly strong support for stringent domestic sustainability regulations aligned with global supply chain standards. This acceptance is driven by perceived benefits (safer production, job creation) outweighing concerns about costs. This demand for ethical sourcing and compliance generates a normative driver for corporations to prioritize social standards, if only for reputational reasons. Additionally, the increasing prominence of the Decent Work norm (which includes fundamental rights, social protection, and social dialogue) creates high **validity** (discursive acceptance) globally, even if facticity (implementation) is low, prompting ongoing debate and structural reform initiatives (Drubel & Mende, 2023).

HRM reform operates at the fraught intersection of economic, legal, and social demands. Drivers include coercive state liberalization efforts (IT, CHRM), the strategic pursuit of innovation and competitive advantage (RBV), and normative pressure from conscious consumers and global governance ideals (ST, TGT). However, reform is consistently undermined by rigid institutional legacies (CHRM), the systematic failure of soft-law enforcement mechanisms (TGT), the ability of digital platforms to execute "regulatory escape" (TGT), and internal organizational deficits (RBV/IT). The fundamental challenge remains shifting the institutional and cultural mindset from viewing labor protection as a cost to viewing comprehensive human resource development and equitable governance as foundational to long-term sustainable competitive advantage, a necessity increasingly demanded by stakeholders globally(van der Straaten et al., 2020).

COMPARATIVE HRM

Labor market regulation varies significantly among developed democracies, with LMEs and CMEs showcasing divergent approaches to managing labor forces and redistribution. In contexts characterized by high government debt and high market inequality, left-wing governments may increase labor market regulation to serve as a tool for non-fiscal redistribution(Aaskoven, 2019).

In contrast, HRM systems in emerging economies often face institutional pressures driving liberalization to attract investment and economic growth. This institutional prioritization frequently translates into precarious working conditions and labor exploitation. For example, Indonesia enacted the Job Creation Law specifically to boost market flexibility by reducing previous worker protections, extending the possibility of fixed-term contracts, and loosening restrictions on outsourcing.

HRM systems in emerging economies suffer from structural deficits in governance and enforcement. Many occupations function within the informal sector (such as domestic work in South Africa), making it difficult to ensure legal and social protections. Where formal legal systems exist, they may lack the capacity for effective enforcement; in Uzbekistan, general courts handling labor disputes suffer from a lack of specialization and expertise, hindering the timely and effective resolution of complex industrial relations conflicts. This institutional divergence results in unique challenges for MNEs navigating these highly heterogeneous environments(van der Straaten et al., 2020).

Regulatory Opportunities in HRM Reform

Regulatory reforms play a catalytic role in shaping the operating environment of private firms, influencing internal management practices, market positioning, and long-term viability by demanding higher standards across multiple dimensions. These mandatory or incentivized institutional changes fundamentally enhance transparency, workforce governance, and sustainability, subsequently translating into improved competitiveness and stronger employer branding.

Enhancing Transparency through Formal Regulation

Regulatory changes directly increase operational transparency by requiring the disclosure of information traditionally held within the private sphere. This shift subjects internal organizational practices to public scrutiny, which is instrumental in driving compliance. For instance, the introduction of labor rights legislation, such as regulations governing domestic service, mandated that these relationships-historically ambiguously situated between the public and private worlds-be brought into the clear domain of the law for accountability purposes. This process converts private conduct into public information legible to courts and inspectorates(Pérez & Canevaro, 2016).

In modern market contexts, transparency is frequently achieved through labeling mechanisms that certify adherence to ethical standards. The proposed 'Quality Agricultural Work' (QAW) ethical label in the Italian fruit sector aims to establish a 'whitelist' of farms compliant with specific labor regulations. This label transforms labor compliance into a recognizable attribute for consumers, thereby exposing producers to market-based judgment. For effective governance of emerging sectors, clarity is also key: identifying and regulating platforms requires addressing the opaqueness of algorithmic management, necessitating rules that mandate disclosure regarding how digital labor processes are controlled and evaluated. Without mechanisms that mandate such disclosure, regulatory oversight remains incomplete(Nilsen et al., 2022).

Improving Workforce Governance and Standards

Regulatory reforms strengthen workforce governance by formalizing employment relationships and institutionalizing protective mechanisms, serving fundamentally to safeguard the weaker party-the employee-against the employer's superior bargaining power. Effective governance is achieved by establishing clear expectations for labor standards and defining enforcement avenues. For example, legal rights legislation ensures that labor relations are situated in the public world, granting entitlements such as mandatory paid vacations, sick leave, and dismissal compensation. Moreover, legislative reforms broaden the scope of worker protection to address new categories of rights. In Argentina, reforms led to the inclusion of maternity and marriage licenses, and family allowances for domestic workers.

Regulation explicitly targets the deficiencies of informal and unfair labor practices, thereby stabilizing employment structures. The Italian QAW network actively tackles undeclared and exploitative labor by creating verified lists of compliant employers Legal frameworks also provide mechanisms for conflict resolution, shifting disputes from informal personal dynamics to formal judicial procedures, as observed with the Tribunal del Trabajo Doméstico (TTD). Even in the face of persistent power imbalances, as often seen in developing economies, regulatory mandates, such as establishing compensation for fixed-term contract (PKWT) workers in Indonesia, enforce minimum standards of accountability for employers. Overall, a supportive legal environment, characterized by functional labor freedom and efficient administration, positively correlates with entrepreneurial stability and new venture creation, suggesting that regulation supports robust human capital formation(Bakkar et al., 2021).

Driving Corporate Sustainability

Regulation is a primary mechanism for fostering Sustainable HRM (SHRM), a conceptual model that shifts management's focus from purely economic performance to long-term organizational survival through resource regeneration. SHRM advocates for considering a multi-dimensional outcome that includes human, social, and environmental concerns, thereby moving beyond the traditional view of employees merely as instruments for profit.

The core characteristics of sustainable HRM, which regulations encourage, include a long-term orientation regarding human resource planning, care of employees, and compliance that exceeds minimum legal standards. The aspect of care of employees includes ensuring a safe working environment, fair remuneration, and managing workload and work-life balance issues. For multinational enterprises (MNEs), the need to maintain an international reputation, coupled with heightened public scrutiny, acts as a powerful institutional force compelling compliance with diversity and equality standards, particularly in developed countries where domestic firms often maintain high standards. Conversely, the absence of sufficient regulation exacerbates sustainability deficits, exemplified by the risks posed to agricultural workers lacking adequate labor regulations and protective gear against chemical exposure. Thus, regulatory influence is indispensable for embedding ethical and regenerative practices into core business strategy(Valencia-Quintana et al., 2023).

Enhancing Competitiveness and Employer Branding

Well-designed regulatory systems, especially those mandating social and ethical compliance, convert potential liabilities into assets, thereby strengthening a firm's market competitiveness and employer brand identity.

Competitiveness

Compliance with certified ethical standards offers a critical competitive edge. Studies show that consumers demonstrate a willingness to pay a high price premium for products, such as fruit, that are certified to have been produced under fair working conditions. This consumer preference effectively translates social compliance into a source of reputational advantage and market differentiation. In the manufacturing sector, compliance with robust labor regulations, coupled with high information technology capabilities, positively impacts enterprise innovation input and output. This dynamic suggests that stability gained through adhering to formal standards facilitates the integration of new technologies and organizational capabilities, leading to performance improvements and sustainable enterprise development.

Furthermore, by establishing predictable and equitable labor practices, companies can better allocate resources, mitigate the risks associated with high turnover, and increase the efficiency necessary to compete effectively.

Employer Branding

A strong regulatory environment supports positive employer branding by affirming the company's commitment to decent working conditions, essential for attracting and retaining high-quality talent. Providing transparency and fairness in compensation and working arrangements is paramount to this appeal. Conversely, the perception of organizational instability or widespread discrimination actively undermines the ability to attract desirable employees, limiting the available workforce pool. MNEs, conscious of their global reputation, are driven toward greater transparency and standardization in their human resource practices to appeal to a broad, international talent market. Therefore, regulation sets the baseline conditions under which private firms can build a legitimate and attractive reputation as employers of choice, making compliance an intrinsic part of securing future human capital(van der Straaten et al., 2020).

Regulatory Opportunities in HRM Reform

Regulatory reforms fundamentally reshape the operational structure of private firms by mandating changes that enhance transparency and formalize workforce governance, ultimately contributing to long-term sustainability, increasing competitiveness, and strengthening employer branding. Traditionally, Human Resource Management (HRM) systems focused predominantly on achieving economic organizational performance, often viewing employees as resources to be consumed rather than developed. The resultant push towards models such as Sustainable HRM (SHRM) necessitates a strategic reorientation, prioritizing long-term organizational survival through resource regeneration, the care of employees, and compliance beyond mere legal minimums.

Regulatory Reforms and Corporate Enhancement

The implementation of protective labor legislation enhances transparency by drawing relationships that exist in the private world, such as domestic service, into the public domain of rights and justice. This legalization counters the pervasive trend of highly precarious and exploitative labor, ensuring that employment relations are subject to judicial and institutional scrutiny.

In terms of workforce governance, SHRM advocates for adopting policies characterized by a long-term orientation, comprehensive care of employees, balancing flexibility with fairness, and ensuring compliance that exceeds minimum regulatory requirements. This involves addressing critical issues such as providing a safe work environment, achieving work-life balance, managing workload, and ensuring fair remuneration. For organizations facing competition, this focus on human resource renewal and development becomes a survival strategy, allowing the organization to secure healthy and productive human resources for the future.

Regulatory and institutional conditions profoundly influence economic competitiveness. In Spain, the trajectory of labor market institutional change moved from a system of employment regulation established during a critical juncture (1976–1983) to a period of institutional dualism (1984–1996) that introduced flexibility at the margin, often through specific temporary contracts. This stratification eventually contributed to deregulation at the core (1997–2019), characterized by easier and cheaper dismissal costs for permanent employees, eroding protected employment. Conversely, rigid labor market regulation, though initially intended to protect workers, can hamper necessary adjustments for adopting new production technologies.

In contemporary emerging economies like China, flexible employment has been shown to positively contribute to sustainable enterprise development by enhancing innovation input and output. This phenomenon is moderated positively by superior information technology capabilities (IT) and strict labor regulations. Flexible employment introduces diverse new talent and innovative ideas, helping enterprises overcome internal rigidity and external knowledge gaps, thereby promoting sustainable innovation (You et al., 2023).

The adoption of robust HRM systems directly supports sustainability goals. SHRM explicitly incorporates the negative externality theory, compelling management to address harms inflicted not just on employees, but also on their families and the environment. By aligning with principles like fostering care of employees and ensuring fair remuneration, SHRM contributes to long-term organizational viability and reinforces the economic component of sustainability. Furthermore, international attention and pressure on Multinational Enterprises (MNEs) compels them to maintain equal opportunity and diversity standards, resulting in an upward harmonization of social practices. The combination of compliance, innovation, and sustainability significantly bolsters employer branding, making the organization an attractive choice for skilled labor.

Transparent HR Systems Strengthen Trust and Compliance

Transparent Human Resource (HR) management systems build trust by ensuring fairness and accountability across the employment lifecycle. In the realm of recruitment, transparency requires the explicit prohibition of discrimination, ensuring equal opportunity for all applicants based on objective criteria rather than extraneous factors like gender, age, or family responsibilities. For vulnerable groups such as women with family responsibilities, specific legislative guarantees are proposed to enable them to combine professional and family duties without facing hiring prejudice.

Appraisal and promotions benefit from formalized HR systems, particularly those established by MNEs, which are often highly standardized to execute global strategy and reduce managerial biases. These formal structures decrease the discretion that might otherwise lead to unequal allocation of pay or resources based on gender or other biases.

When disputes arise, access to transparent grievance systems and judicial protection mechanisms is crucial for restoring labor rights and building trust. Historically, court mechanisms like the Tribunal del Trabajo Doméstico (TTD) have been vital in transforming ambiguous relationships in the private world into formalized legal claims subject to public judicial review. However, the efficacy of these systems is critically dependent on institutional capacity. In countries like Uzbekistan, legal protections are undermined by a lack of specialized judicial competence, resulting in complex and slow resolution procedures that inhibit workers' access to justice. Trust in the system thus hinges both on the legal clarity and the reliable effectiveness of enforcement(Musakhonovich et al., 2024).

Regulatory Compliance, Corporate Reputation, Risk, and ESG Performance

Regulatory compliance is directly correlated with enhancing corporate reputation and bolstering ESG performance. The "S" (Social) component of ESG criteria emphasizes adherence to internationally recognized human rights, with International Labour Standards (ILS) providing a core foundation for measuring a company's sustainability and societal impact. Given the global prominence of MNEs, compliance serves as an essential tool to manage their public image and address legitimacy concerns regarding labor infringements.

Effective compliance significantly reduces risk, mitigating potential legal and financial liabilities. Investment tribunals are increasingly willing to impose accountability on investors for human rights, labor, and environmental violations associated with their projects. The level of due diligence conducted by an investor in a host state is now considered a factor when tribunals assess claims for protection under substantive investment agreements, such as the Fair and Equitable Treatment (FET) standard. Failure to assess risks properly, especially in contexts characterized by instability or non-compliance, can jeopardize an investor's ability to claim protection. Finally, global standards, such as the Global Reporting Initiative (GRI), require public disclosure of the management approach taken toward material social issues, linking internal performance results (e.g., grievance mechanisms, auditing) directly to declared ethical commitments(Waas, 2021).

AI, Automation, and HR Analytics Support Compliance Monitoring and Strengthen HR Decision-Making

The integration of AI, automation, and HR analytics into HR processes fundamentally strengthens decision-making and enhances compliance capabilities. HR Information Systems (HRIS) modernize HR functions by providing a steady stream of generated data that reduces uncertainty in labor planning and serves as a reliable basis for managerial decisions. In recruiting, sophisticated intelligent search systems utilize ontologies to model job descriptions and candidate CVs, facilitating efficient matching of individual skills to organizational needs. This process is key to ensuring the appropriate allocation of human capital.

For compliance monitoring and legal guidance, integrated systems incorporating AI and analytics can host legal knowledge domains. These models represent the semantics and relationships within complex legal documents (such as labor codes). This allows users (both employers and employees) to quickly query information regarding specific regulations, such as unemployment or healthcare benefits, ensuring adherence to legal standards. However, this digital transformation introduces vulnerabilities related to control. In platform-mediated work, algorithmic management automatically assigns, optimizes, and evaluates work using tracked data fundamentally transforming employment relations into standardized, taskified transactions, The inherent opaqueness of algorithmic control presents challenges to regulatory bodies, allowing platform companies to maximize profits while obscuring accountability for labor conditions(Nilsen et al., 2022).

Certifications, Codes of Conduct, and Supply Chain Audits Enforce Labor Standards across Global Production Networks

Certifications, Codes of Conduct (CoCs), and supply chain audits constitute essential components of private governance mechanisms intended to enforce labor standards in global production networks (GPNs). Audits, commonly commissioned by MNCs, are typically conducted to monitor compliance with CSR codes. However, empirical evidence suggests that repeated, long-term auditing often fails to generate statistically significant improvements in working conditions over time. Instead, the auditing process often acts more effectively as a filtering mechanism that is utilized to identify and remove the poorest performing factories from the GPN, rather than as a mechanism designed for achieving substantive, sustained reform(Sanders et al., 2018).

A critical barrier to the effectiveness of monitoring systems is related to worker behavior. Workers may willingly collaborate with management to deceive auditors and conceal non-compliance practices. This intentional concealment may stem from an expectation of reciprocal exchange, where workers support management in the short term under the assumption that management will return the favour by addressing their core demands regarding pay or working conditions. Conversely, certifications and ethical labels operate via market incentives, leveraging consumer purchasing power to drive compliance. The establishment of ethical labels, such as Italy's 'Quality Agricultural Work' (QAW) label, creates a recognizable certification for fair working conditions. Consumer studies affirm a strong willingness to pay a high price premium for certified products, making compliance a tangible business advantage that encourages producers to adhere to stipulated labor regulations(Rossi et al., 2024).

RISKS AND CHALLENGES

The contemporary labor market is defined by structural transformations driven by accelerating technological change and shifting global economic imperatives, leading to endemic challenges centered on regulatory fragmentation, enforcement gaps, gig-work vulnerabilities, and the ethical risks of digital HRM systems. Globalization and increasing economic competition have historically constrained the ability of states to act as strong regulatory actors, advocating for policy strategies that prioritize flexibility over traditional labor protection in an effort to maintain competitiveness. This institutional retreat creates a fundamental dilemma: traditional labor law is built upon the assumption of a clear, dyadic employment contract, a framework that is increasingly inadequate for achieving socially just outcomes in a world characterized by diverse, often precarious, forms of work.

This fragmentation is acutely exploited by digital labor platforms, which thrive by engaging in regulatory arbitrage, strategically defining their workers as independent contractors to shed traditional employer responsibilities such as social security and occupational safety. The nature of platform-mediated work (PMW)-characterized by a triangular, transient relationship and the taskification of labor-facilitates gig-work vulnerabilities. Platforms deliberately withhold operational information to avoid scrutiny and labor standard compliance. In vulnerable sectors, such as domestic work in South Africa, these platforms capitalize on the historical undervaluation of marginalized women's labor, embedding exploitation into their operating model. The consequence is widespread persistent precarious employment, lacking fundamental protections, social nets, and collective bargaining mechanisms.

Simultaneously, digital platforms introduce new forms of control through algorithmic management, a distinguishing feature that transforms work monitoring and distribution. Algorithms automatically assign, optimize, and evaluate human tasks using tracked data, cloaking platform accountability beneath a "black box" of technological opacity. The resulting labor environment subjects workers to ethical risks associated with digital control, notably evolving into a "system of permanent probation" based on measurable output and digital reputation. Even when implemented in the public sector, the introduction of Human Resource Information Systems (HRIS), often driven by coercive institutional pressures, may fail to generate desired outcomes like innovation, indicating that the technology itself cannot compensate for deeper deficits related to employee ability, motivation, and opportunity (AMO) (Satispi et al., 2023).

These internal firm strategies intersect with pervasive enforcement gaps across global governance systems. Within global production networks (GPNs), compliance is hindered by intricate, multi-layered subcontracting structures that allow multinational corporations (MNCs) to deny formal responsibility when transgressions occur. Voluntary corporate governance mechanisms, such as Corporate Social Responsibility (CSR) codes and factory audits, often prove insufficient against relentless economic pressure and are commonly used to mitigate legal liability or protect brand reputation rather than ensure genuine, sustained reform. Auditing frequently operates merely as a filtering mechanism designed to purge the worst offenders, not to promote continuous improvement. Enforcement failures are compounded by worker agency, as employees sometimes collaborate with management to hide non-compliance, viewing buyers' demands as hypocritical and fearing job loss if contracts are terminated(Hoang, 2019).

For digital platforms, the regulatory challenge is compounded by four specific, interconnected governance gaps: a lack of *oversight* (due to missing data and hidden enterprise registration), *hindsight* (inability to learn from diffused accidents and underreporting), *resight* (discontinuous improvement due to high worker turnover), and *foresight* (inability of traditional regulatory models to anticipate technologically emerging risks). Taming these powerful digital entities, which utilize symbolic power to frame their evasion of responsibility as "disruptive technology" and "flexibility", requires regulators to expand their purview beyond traditional command-and-control rules to encompass all forms of social and economic influence. Ultimately, the persistence of these intersecting challenges demonstrates a political failure to address fundamental distributional problems in the contemporary labor market(Khan, 2018).

Inconsistencies Between National and International Labor Rules Complicate Compliance

The disparity between international labor standards and national regulations poses significant complications for consistent compliance, often stemming from the transformation of labor law under global economic pressure. International bodies like the International Labour Organization (ILO) promote a vision of Decent Work, universally applicable and structured around core labor rights, employment creation, social protection, and social dialogue. However, in practice, national governments often adopt regulatory strategies emphasizing flexibility over protection in response to global economic competition. This shift undermines the legal and institutional framework needed for robust worker protections.

Compliance is further complicated by the fact that traditional labor law is built around the concept of an employment contract, which is increasingly insufficient for regulating modern, diverse forms of work that fall outside this framework. This results in a persistent gap between protected and unprotected workers. For example, despite Kazakhstan's ratification of core ILO Conventions, the effectiveness of these commitments is curtailed by weak law enforcement and insufficient implementation in domestic practice. Specific inconsistencies noted by the ILO supervisory bodies include Kazakhstan's failure to consolidate an adequate legal definition of "wages," adequately implement protections for workers with family responsibilities, and ensure the burden of proof rests with the employer in discrimination cases(Khamzina et al., 2022). Furthermore, regional governance mechanisms demonstrate this tension, such as in the EU, where the right to collective bargaining and industrial action (a component of freedom of association) is limited when balanced against the employer's fundamental economic freedoms. These inconsistencies reveal that economic interests often supersede the universal principles of social justice and fundamental labor rights.

The Tensions Between Cost Pressures and Adherence to Labor Standards

Firms operating in competitive global markets face inherent tensions between managing costs for profitability and adhering to mandated labor standards, which often dictate higher compliance expenses. Strict Employment Protection Legislation (EPL) protecting regular workers significantly increases the financial and administrative burden on firms, including costs associated with firing, overall compliance, and adjusting the workforce to fluctuating market conditions. In response to these cost pressures, companies often rely excessively on temporary contract workers as a low-cost, flexible means to adjust their workforce rapidly, thereby circumventing the extensive firing and compliance costs associated with permanent contracts. This approach risks sacrificing long-term stability and future innovation benefits in favor of immediate financial gains through cheap labor.

At the governmental level, managing this cost-versus-welfare tension is a key political economy challenge. Left-wing governments, constrained by high government debt and faced with rising market inequality, may deploy labor market regulation (such as minimum wage laws or hiring restrictions) as a nonfiscal redistribution tool. This approach is used to secure worker welfare when direct fiscal transfers are fiscally impossible. While adhering to strong labor standards can induce firms to seek value-enhancing process innovation to restore productivity and foster worker commitment, the dominant reality remains that high costs often lead firms to seek mechanisms, legal or otherwise, to reduce their burden(Sapkal, 2016).

The Misclassification Issues, Vulnerabilities, and Lack of Protections Faced by Platform and Gig Workers

The platform economy is intrinsically linked to misclassification, leveraging it as a core business strategy to maximize profits while externalizing risks onto workers. Platform-mediated work (PMW) transforms labor relationships into a transient, standardized exchange of atomized tasks mediated by an app. By classifying individuals as independent contractors, platforms engage in regulatory arbitrage, effectively shielding themselves from employer obligations, such as providing social protection, occupational safety, and benefits.

This misclassification directly creates acute vulnerabilities for gig workers. Lacking traditional protections, these workers, who are often migrants or young individuals, fall through legal safety nets. The resulting condition of persistent precarious employment (lasting 12 months or longer) is linked to significant negative health outcomes, increasing the odds of developing symptoms of poor mental health (OR 1.44) and poor self-rated general health (OR 1.53) compared to those in stable employment. Control is maintained not by human managers but by algorithmic management, which assigns, evaluates, and optimizes jobs using tracked data. The lack of transparency surrounding these algorithms-the "black box"-exacerbates the power imbalance, leaving workers without recourse against punitive rating and ranking systems. Workers are often compelled by economic necessity to accept these conditions, including low pay (as seen in domestic work in South Africa)(Hunt & Samman, 2020), leading to a deeply ingrained sense of individual responsibility for safety despite external control mechanisms. The inherent design of the platform model perpetuates precarity by ensuring minimal security and rights.

Why Accountability Weakens in Global Supply Chains and Why Enforcement Often Fails Internationally

Accountability in global supply chains (GPNs) is fundamentally compromised by the intricate, multi-layered structure of sourcing and production that grants capital mobility while undermining regulatory enforcement. Enforcement often fails because voluntary governance mechanisms, particularly Corporate Social Responsibility (CSR) standards and factory audits, are insufficient barriers against market pressures. These audits are criticized as tools primarily designed to protect the buyer's brand and mitigate legal liability, operating merely as a filtering mechanism to identify and shed the worst-offending suppliers rather than ensuring sustained, positive reform. This problem is compounded by a lack of transparency in contracting. Brands frequently lack or deny a formal contractual relationship with subcontractors in deep layers of the supply chain, allowing them to evade direct responsibility for violations. Furthermore, workers and management sometimes collude to hide non-compliance from auditors. This tactical deception is often driven by workers' expectations of reciprocal exchange (hoping management will address core demands later) and the belief that reporting violations will only lead to the cancellation of contracts, resulting in job loss. Ultimately, transnational labor governance fails because its focus is too narrow, emphasizing fundamental rights but neglecting the deep-seated distributional problems of labor arising from deregulation.

AI bias, worker surveillance, and data-privacy concerns within DIGITAL HRM SYSTEMS

Digital HRM systems introduce significant ethical risks related to AI bias, pervasive surveillance, and data-privacy violations. The systems rely on automated decision-making and are built on knowledge bases, such as those used in intelligent search systems for job matching, which inevitably carry potential biases from the underlying data. These algorithmic biases risk exacerbating existing inequalities, including gender discrimination in employment access or pay.

Pervasive worker surveillance is integral to digital management, enabling a system of control based on measuring performance and tracking workers. High-skilled workers are subjected to a "system of permanent probation" linked to their digital reputation, raising serious concerns about autonomy and work-life balance. This extensive monitoring is maintained, especially in remote work settings, where management focuses on continuous performance feedback. The lack of clarity regarding how information is handled and retained heightens data-privacy **concerns** and the risk of psychological fatigue and burnout due to the blurring of boundaries between professional and private life(Sheveleva & Rogov, 2021).

INTEGRATED CONCEPTUAL MODEL

The model begins with Regulatory Inputs originating across governance scales. At the Global level, inputs include universal standards established by bodies like the International Labour Organization (ILO), emphasizing core labor rights (e.g., freedom of association) and the Decent Work Agenda. These translate to Macro inputs, such as national labor codes (e.g., Indonesia's Job Creation Law), deregulation policies, and economic priorities like market liberalization or fiscal constraints. Meso inputs involve industry-specific regulations (e.g., agricultural standards or trade agreement labor chapters) and prevailing local neighborhood norms. Micro inputs are derived from firm-level compliance mechanisms, particularly Corporate Social Responsibility (CSR) Codes of Conduct set by Multinational Enterprises (MNCs)(Sanders et al., 2018).

The HRM Processes translate these inputs into internal operations. These processes encompass fundamental functions such as compensation and dismissal policies, employee development, and working hour regulations. A critical process involves the adoption of non-standard work arrangements, including flexible employment (FE) and outsourcing, often facilitated by Information Technology (IT) capabilities or HR Information Systems (HRIS).

The Organizational Outputs are multifaceted. They include economic outcomes like organizational profitability and overall labor productivity, and employee-level outcomes such as health and mental well-being, job precarity, or skill accumulation(You et al., 2023). Feedback Loops occur when these outputs influence subsequent regulatory cycles; for instance, observed compliance deficits or increased worker precarity (Outputs) trigger calls for stronger enforcement or the creation of new international or national legislation (Inputs).

FUTURE DIRECTIONS & RESEARCH AGENDA

The integrated conceptual analysis outlines crucial forward-looking research directions, emphasizing the intersection of digital transformation, sustainability, transnational regulation, and human resource management practices.

Future research should focus on how the pervasive expansion of capitalist structures into the "information space" influences the formal and regulated social system of labor, interpreting the phenomenon as a new stage of capitalist *Landnahme*. Specifically, researchers need to analyze how corporate strategies use the global information space to integrate diverse forms of societal work and private activity into value-added processes, effectively subjecting them to *de facto* wage labor arrangements without applying legal labor norms. This demands an urgent agenda examining how regulation can establish protective rights linked to the employee status, which are currently being undermined by the flexible and industrialized production methods enabled by digitalization, presenting challenges for labor law and social security systems(Boes et al., 2017). Regulatory fragmentation arises as states emphasize flexibility over protection, often aligning regulatory strategies with economic competition rather than workers' welfare. A pathway to harmonization requires adopting an inclusive view of work, such as the ILO's Decent Work concept, which applies standards beyond traditional employment contracts. Harmonization efforts must address the growing vulnerabilities stemming from globalization and complex changes in work organization, recognizing that traditional labor law frameworks are insufficient to tackle issues like informal work or atypical employment. To counter the decline in collective bargaining coverage and institutional changes pushing decentralization, future regulation needs to build inclusive frameworks that strengthen fundamental rights universally across different legal and social contexts, encouraging multilateral trade and investment negotiations to enforce these standards. This approach ensures protection is extended to all working individuals(Liukkunen, 2020).

KEY RESEARCH NEEDS RELATED TO ALGORITHMIC FAIRNESS, AI ETHICS, AND DIGITAL LABOR RIGHTS

Key research is needed into how algorithmic management, which assigns, optimizes, and evaluates work through tracked data and opaque algorithms, impacts working conditions and safety. Scholars must investigate the lack of transparency surrounding platform technology, which contributes to work pressures and cloaks platform accountability. Research should explore the mechanisms platforms use to exert symbolic power, framing practices like externalization of responsibility as technological innovation or flexibility, thereby navigating regulatory grey areas. Furthermore, given platforms' enormous data gathering capability, studies must address issues of data ownership, how information is used, and how to build regulatory competence in digital technology to impose platform transparency, ensuring the protection of fundamental labor rights in this digital ecosystem. This inquiry is vital due to the ease with which platforms classify workers to avoid detection and liability.

CONCLUSION

Transnational Human Resource Management (HRM) governance faces significant structural challenges rooted in globalized production methods and digitalization, necessitating coordinated policy and ethical responses. A crucial insight is the challenge posed by transnational actors engaging in regulatory escape, notably amplified by digital platforms. Companies increasingly structure their operations, such as cloudsourcing and crowdsourcing, to bypass traditional employer–employee relationships, effectively subjecting societal work to *de facto* wage labor arrangements without adhering to necessary legal labor regulations. This flexible model contributes directly to persistent precarious employment, characterized by unstable contracts and low material rewards, which available evidence consistently links to serious adverse health outcomes, particularly symptoms of poor mental health and low self-rated general health.

Furthermore, attempts to ensure compliance through private governance mechanisms are often undermined at the operational level. While multinational corporations (MNCs) adopt voluntary Corporate Social Responsibility (CSR) Codes of Conduct and auditing regimes to monitor global production networks (GPNs), these efforts are frequently nullified by *compliance deception*, where local management and workers actively collaborate to conceal non-compliance from visiting auditors. This highlights the unreliability of relying solely on external checks. Moreover, domestic labor disputes, particularly concerning highly vulnerable workers such as domestic employees, demonstrate a persistent pattern where employers attempt to relocate conflicts from the public realm of legal rights back into the private sphere of familial or quasi-familial relations, thereby compromising formal rights protection.

REFERENCES

Aaskoven, L. (2019). Redistributing under fiscal constraint: Partisanship, debt, inequality and labour market regulation. *Journal of Public Policy*, *39*(3), 423–441. DOI: 10.1017/S0143814X18000193

Bakkar, Y., Durst, S., & Gerstlberger, W. (2021). The Impact of Institutional Dimensions on Entrepreneurial Intentions of Students—International Evidence. *Journal of Risk and Financial Management*, *14*(4). Advance online publication. DOI: 10.3390/jrfm14040174

Boes, A., Kämpf, T., Langes, B., Lühr, T., & Ziegler, A. (2017). Cloud & crowd: New challenges for labour in the digital society. *TripleC*, *15*(1), 132–147. DOI: 10.31269/triplec.v15i1.760

Cárdenas, L. (2023). Trajectories of Labour Market Liberalisation in Spain: An Empirical Approach to the Historical Evolution of Institutional Change. *Revista Española de Investigaciones Sociológicas*, *183*, 121–132. DOI: 10.5477/cis/reis.183.121

Drubel, J., & Mende, J. (2023). The hidden contestation of norms: Decent work in the International Labour Organization and the United Nations. *Global Constitutionalism*, *12*(2), 246–268. DOI: 10.1017/S2045381722000259

Hoang, D. (2019). Labour standards in the global supply chain: Workers' agency and reciprocal exchange perspective. *Societies (Basel, Switzerland)*, *9*(2). Advance online publication. DOI: 10.3390/soc9020038

Hunt, A., & Samman, E. (2020). Domestic work and the GIG economy in South Africa: Old wine in new bottles? *Anti-Trafficking Review*, *2020*(15), 102–121. DOI: 10.14197/atr.201220156

Jalón Aymerich, F. B., & Herce, J. A. (2020). Countercyclical labor productivity: The case of Spain. *Cuadernos de Economía (Santiago, Chile)*, *43*(122), 105–118. DOI: 10.32826/cude.v42i122.194

Khamzina, Z., Buribayev, Y., Taitorina, B., Yessengazieva, A., & Kuttygalieva, A. (2022). Towards Nondiscrimination and Gender Equality: The Role of International Labor Standards. *Sustainability (Switzerland)*, *14*(9), 1–14. DOI: 10.3390/su14095349

Khan, Z. (2018). Transnational Labour Governance: A Critical Review of Proposals for Linkage through the Lens of the Rana Plaza Collapse in Bangladesh. *Canadian Journal of Law and Society*, *33*(2), 177–197. DOI: 10.1017/cls.2018.12

Kumar, M., Dagar, M., Yadav, M., Choudhury, T., & Luu, T. M. N. (2025). Navigating the future: Challenges and opportunities in intelligent RPA implementation. In *Intelligent Robotic Process Automation: Development, Vulnerability and Applications* (pp. 393–420). IGI Global. https://doi.org/DOI: 10.4018/979-8-3693-4365-4.ch015

Kumar, M., Jain, A., Mittal, A., Gera, R., Biswal, S. K., Yadav, M., Hung, T. H., & Priya Srivastava, A. (2024). Inclusion of Neural Networks in Higher Education: A Systematic Review and Bibliometric Analysis. *2024 4th International Conference on Innovative Practices in Technology and Management (ICIPTM)*, 1–6. https://doi .org/DOI: 10.1109/ICIPTM59628.2024.10563852

Kumar, M., & Yadav, R., Sushma, & Yadav, M. (2025). Investigating the influence of digital and social media marketing on university brand equity: An in-depth literature review and bibliometric study. *Global Knowledge, Memory and Communication*, •••, 1–26. DOI: 10.1108/GKMC-07-2024-0426

Liukkunen, U. (2020). The ILO and transformation of labour law. In *International Labour Organization and Global Social Governance*. https://doi.org/DOI: 10.1007/978-3-030-55400-2_2

Musakhonovich, M. M., Esirgapovich, E. A., Jaelani, A. K., Wan Khairuldin, W. M. K. F., & Luthviati, R. D. (2024). The Protection of Labor Rights on the Court System. *Journal of Human Rights. Culture and Legal System*, *4*(3), 742–764. DOI: 10.53955/jhcls.v4i1.115

Nguyen, T. B., Kumar, M., Sahoo, D. K., Nain, N., Yadav, M., & Dadhich, V. (2025). Mapping the landscape of women entrepreneurs in micro and small enterprises: Trends, themes, and insights through systematic review and text mining. *F1000Research, 14*. https://doi.org/DOI: 10.12688/f1000research.163030.1

Nilsen, M., Kongsvik, T., & Antonsen, S. (2022). Taming Proteus: Challenges for Risk Regulation of Powerful Digital Labor Platforms. *International Journal of Environmental Research and Public Health*, *19*(10). Advance online publication. DOI: 10.3390/ijerph19106196 PMID: 35627735

Pérez, I., & Canevaro, S. (2016). Entre lo público y lo privado: Empleadores y trabajadoras domésticas frente al Tribunal del Trabajo Doméstico de la ciudad de Buenos Aires. *Politica y Sociedad*, *53*(1), 169–186. DOI: 10.5209/rev_POSO.2016. v53.n1.45274

Policies, P. (2023). *Latin America and the Caribbean ' s Productivity : The Role of.*

Pulford, A., Thapa, A., Thomson, R. M., Guilding, A., Green, M. J., Leyland, A., Popham, F., & Katikireddi, S. V. (2022). Does persistent precarious employment affect health outcomes among working age adults? A systematic review and meta-analysis. *Journal of Epidemiology and Community Health, 76*(11), 909–917. DOI: 10.1136/jech-2022-219292 PMID: 36137738

Rossi, E. S., Cacchiarelli, L., Severini, S., & Sorrentino, A. (2024). Consumers preferences and social sustainability: A discrete choice experiment on 'Quality Agricultural Work' ethical label in the Italian fruit sector. *Agricultural and Food Economics, 12*(1). Advance online publication. DOI: 10.1186/s40100-024-00307-9

Sanders, S. R., Cope, M. R., & Pulsipher, E. R. (2018). Do factory audits improve international labor standards? An examination of voluntary corporate labor regulations in global production networks. *Social Sciences, 7*(6). Advance online publication. DOI: 10.3390/socsci7060084

Sapkal, R. S. (2016). Labour law, enforcement and the rise of temporary contract workers: Empirical evidence from India's organised manufacturing sector. *European Journal of Law and Economics, 42*(1), 157–182. DOI: 10.1007/s10657-015-9514-z

Satispi, E., Rajiani, I., Murod, M., & Andriansyah, A. (2023). Human Resources Information System (HRIS) to Enhance Civil Servants' Innovation Outcomes: Compulsory or Complimentary? *Administrative Sciences, 13*(2). Advance online publication. DOI: 10.3390/admsci13020032

Sheveleva, A., & Rogov, E. (2021). Organization of remote work in the context of digitalization. *E3S Web of Conferences, 273*. https://doi.org/DOI: 10.1051/e3sconf/202127312042

Stankevičiute, Ž., & Savanevičiene, A. (2018). Designing sustainable HRM: The core characteristics of emerging field. *Sustainability (Switzerland), 10*(12). Advance online publication. DOI: 10.3390/su10124798

Valencia-Quintana, R., Milić, M., Bonassi, S., Ochoa-Ocaña, M. A., Campos-Peña, V., Tenorio-Arvide, M. G., Pérez-Flores, G. A., & Sánchez-Alarcón, J. (2023). Effect of Pesticide Exposure over DNA Damage in Farmers from Los Reyes, Michoacan in Mexico. *Toxics, 11*(2), 1–11. DOI: 10.3390/toxics11020122 PMID: 36850997

van der Straaten, K., Pisani, N., & Kolk, A. (2020). Unraveling the MNE wage premium. *Journal of International Business Studies, 51*(9), 1355–1390. DOI: 10.1057/s41267-019-00285-x

Waas, B. (2021). The "S" in ESG and international labour standards. *International Journal of Disclosure and Governance*, *18*(4), 403–410. DOI: 10.1057/s41310-021-00121-5

Yadav, M., Kumar, M., Goswami, A., Tiwari, N. K., Amoozegar, A., & Rani, P. (2025). Innovating under constraints: A bibliometric and systematic review of frugal and inclusive innovations in start-up ecosystems. *International Journal of Business Innovation and Research*, *38*(8), 31–55. DOI: 10.1504/IJBIR.2025.150148

Yadav, M., Kumar, M., Sahoo, A., & Rathnasiri, M. S. H. (2024). AI and the evolution of artistic expression: Impacts on society and culture. In *Transforming Cinema with Artificial Intelligence* (pp. 15–36). IGI Global., DOI: 10.4018/979-8-3693-3916-9.ch002

Yadav, M., Mittal, S., Kumar, M., Sahoo, A., Jayarathne, P. G. S. A., Yadav, M., Mittal, S., Kumar, M., Sahoo, A., & Jayarathne, P. G. S. A. (2024). From Textbooks to Teamwork:The Importance of Collaboration Skills in Workforce Preparation. In https://services.igi-global.com/resolvedoi/resolve.aspx?doi=10.4018/979-8-3693-3856-8.ch011 (pp. 333–352). IGI Global Scientific Publishing. https://doi.org/DOI: 10.4018/979-8-3693-3856-8.ch011

You, C., Qiu, H., Pi, Z., & Yu, M. (2023). Sustainable Enterprise Development in the Manufacturing Sector: Flexible Employment and Innovation in China. *Sustainability (Switzerland)*, *15*(10), 1–30. DOI: 10.3390/su15108180

Chapter 8
Role of Legal Frameworks in Promoting Sustainable HR Practices

Xuan-Hoa Nghiem
https://orcid.org/0000-0003-2292-0257
International School, Vietnam National University, Hanoi, Vietnam

Mananage Shanika Hansini Rathnasiri
https://orcid.org/0000-0002-6496-5106
Department of Marketing Management, Faculty of Management Studies, Sabaragamuwa University of Sri Lanka, Sri Lanka & Qasim Ibrahim School of Business, Villa College, Maldives

Preet Kanwal
https://orcid.org/0009-0006-5114-8381
Lovely Professional University, India

Gunjan Mohan Sharma
https://orcid.org/0000-0003-2272-7385
JGBS, O.P. Jindal Global University, India

ABSTRACT

This chapter explores the role of legal frameworks in promoting sustainable human resource (HR) practices within organizations. As businesses increasingly recognize the importance of sustainability, effective legal regulations serve as critical tools for fostering ethical labor practices, diversity and inclusion, and employee well-being. This study examines global legal trends in HR sustainability, legal requirements for diversity, and the relationship between employment rights and well-being initiatives. Additionally, it highlights the importance of sustainable talent development, labor

DOI: 10.4018/979-8-3693-5390-5.ch008

laws concerning environmental sustainability, and the integration of corporate social responsibility (CSR) into HR policies. Despite existing challenges such as enforcement gaps and resistance to change, the future of legal frameworks will likely evolve to address these issues through technological innovations and multi-stakeholder collaborations.

INTRODUCTION

Sustainability refers to environmental concerns but has since been broadly placed on social and economic dimensions. Within this context, HR activity is increasingly seen as a critical area for promoting sustainability. The above definition indicates that sustainable HR practices include a portfolio of activities that aim at fostering long-term employee wellbeing and diversity, ethical employment, and responsible talent management. These practices contribute toward an organization's resilience and contribute to the betterment of society at large. The effectiveness of these practices, however, is one that is grown by laws prescribing and enforcing standards and guidelines that organizations should follow.

Legal frameworks provide scope for sustainable HR practices to develop based on minimum standards created about rights at work, equality, wellbeing, and ecological responsibility in the workplace. Labor rights, anti-discrimination, occupational safety, and corporate social responsibility are but a few of the main instruments guiding how organizations manage human capital sustainably. If this set of regulations were nonexistent, most of the above-noted dimensions-most notably, employee wellbeing, fair hiring, and long-term development-would probably remain underdeveloped.

As business concerns realize the value of sustainability in their operations, they focus on the need for legal mandates that would ensure even the HR practices are bringing them closer to social equity, economic resilience, and environmental stewardship. Local labor legislation is generally aligned with international instruments such as ILO conventions and UN SDGs, which affect the policies of businesses worldwide to be more sustainable in their operations. This chapter discusses how the legal framework enables and promotes practices of sustainable HR, keeping in view the fact that these frameworks play a critical role to shape the future-oriented and socially responsible workforce.

WHAT ARE SUSTAINABLE HR PRACTICES?

Concept of Sustainable HR

Sustainable HR practices place themselves midway in between short- and long-term interests of organizations and its employees so that workforce management works to support the overall sustainability goals of the enterprise. Thus, these practices encompass more than the usual recruitment and payroll activities of HR; they must also consider environmental impacts, social equity, and economic viability. Sustainable HR promotes a workplace culture that focuses on employee wellbeing, diversity, professional growth instead of organizational growth and competitiveness.

Key Elements of Sustainable HR

Sustainable HR practices embed several practices toward helping an organization have long-run success while being socially and environmentally sustainable. These may include the following:

- Employee Wellbeing: Polices such as flexible working hours, mental health programs, and work-life balance aim at supporting the overall wellbeing of employees in terms of their physical, mental, and emotional health. Productivity goes up along with employee retention.
- Diversity and inclusion: Sustainable HR aims at developing an efficient workforce by giving contributions toward a wide variety of backgrounds, perspectives, and experiences, which is very much beneficial for driving innovation and leading to better decision-making.
- Long-term Workforce Planning. Long-term workforce planning would reflect strategic efforts to develop and retain talent that offers the potential of reducing turnover in an organization and enhancing organizational resilience. Sustainable HR stands for learning and skill development in continuous chains, preparing employees for the future needs of the organization and changes in the market.
- Ethical and Fair Employment Practices: Ensuring the fair treatment of employees, with respect to wages, promotion opportunities that are clear and transparent, and labor conditions that are ethical. This also includes being on the right side of labor laws and upholding human rights.

Linking Sustainability with HR Functions

Sustainable HR practices are not standalone activities but integral to the core HR functions within an organization. Recruitment strategies need to attract talent linked to the company's sustainability objectives: a person who holds diversity and/or innovation and environmental responsibility close to his/her heart. The performance management systems need sustainability to provide a platform for employees to contribute to these greater organizational goals.

In talent management, sustainable HR maintains an effective balance of organizational development and employee satisfaction by creating a learning culture of continuous improvement, urging the employees toward lifelong learning and development. Sustainable HR reflects sustainability as one of the core elements of HR functions to help organizations develop a work environment with future-ready and socially responsible employees.

Role of Technology in Sustainable HR

Technology plays a significant role in advocating for the expression of sustainable HR practices. Digital technologies include AI-based recruitment systems and employee wellness apps, which have streamlined processes and made it easier for organizations to support sustainability goals. Data analytics may also enable the HR teams to assess the future implications of their practices on employee satisfaction, diversity, and productivity. Sustainable HR practices exploit technological resource efficiencies in the workplace to improve workforce management with reduced environmental impacts, thereby reducing carbon footprints through remote work.

While defining and integrating sustainability into the functions of HR, companies do not only contribute to a fairer and more responsible world but also to long-term organizational viability. Sustainability-embedded HR practices, in conjunction with sound legal frameworks, drive the growth of socially aware and forward-thinking workforces.

GLOBAL LEGAL TRENDS IN HR SUSTAINABILITY

The Growing Influence of International Labor Standards

Probably, international labor standards initiated by organizations like the ILO and the United Nations remains a basic source that has been influential in shaping the pattern of development for sustainable HR practices in the world. Through ILO conventions and recommendations, this sets the international benchmark for working conditions, fair wages, occupational health and safety, and the rights of employees. These conventions provide a legal framework that various countries incorporate within their respective national labor laws. Therefore, the sustainable HR practice will be in conformity with the international standards. For instance, conventions of ILO concerning equal rights of men and women at work place, minimum wage, and fair labor standard formed an international platform for generating inclusive and equitable HR policies and practices in organizations.

The other basic principle is that embodied in the United Nations' Sustainable Development Goals, especially the eighth one: Decent Work and Economic Growth. Here, it aims at promoting sustained, inclusive, and sustainable economic growth; full, productive, and decent employment for all; and decent work conditions. These are guiding principles in developing a country-specific set of labour laws supposed to be used with the aim of upholding sustainability in HR practices. More and more businesses are coming to align their operations with SDGs, which changes legal frameworks to oblige such an alignment to principles of fair wages, ethical recruitment, and respect for workers' rights.

Regional Legal Directions Driving Sustainable HR

Various regions have standardized all-inclusive legal directions which have driven sustainable HR practices, especially in Europe, North America, and some parts of Asia. These include fair wages, gender equality, and workers' safety. The European Pillar of Social Rights also set out 20 key principles and rights for fair and well-functioning labor markets. The European Green Deal emphasizes the role of social sustainability in its goals by trying to integrate the environmental considerations into workplace regulations and encouraging companies to include green HR practices, such as remote working and environmentally responsible operations.

It is, therefore, in North America that laws like the FLSA of the United States and the Employment Equity Act of Canada will work towards nurturing the practice of fair labor and fair workplace equity. Together with the complementary effect of environmental regulations, these laws empower firms to embark on the process of sustainability in their HR functions-from decreasing workplace discrimination, for example, to helping corporate cultures promote environmental stewardship. For instance, in Japan and South Korea, the focus is shifting to a work-life balance culture as well as reducing overwork. It led to a more sustainable working environment (Kramar, 2014; Pfeffer, 2010).

Corporate Social Responsibility (CSR) and Legal Mandates

Corporate social responsibility ties into CSR requirements, which many countries are mandating as part of the principles for maintaining sustainability in businesses. Countries like India have enacted the Companies Act 2013, which compels large-scale corporations to spend 'CSR expenditure' against which various companies spend their profits on social and environmental activities. Such legal push towards CSR ensures that companies make sustainable HR practices, such as community engagement and hiring people from diverse backgrounds, and it also ensures well-being programs for its employees (Wright & McMahan, 2011; Malik, 2018).

Europe requires large companies to report non-financial information as detailed in the Non-Financial Reporting Directive. This non-financial information is related to the company's impact on the environment and the social areas, its policies on diversity, and respect for human rights. Firms were encouraged under this directive to promote sustainable HR practice through larger corporate sustainability strategies so that the priorities of diversity, equity, and employee development are treated as legal obligations that the HR departments should internalize.

Legal Frameworks Supporting Workplace Diversity and Inclusion

Workplace diversity and inclusion are some of the major legal trends that promote sustainable HR practices. In most countries, legislation has been established to force organizations to establish and work toward an environment at workplaces free from discrimination of any form based on gender, race, age, or disability. In America, for instance, the EEOC is the body responsible for upholding the federal laws against the discrimination at the workplace. Such organizations are compelled to develop policies, as well as sustain them which create equal opportunities for all employees (De Stefano et al., 2018).

The European Union requires organizations to take diversity and inclusion measures through the doctrine of Equal Treatment and the Anti-Discrimination Directives, which bring legal protection against workplace discrimination in the European Union. In Australia, the Workplace Gender Equality Act implores companies toward better gender balance and transparency in hiring and promotion. These legal frameworks celebrate diversity as a core element of sustainable HR; this promotes responsible operation of businesses while reaping the benefits of a diverse workforce.

Emerging Legal Frameworks for Employee Wellbeing

Employee wellbeing is increasingly becoming recognized as an essential part of sustainable HR. Moreover, evolving legal frameworks continue to protect mental health and push for work-life balance. Countries like Sweden and Finland have passed progressive legislation that has attempted to work on stress in the workplace to address the welfare of employees. For example, in Sweden, the Work Environment Act specifies requirements for employers to take preventive measures against workplace stress, among others, to eliminate psychosocial hazards. Laws like these focus attention on employee welfare and encourage healthier work environments among organizations.

Likewise, nations such as Japan, which are famous for their long working hours and the high rate of burnout, have even enacted laws such as the Work Style Reform Act to cope with too many hours at work and the well-being of workers. Such legal reforms focus on keeping a good balance between work and life, reducing working hours, and flexible arrangements of work, which accordingly place wellbeing at the very heart of sustainable HR practices.

Challenges in Global Legal Compliance

Despite the building momentum in legal frameworks that support sustainability in human resources, it proves very challenging in compliance, especially for multinationals that operate in different legal environments. Inconsistent national regulation and mechanisms of enforcement often result in uniformity in adapting sustainable HR practices in global operations. For instance, while most European countries are proponents of strict legislation regarding the well-being of the employee and diversity issues, other geographies are less strict on the enforcement mechanism, and thus disparities occur in how an organization adapts such practices.

Businesses have to adapt to a changing legal landscape for which there is no real precedent in terms of emerging legislation on environmental responsibility and about protecting employees. There is constant vigilance that needs to be exerted with regards to local and international changes in the regulatory framework so that no violation of those laws at the behest of the company will be borne by it if not corrected (ILO, 2019; European Commission, 2020; OECD, 2020).

The International influence towards further sustainability in HR practices would include labor rights, diversity mandates, CSR obligations, and wellbeing initiatives. International standards, regional directives, and emerging national laws are creating a sustainability approach to workforce management, holding businesses in socially and environmentally responsible ways of operating. However, legal compliance definitely is one of the challenges which an organization faces when in a globalized economic aspect where regulations are imposed differently by jurisdictions. As legal frameworks evolve, business matters must also adapt to the global push for sustainability.

LEGAL REQUIREMENTS FOR DIVERSITY AND INCLUSION

The Importance of Diversity and Inclusion in Sustainable HR

Diversity and inclusion (D&I) top the cornerstones of sustainable HR practices. Organizations now widely focus on making sure that the workplace culture instills feelings of value and equity toward employees with various backgrounds, perspectives, and identities. Diversity and inclusion in the workplace has become, in the current global economy, not just a matter of morality, but also a business requirement. A number of different studies reveal that diverse teams will promote more innovation, better decision-making, and develop employee engagement. Diversity and inclusion-friendly legal frameworks help in enforcing these practices and create settings where everybody working under their auspices will be able to enjoy equal opportunities in growing and excelling.

Anti-Discrimination Laws

One of the basic building blocks for promoting diversity and inclusion in the workplace is anti-discrimination legislation. Countries have passed various laws that are aimed at stamping out discrimination on race, gender, age, disability, religion, and many other protected characteristics. Such law protections ensure that hiring and promotion decisions as well as pay levels and all forms of considerations within employment are made equitably and rather meritoriously.

Title VII under the Civil Rights Act of 1964 in the United States forbids a general provision against the discrimination of employees based on race, color, religion, sex, and national origin. The Americans with Disabilities Act or ADA and Age Discrimination in Employment Act or ADEA are special legal protections against people with disabilities and older workers, respectively. The laws institute equal opportunities when it comes to recruitment, hiring, promotions, as well as the workplace policies so that employees are provided with a chance to work without biased treatment against them as individuals.

The Equal Treatment Directive and the Race Equality Directive establish a legal framework between the member states of the European Union. The directives eliminate discrimination in the workplace regarding gender, race, religion, disability, as well as other discriminatory forms. These provisions provide equal opportunity policies for organizations to implement, preventing discrimination in the workplace, as well as ensuring victims of discrimination have recourse. Similar anti-discrimination laws exist in countries like Australia, which are stipulated by the Racial Discrimination Act and Sex Discrimination Act to ensure fair treatment for all employees irrespective of race (Gond et al., 2011; Brammer et al., 2012).

Gender Equality in the Workplace

Legal frameworks that particularly focus on gender equality have helped greatly in integrating women into the workforce. The countries have enacted laws that will eventually close the gender pay gap, prevent sexual harassment, and advance women into leading roles.

In the European Union, the Gender Equality Directive obligates equal pay for equal work and prohibits gender-based discrimination in employment. Member states should encourage policies in this regard of work-life balance. This is fundamentally critical to support women who may face obstacles in balancing time for caregiving responsibilities and career advancement. Some EU countries, like Norway and France, have implemented gender quotas for their corporate boards.

In the United States, one of the early legislation that was enacted to fight discrimination towards a gender pay gap is the Equal Pay Act of 1963. This established that the employers must pay men and women equally when they perform the same work. Like the Pregnancy Discrimination Act of 1978, the FMLA has provided pregnant women and parents with equal opportunities regarding hiring, promotions, and the retention of jobs due to family obligations.

Legal Protections for Individuals with Disabilities

The cardinal principle of inclusive HR practices is equal access to employment for workers with disabilities. Most countries have already enacted legal provisions that require employers to accommodate workers with disabilities and are working to make employment environments more accessible, in the process eradicating discriminatory practices.

Similarly, in the United States, with the Americans with Disabilities Act, employers are statutorily bound to make reasonable accommodations for employees with disabilities, from modified workspaces to flexible schedules or assistive technologies when it does not cause an undue hardship on the business. Similarly, in the European Union, the Employment Equality Directive makes it illegal to discriminate against persons with disabilities and obliges employers to provide accommodations that allow disabled persons to perform their jobs effectively.

Other countries have implemented equal laws. As for example, Australia's Disability Discrimination Act prohibits discrimination against people with disabilities at all levels of employment from hiring, training, up to promotion. The act also requires employers to make such reasonable adjustments at the workplace in order to make the working environment accessible and provide support where necessary for the employees with disabilities.

Promoting Ethnic and Cultural Diversity

The legal framework enforces ethnic and cultural diversity in the workplace by providing general prohibition against the acceptance of racial and ethnic discrimination while protecting equal opportunities for the underrepresented groups. Building work environments that are reflective of diverse societies and leverage the unique perspectives of employees from all walks of life call for these laws.

Title VII of the Civil Rights Act of 1964 is one of the basic enacting statutes in the United States anti-discrimination law. This made prohibition against race, color or national origin discrimination by employer's illegal. The Immigration Reform and Control Act of 1986 generally prohibits citizenship status and national origin discrimination, so immigrant workers are assured not to be discriminated upon at the workplace. Employers are obligated to exclude discrimination in hiring and ensure equal opportunities among all workers with different backgrounds (Shen & Benson, 2016; Guest, 2017).

On a similar trend, in the European Union, the Racial Equality Directive outlines detailed legal protections against discrimination based on racial or ethnic origin. While calling for employers to guarantee and promote equal treatment in employment, training, and working conditions while offering avenues where they can pursue legal remedy for those applicants who experienced discrimination.

Inclusive Hiring and Recruitment Practices

Legal frameworks increasingly push organizations to adopt inclusive hiring and recruitment practices that go beyond avoiding discrimination. At present, affirmative action policies and diversity quotas are being enforced in the majority of countries for providing equal employment opportunities to the underrepresented groups (Paillé et al., 2014; Armstrong & Taylor, 2020).

For example, affirmative action programs in the United States, generally initiated and overseen by the EEOC, require employers to engage in expansive hiring of historically underrepresented minority groups in the labor force. In South Africa, equivalent programs operate under the Employment Equity Act and are geared toward redressing apartheid's legacy through the increased hiring and promotion of black South Africans, women, and people with disabilities.

This is complemented by diversity and inclusion legal obligations in other parts of the world, such as the European Union. For example, the Public Sector Equality Duty in the United Kingdom requires public sector employers to end discrimination and foster equality in their recruitment, employment policies, and service delivery.

Legal requirements for diversity and inclusion must be a driver toward sustainable HR practices toward accomplishing equitable workplaces. Anti-discrimination laws, gender equality mandates, protections for people with disabilities, and frameworks for ethnic and cultural diversity all contribute to diversifying the workforce towards equality. These legal protections not only guarantee rights to employees but also enhance organizational performance by making sure that diverse talent is recognized and supported. Indeed, this requires that organizations keep looking over their shoulders at these laws and how they can be integrated into practical HR strategies for a more sustainable and socially responsible workplace.

EMPLOYMENT RIGHTS AND WELLBEING INITIATIVES

The Link Between Employment Rights and Wellbeing

Employee wellbeing is one of the critical points of the sustainable human resource practice developed by organizations as they are increasingly coming to realize that a healthy and involved workforce will contribute to higher productivity and retention. Legal frameworks protecting employment rights play an important role in promoting the wellbeing of the employees. As they address minimum standards for conditions of work, fair treatment, and consideration of mental and physical health of workers, employers' moral and social responsibility to promote wellbeing has been transformed into legal obligation under many jurisdictions (European Commission, 2020; ILO, 2016).

This foundation in the form of protection of employees' rights, such as fair wages, working hours, and safe work conditions, is important for the creation of the kind of context in which they will be well. Wellbeing initiatives often encompass a range of programs and policies in respect to positive mental health, work-life balance, physical health, and engagement. The emerging trend of HR sustainability spotlights the connection between robust employment rights and effective wellbeing initiatives.

Legal Protections for Mental Health and Work-Life Balance

Workplace wellbeing initiatives often concentrate on mental health since awareness of how stressful, anxious, and burned out employees cannot work effectively is high. Everywhere, legal frameworks protect workers' mental health and place obligations on employers to help them in this respect (Ulrich et al., 2020; Brammer et al., 2012).

The Framework Directive on Health and Safety at Work of the European Union calls upon employers to provide a safe and healthy working environment. Eliminating risk and effects of stress at work and measures regarding psychosocial risks are thereby covered. In Australia and the UK, for instance, the Workplace Health and Safety Act requires an assessment and elimination of employees' risks at their working place. They adopt policies to encourage programs that foster wellness in the workplace, cutting down stress at work, have positive working environments, and offer mental health services like counselors and support services.

Provisions for work-life balance legislation become essential for employees' welfare. A policy to reduce working hours, provide flexibility at work, and generous parental leave has been a preference in Sweden and Denmark. The Right to Disconnect law of France enables workers to disconnect from e-mails and calls outside of work hours, avoiding burnout and ensuring more effective work-life balance. Such legal constraints ensure that employees can maintain a better balance between life at work and personal life, a critical element of wellbeing.

Occupational Health and Safety (OHS) Laws

OHS legislation provides much of the framework for protecting workers' physical well-being by not allowing workplaces to have hazards that can cause injury or illness. Legal requirements for workplace safety in many countries are rather all-inclusive, having to account for everything from physical conditions of the workplace to personal protective equipment (PPE) (WHO, 2021; United Nations Global Compact, 2020).

The OSHA, or Occupational Safety and Health Act, in the United States sets the standards for safe working conditions and requires employers to prevent work accidents and illnesses through instruction, risk assessment, and safety programs. The European Framework Directive on Safety and Health at Work can set the roles of employers in preventing occupational risks and ensuring the safety and health of workers. These legal obligations are the foundation of most corporate wellbeing programs, which marry OHS requirements with other, more general initiatives, such as fitness programs, ergonomic working conditions, and wellness check-ups.

Moving beyond the most basic aspect of safety, developing legal frameworks now encompass employee well-being in a holistic sense. The Stress Check Program in

Japan requires companies to check their employees' stress levels and take measures to reduce workplace stressors periodically. In this manner, laws encourage employers to watch and improve the conditions and factors that boost both physical and mental health (Kapoor & Narayan, 2021; ILO, 2016).

Employee Wellbeing and the Role of Fair Compensation

Fair compensation is one of the most critical employment rights that directly relate to the wellbeing of the employee. There are minimum wage, overtime pay, and equal pay for equal work laws enacted to make sure the laborers are justly compensated and thus protected financially in their working lives (Armstrong & Taylor, 2020; Paillé et al., 2014).

Many countries around the world have minimum wage laws playing a very central role in protecting workers from exploitation. For instance, in the United States, the Fair Labor Standards Act ensures federal minimum wages, overtime pay, and child-labor protections. The Minimum Wage Directive, found in the European Union, gives a direction on ensuring that all workers receive adequate remunerations for wages expected to meet a standard standard of living, thereby supporting their welfare. In this view, it is evident that fair wages not only boost their confidence about financial security but also reduce economic-related stress, thereby allowing them to channel more time towards work and personal development.

Pay equity legal frameworks include the Equal Pay Act in the United States and the Gender Equality Directive in the European Union, focusing on wage discrimination based on gender, race, amongst others. Through equal pay for equal work, these laws would advance social justice, enhancing an inclusive and sustainable workplace culture and further employee wellbeing.

Flexible Work Arrangements and Legal Support

Demand from the workforce as well as legislation have driven this shift toward flexible work arrangements, which are well within the mainstream approach to address work-life balance and employee well-being.

In the United Kingdom, the Flexible Working Regulations indicate that employees who have at least 26 weeks of continuous service have the right to apply for flexible working arrangements in terms of work hours, schedules, or locations. Employers must take such application seriously and accept it only for specific and valid reasons. The Fair Work Act, similarly, in Australia, identifies the right of the employee to request a flexible work arrangement especially for parents, caregivers, and individuals with disabilities (World Economic Forum, 2022; OECD, 2020).

The COVID-19 pandemic has forced many countries to expand the legal protections that surround telecommuting, since it reduces commuting stress and allows for better work-life integration but also offers much greater autonomy. For instance, with the Flexible Working Act, which promotes telecommuting and flexible working hours in the Netherlands, worker's regulation power is over their professional and personal lives. These legal frameworks further empower workers to determine the work arrangement that best facilitates health and well-being, thus making flex work a universal cornerstone of sustainable HR practices (Guest, 2017; WHO, 2021).

Legal Mandates for Employee Assistance Programs (EAPs) and Wellness Initiatives

Most of the large corporations, for instance, now supplement their corporate wellbeing strategies with employee assistance programs and wellness initiatives in support of employees who face personal or professional turmoil. Many jurisdictions also impose legal responsibilities on employers to provide EAPs by fulfilling their duty of care to workers.

In Canada, the Occupational Health and Safety Act provides that employers have a duty to the utmost degree to ensure that a mental health condition is dealt with within the workplace. Therefore, most firms have adopted EAPs, which provide confidential counselling, stress management resources, and crisis intervention services. In Australia, the Work Health and Safety Act encourages the use of EAPs in terms of helping workers address their mental health issues.

Increasingly valued as truly important to the promotion of long-term employee wellbeing are wellness programs that might include a mix of fitness initiatives, smoking cessation programs, health screenings, and nutrition education. Such legal frameworks often concentrate on preventive care, where the regime recommends practices adopted by companies to improve both the mental and physical well-being of their workforce.

The employment rights and wellbeing initiatives are intricately linked, and through laws, it is ensured that the primary directions and concerns of an organization are toward the health of its employees-be it physical health, mental health, or emotional well-being. Such laws-to protect the employment rights ensure more sustainable and supportive working conditions by promoting guarded mental health, work-life balance, a fair wage, and flexible work conditions. Embedding wellbeing initiatives into legal mandates will ensure long-term success in the sustainability of a healthy, engaged, and productive workforce.

SUSTAINABLE TALENT DEVELOPMENT AND RETENTION

The Role of Legal Frameworks in Talent Development

Sustainable talent development is an integral part of human resources practice aimed to cultivate long-term organization growth and employee engagement. Legal frameworks surrounding training, skill development, and employee progression feed into achieving this objective since all employees have equal access to career development opportunities. Laws motivate organizations to put effort into their employee skills, promoting a culture of continuous learning and development vital in retaining the best talent (Wright & McMahan, 2011; WHO, 2021).

In many countries, labor laws and regulations oblige the implementation of employees' training and development programs. For instance, this Directive of the European Union makes employers take up the obligation to provide employees with opportunities for training that can increase their skills and qualifications, especially in fields where new competencies are required to meet the effects of technological and regulatory changes. Similarly, in the United Kingdom, there is the Apprenticeships, Skills, Children and Learning Act that encourages skills building by promoting companies to engage in apprenticeship and vocational training of advancing people's careers (Armstrong & Taylor, 2020; OECD, 2020).

Those legal requirements would ensure that the organizations focus their efforts on up-skilling to build the workforce in a manner that aligns with the growth of individuals while ensuring long-term sustainability for an organization. With these sets of talent development in place and embedding it within legislation, countries attempt to form labor markets that are dynamic, responsive to changing economic needs, to keep employees in the workplace today.

Legal Requirements for Lifelong Learning and Skills Development

The concept of lifelong learning is gradually becoming part of labor laws as a component that is deemed necessary for sustainable talent development. Legal mandates for continuous training and education ensure employees hold onto the competitive edge within a rapidly shifting job market while making way for organizational flexibility in new technologies and global competitiveness.

For example, European Social Charter identifies the right to education and vocational training as a fundamental career step, which highlights the employer's responsibility towards availability of training and professional growth at all stages of an employee's career. Likewise, in Singapore, SkillsFuture provides for the legal basis and focus on reskilling or up-skilling workers at all stages of their careers.

This framework challenges the employees to go through proper training programs that the employer initiates to acquire new skill sets related to industry requirements (ILO, 2019; OSHA, 2020).

Some such legal frameworks not only encourage sustainable talent development but also help in improvements in employee retention, because it creates a line of career growth. As a result, the organization will have talented employees who are stable and willing to stay with the organization for a longer period.

Legal Frameworks Promoting Employee Engagement and Retention

Employee engagement, job satisfaction, and career development are some of the best retention strategies for a sustainable HR practice. As far as legal frameworks go, they ensure that adequate standards are met in delivering services to staff fairly, equitably recompensing them, and appropriately considering employee well-being- all of which imply higher retention rates.

For example, laws regarding the issuance of performance appraisal and promotion calls for a definite recognition and reward system for employees' contributions. Equal Pay Acts and Anti-Discrimination Acts in most countries target to get rid of biases in performance reviews, promotions, and even in rising salaries, giving each employee equal chances of advancement in the workplace. These legal protections promote fairness and transparency that are very essential in building trust between an organization and its workforce- an important determinant of retaining the right talent.

Additionally, labor laws covering work-life balance and leave for family purposes will ensure retention of employees because they enable greater balancing of work and personal responsibilities among workers. For example, in the United States, the Family and Medical Leave Act provides that a worker is legally safeguarded to be absent from work to care for any family member or to recover from illness without this impacting their security at work. The European Union has ensured that an employee has the right to be absent from work for such parental responsibilities without losing career progression opportunities because of the Parental Leave Directive. These policies help retention because they make the workplace an accommodating place for employees in any life situation, thus making them stay longer in their jobs while dealing with family or health issues.

Employer-Funded Education and Retraining Programs

Legal frameworks in some countries, however, encourage or mandate employers to pay for education and training courses- significant in industries where serious skill shortages exist, or technology changes at an acute rate. These then qualify employees on the job while at work, reducing the turnover rate and enhancing organisational commitment.

For example, in Germany, by the Vocational Training Act, companies are required to provide methodical training and education to apprentices, thus providing a supply of skilled manpower for future use. In Australia, the Fair Work Act is said to foster employers to engage their employees in training and development programs because it may act as a retention tool for them, particularly in those industries that experience a considerable skills gap.

In addition to a skilled workforce, employer-funded education helps firms keep satisfied employees by demonstrating that the organization cares about the employee's own professional life. The investment in training is highly critical for higher potentials because it aligns organizational needs with the personal aspirations of an individual for a career, and that has been shown to create interdependent relationships that ensure loyalty of the employee in the long run (Kim & Fernandez, 2017; European Commission, 2020).

Retaining Diverse Talent through Inclusive Legal Practices

Law on diversity and inclusion is also relevant to talent retention. A diverse workforce requires inclusive HR practices to provide equal opportunities for growth and development by the employee regardless of their background. Diverse hiring, training, and promotions contribute towards laws that support such diversity. Valuing and supporting employees no matter their origin plays a great role in determining how long they stay.

Employment Equity Acts, such as those enacted in countries like Canada and the United Kingdom, oblige organizations to actively promote the representation of underrepresented groups-including women, minority groups, and disabled people-and to create an all-embracing holistic approach in every aspect of employment, including talent development programs. Such frameworks encouraging the legally enforced action of diversity and inclusion practices motivate organizations to offer more friendly environments toward diverse talent, lower turnover, and increase engagement by traditionally marginalized groups.

Legal mandate to ensure gender pay equity exists, such as the Equal Pay Act, which is equivalent to laws like the European Union law, would be very effective and play a great role in retaining female talent where women are adequately paid and provided with comparable opportunities for career advancement. Legal protections help create a level playing field: such that organisations can have a more representative workforce while promoting equity and inclusion in cultures.

Because of the laws within the framework, sustainable talent development and retention strategy ensures that companies are not wasting time, effort, and resources on developing, maintaining, and treating employees fairly. Legal aspects that protect diversity and inclusion underscore what was previously only a number of lifelong learning mandates and employer-funded education programs. These legal frameworks help organizations in the long run to develop skilled, engaged, and loyal workforces. By aligning these with legal requirements, companies can create sustainable talent pipelines and work environments that support long-term employee retention.

LABOR LAWS AND ENVIRONMENTAL SUSTAINABILITY

The Intersection of Labor Laws and Environmental Goals

Labour laws have recently been acknowledged to play a role in underlining the promotion of environmental sustainability. Traditionally, labor laws emphasized protection of the rights of labourers, wages, fair work conditions, and safety at the work site. Labor laws are changing now to support evergreen practices that involve responsible environmental care at work.

This integration of labor and environmental objectives reflects a larger movement toward sustainable development with a balance toward economic growth, social equity, and environmental protection. Through the inclusion of environmental standards in labor laws, the government and organizations can promote sustainable work environments where employees work to promote economic and social well-being and reduce impacts on the environment.

Similar examples can be mentioned about countries like Germany and Scandinavian states which, under the rubric of employment policies, standardized labor standards in terms of environmental goals where manufacturing is a significant use of the sources and energy usage. For instance, as a move to enforce greener practices in reducing pollution emission and conserving its resources, these policies also develop competent workforces through education and ensure workers' job security as industries move activities towards environmental sustainability (WHO, 2021; Malik, 2018).

Green jobs and legal protection for workers in green industries

A green economy transition created “green jobs,” roles that contribute to environmental protection, resource efficiency, and sustainability. The labor laws of most countries are evolving to protect workers in these new sectors by providing statutory protection on fair treatment and equitable working conditions in areas like renewable energy, sustainable agriculture, and green manufacturing (Ulrich et al., 2020; Malik, 2018).

For instance, the European Union's Green Deal has policy measures that promote the development of green jobs and outlines provisions for training and reskilling in sustainable industries. Likewise, while promoting the development of environmentally sustainable industries, the US Green Jobs Act also gives jurisprudential support to job training and workforce development programs. This ensures that workers involved in this green economy are not only geared for the change but also protected under fair labor laws (Eurofound, 2019; OECD, 2020).

These protections are vital because a shift in green jobs is very often accompanied by significant changes in the work force, with traditional industries like coal or oil gradually giving way to renewable energy industries. Labor laws can help offset some of the negative impacts this transition may bring about by ensuring the workers in such jobs that contribute toward environmental sustainability also receive their equal rights and benefits under the law.

Labor Laws Encouraging Sustainable Workplace Practices

Labor laws can directly make organizations embrace environmentally sustainable workplace practices by requiring them to enact policies on efficiency in energy use, waste reduction, and responsible handling of resources. Some countries have labor regulations that require organizations to establish work environments that encourage environmental sustainability, thus linking workplace standards with wider ecological objectives.

In France, for example, the labor law requires companies of a given size to form committees of environmental and social responsibility within the companies. The employee committees would involve the workers in decision-making on the type of policies on the environment within the organization to enhance teamwork among workers and management towards sustainable ways. The Sustainable Development Strategy of the European Union incorporates provisions of labor law into environmental goals through the requirement of companies to implement different green technologies and processes that cause minimal damage to the environment.

At present, more OHS laws also contain environmental provisions to ensure that the workplaces not only safe for employees are also environmentally responsible. For instance, rules on exposure to hazardous materials or industrial wastes' disposal include aspects not only of labor interests but also environmental considerations. The dual approach thus provides a measure of protection to employees from adverse exposure while waste disposal is carried out in an environment-friendly way (Guest, 2017; Wright & McMahan, 2011).

Legal Incentives for Sustainable Supply Chains

A third area is through labor standards that regulate supply chains, particularly in industries where the environmental impacts are significant. In doing so, the government can be able to influence business decisions in incorporating environmental-friendly practices. This is particularly important for supply chains involving global activities, where the attendant consequences are often suffering working conditions and bad environmental conditions (OECD, 2020; World Economic Forum, 2022).

Many countries have enacted laws that require organizations to ensure that their suppliers operate according to environmental and labor standards. For example, the UK's Modern Slavery Act and California's Transparency in Supply Chains Act require companies to report about the efforts made toward the elimination of forced labor and environmental harm in their supply chains. Such laws motivate companies to adopt environmentally friendly procurement practices, to treat overseas laborers fairly, and to use non-toxic materials and clean technologies in the production process.

With the relationship between labor standards and the environmental objectives of sustainable development, these laws become means both of defending workers' rights and of driving down the total environmental impact of industries at the same time. This is quite relevant in industries where environmental sustainability and the rights of the workers are often intertwined with such trends, including those in the fashion, electronics, and agriculture industries.

The Role of Corporate Social Responsibility (CSR) in Labor and Environmental Sustainability

Labor laws and the relationship of Corporate Social Responsibility with labor rights and environmental sustainability nowadays are more intertwined than ever. Most jurisdictions nowadays require that organizational reports regarding their CSR activities be sent across to them in terms of both labor and environmental issues. This system would push most companies to adopt a more holistic approach regarding the concept of sustainability, where the well-being of workers and the environment are interlinked (Zaid et al., 2018; European Commission, 2020).

As illustrated in the case of the Non-Financial Reporting Directive issued by the European Union, which obliges large enterprises to report on their environmental, social, and labor-related activities, including efforts to make their operations sustainable, accountability is made upon reporting. In such cases, the enterprises can be held responsible for their impact on employees and the environment, motivating them to introduce more sustainable labor practices.

CSR initiatives may include an attempt to reduce the carbon footprint, minimize wastefulness, and ensure better labor practice within the entire chain of the supply.

Organizations may use this opportunity of alignment of such initiatives with legal requirements in a manner that meets the confluence between sustainable business models and protection of employees and the planet. This approach will benefit the employee, ensuring that they are treated fairly and work under safe conditions, and will also contribute to long-term environmental sustainability (United Nations Global Compact, 2020; OECD, 2020).

Labor laws have taken the center stage in advocating for environmental sustainability by utilizing those aspects as a gateway. This is because of recognition that there is an increasingly strong linkage between workers' well-being and environmental conditions. In this light, the general framework of law that is emerging to grapple with the future that is sustainable promotes the growth of green jobs, encourages sustainable workplace practices, and regulates supply chains. Environmental objectives can be integrated into labor policies, thus a facilitation technique for governments and organizations to develop more just, responsible, and sustainable working environments that nurture people and the planet (Gond et al., 2011; Brammer et al., 2012).

CORPORATE SOCIAL RESPONSIBILITY (CSR) AND HR POLICIES

The Role of CSR in Shaping HR Policies

CSR, as a concept, is vital to modern business strategy. In one sense, it affects how companies deal with external constituencies; on the other hand, this new era of responsibility is expressed directly through the policies of human resources relating directly to companies. CSR effort refers to that of a company in terms of its ability to operate ethically, in a sustainable way, while maintaining a focus on social and environmental responsibilities (Guest, 2017; Malik, 2018). HR policies that incorporate the principles of CSR offer a chance for ethical, inclusive, and sustainable workplaces that bring into better alignment employee welfare with more profound societal and environmental outcomes.

Incorporating CSR into HR policies may help organizations improve employee engagement-an important factor in growing their strength as an employer of choice and helping to make a positive difference to the welfare of communities. For example, work-life balance, diversity and inclusion, environmental sustainability in the workplace, and employee volunteerism are some of the CSR-influenced HR policies. These are areas where companies are dedicated to ethical business practices and social responsibility, which thus enable them to attract and retain talent considerably among the younger generation who put a higher emphasis on work for socially responsible employers (Shen & Benson, 2016; OECD, 2020).

In addition, alignment of CSR and HR policies allows organizations to deal with issues on wages, ethical labor practices, and workplace health and safety. In doing so, the organizations demonstrate compliance in meeting the legal requirements and societal expectation. As CSR turns out to be a vital benchmark of corporate success, the role of HR is highly relevant in upholding the commitment of the company's internal policies reflecting its external commitment on social responsibility and environmental issues.

CSR and Employee Wellbeing Initiatives

The most direct impacts of CSR on HR policies occur through employee wellbeing initiatives. Companies focused on CSR most frequently have their HR policies formulated to work toward the physical, mental, and emotional health and wellbeing of employees. Such wellbeing initiatives-not only improving the causes of employee satisfaction and productivity-would align with the company's overall missions to impact society in positive ways.

For instance, employee-centric HR policies may include health and wellness programs that major on preventive healthcare, mental wellbeing, and work-life balance. Organizations such as Patagonia and Unilever, which have a very commendable CSR record, ensure generous leave policies, work flexibilities, and wellness resources in their HR policies. This marks a much broader understanding of sustainability-not merely the environmental sense but also of the long-term health and wellbeing of the workforce.

It also witnesses many organizations incorporate volunteerism and community engagement into their human resources policies by creating policies such as paid time off for staff to be involved in community service or charity work. In addition to its impact on society, it enhances job satisfaction and retention among employees since it has given them a reason for being part of something. Such policies, as part of CSR-driven HR policies, guarantee employee support and welfare by first and foremost putting the employees and investing in the community.

CSR and Ethical Labour Practices

Another important place where CSR overlaps with HR policies is in the promotion of ethical labor practices. Businesses that adhere to CSR engage in HR policies more than just codifying into law and ensuring fair and ethical treatment among employees in a workplace environment. Such policies would normally depict the fields of fair wages, anti-discrimination laws, equality between genders, and workplace safety measures as guiding principles. These are global considerations on human rights and labor rights.

For example, more and more firms nowadays establish HR policies in alignment with the United Nations Global Compact principles, which suggest that business organizations respect human rights, adopt a policy of no use of forced labor, and respect collective bargaining rights. Companies further protect their employees through such policies integrated into their HR practices, thus enhancing reputation for ethical leadership-a trait becoming increasingly important for today's socially conscious marketplace.

It also extends this ethical labor practice to its supply chain. Such CSR-oriented organizations enforce HR policies obliging their suppliers to follow similar best labor practices, especially in industries where the likelihood of exploitation and working conditions are unhealthy. For example, Nike and Adidas have stern CSR frameworks implemented throughout their global supply chains. These include labour problems such as child labor, wages, and working conditions. By integrating these standards of ethics into the company's HR policies, companies like Nike and Adidas not only maintain fairness and accountability within their labor force but also along their business spectrum.

CSR and Diversity, Equity, and Inclusion (DEI) in HR

DEI is a primary aspect of CSR, with the potential to significantly impact HR policies. An organization's robust commitment to CSR often pushes them to develop these HR policies with the objective of making their work environments more diverse and inclusive because an array of people in the company not only helps maintain social equity but also ensure organizational success. CSR motivated HR policies in this sphere of activity tend to contribute to the establishment of fair workplace environment wherein employees from different sectors get equal opportunity to achieve success.

CSR-inspired HR policies would outline practices in regions of diversity hiring, pay equity audits, and anti-discrimination training programs. For instance, it is leaders like Microsoft and Intel that establish a wide-ranging DEI policy through their Human Resources departments in an effort to build greater numbers of women, underrepresented people of color, and other subgroups into leadership positions. These programs align with the CSR goals of these companies and fuel innovation and competitiveness by bringing diversities of perspectives and ideas.

In addition, effective companies with strong CSR policies look at doing a good job in hiring practices and all employees once hired feel valued and included. In this context, HR policies aim to promote equal pay for equal work while, at the same time, establishing use of mentoring programmes for underrepresented groups and developing leadership to foster a more inclusive corporate culture. Through embedding DEI in HR policies, companies create an equitable and inclusive workplace that breeds satisfaction and retention of the workforce.

The Role of CSR in Talent Attraction and Retention

CSR is increasingly becoming recognized as a valuable lever for attracting and retaining talent, specifically in millennials and Gen Z employees, who would more likely choose working for organizations that are socially responsible. Thus, the HR policies reflecting a company's commitments to CSR can be a key differentiator of organizations in the competitive marketplace of talent and is an enabler for companies to attract top talent at the same time as it enables the development of employer branding.

Businesses exemplifying a commitment to CSR could offer significantly more than just competitive pay and benefits—the potential to have value-added work that enables the employee to contribute toward the betterment of society. In this context, HR policies that encourage engagement in sustainability initiatives or community outreach programs or social impact initiatives tend to make people feel responsible for creating value, in so doing, drive loyalty to stay at the job.

Companies with very strong CSR policies would keep most employees for a long time. When employees feel that their work is in tandem with their values, and they are part of a company doing some good in the world, they tend to stay much longer with the organization. Such values alignment of individual and corporate is of greater importance to the younger workforce, which increasingly seeks employers who embody their values of social and environmental responsibility.

CSR impacts HR policies by constantly reshaping how organizations develop strategies to promote wellbeing among employees, ethical labor practices, and diversity and inclusion. Integrating CSR principles in HR practices not only enhance the company's social and environmental effect but also contribute toward creating more interested, satisfied, and loyal workforce. As CSR continues to evolve, the role of HR departments is going to play an increasingly important role for companies to meet their social responsibilities through sustainable long-term success at the workplace.

CHALLENGES AND LIMITATIONS OF LEGAL FRAMEWORKS

Complexity and Fragmentation of Legal Systems

Among the various causes, one major obstacle to promoting sustainability within legal contexts is the intricacy and dispersion of legal regimes within diverse regions and sectors. Labor legislations and regulations are quite different between countries and even across jurisdictions posing vast challenges for multinational organizations when looking to standardize HR practices that align with all applicable laws. This trend is very fragmented creating uncertainty about the law. This can be particularly challenging for multinationals in implementing sustainable HRM strategies that cut across local and international legal laws.

For instance, while some other country has a well-defined legal system supportive of sustainability principles, others have a lack thereof on major areas such as labor rights, environmental, and diversity or inclusion themes. Companies that operate within such diverse legal landscapes will be challenged by harmonizing their HR policies under a vast umbrella of local regulations whilst, at the same time, striving to maintain a uniform corporate culture that subscribes to sustainability. This calls for substantial resource and legal expertise in order to navigate through these complexities, often placing such a great burden on the HR departments.

This also implies that not every region may realize a quick shift toward embracing sustainability-led HR practices; hence, the extent of change is very much constrained. For example, while labor and environmental laws are quite stringent in Europe, the same cannot be said of developing nations. As such, developing nations have insufficient legal measures to ensure compliance with sustainable practices, and this leads to wide disparities between labor and environmental standards in the supply chain.

Enforcement Gaps and Lack of Accountability

The other significant weakness of legal frameworks is the lack of enforcement. Despite the presence of laws that support sustainable HR practices, weak enforcements may melt down the positive impact of such laws. Most prominently, countries whose labor inspections suffer underfunding or are strangled by corruption and political instability where legal protections are not implemented have been known to suffer this.

For instance, while the codes of many nations prohibit exploitation, unsafe work conditions, and environmental degradation, the enforcement in most cases is less vigorous because the resources are missing or there is a lack of political will. Workers consequently continue to endure unsafe conditions of employment and unsustainably hazardous conditions in agriculture, manufacturing, mining industries among others, even though such work is legally protected, because enforcement is weak. Legal frameworks might then become purely symbolic and not transformative.

Companies will face challenges in ensuring compliance with regulations on sustainability and labor by the suppliers in transnational supply chains. Although the UK has the Modern Slavery Act, or even EU's Due Diligence Directive that obligates companies to ensure the conformance of their suppliers to human rights and environmental conditions, enforcing this broadly across supply chains across other countries poses a very difficult problem. Most companies rely on third-party audits, which may not capture all non-compliance issues, thus leaving some loopholes in accountability and transparency.

Balancing Business Interests and Legal Compliance

One of the major integration challenges of legal frameworks into sustainable HR practices is balancing business interests against complying with legal requirements. Companies at times face the difficulty of fitting profitability, competitiveness, and sustainability-driven legal mandates. This may evidently affect small and medium-sized enterprises (SMEs) mainly because they lack resources for complete compliance with increasingly complex legal requirements.

For instance, environmental sustainability legal mandate - such as reduction in carbon emissions or management of waste - can be a factor that forces upfront costs on firms. Large firms alone are financially capable to invest in green technologies or sustainable HR initiatives; however, small organizations with tight profit margins may face a challenge in order to allocate resources to meet legal mandates without diminishing their profitability levels (Tayal et al., 2021).

Businesses in intensely competitive industries might be forced to concentrate on short-term financial results rather than using such legal demands for long-run sustainability. This could limit the full integration of legal demands into their HR policies. Companies might, at times, regard compliance as bureaucratic and not a strategic advantage; therefore, with minimal effort put, there cannot be effective implementation of sustainability practice. This tension underlines the need for an institutional framework that not only necessitates compliance but also provides incentives, such as tax benefits or financial assistance, for businesses to ensure that they adopt sustainable HR practices without risking their financial bottom lines (Ahmad, 2015; Armstrong & Taylor, 2020).

Ambiguity in Legal Definitions and Standards

Legal ambiguity and standards limitation: In any legal definitions and standards about the existing laws concerning sustainability, ambiguity or vagueness always creates a major limitation in the effective practice of sustainable HR practices. Much of the wordings used in the existing law concerning issues on sustainability problems, particularly topics like climate change, diversity, and corporate social responsibility, have ended up being either too vague or ambiguous so that they leave a lot of scope for interpretations. On other occasions, ambiguity can lead to a situation where there is inconsistent application of the law. This, therefore, makes it difficult for various organizations to apply clear and measurable HR policies (Choudhary et al., 2024).

For example, "sustainable development," "fair labor practices," or "green jobs" are buzzwords used in legal texts without well-defined meanings. This leaves unanswered questions about the natures of compliance. Ambiguity results in companies, regulators, and courts interpreting these blurry concepts differently often, hence making attempts to formulate unified and enforceable HR policies difficult. Sometimes, there is also uncertainty in measuring the effectiveness of sustainability efforts made by businesses and ensuring that they actually comply with the established law.

Other emerging fields, such as AI in HR or the gig economy, are raising new concerns. Existing labor laws either become outdated or ineffective in their application to new contexts. Technological advancements are often too rapid to allow for full protection of workers within the legal framework. Unclear legal standards in this respect could pose problems for businesses that are attempting to integrate sustainable HR practice, especially with respect to matters like workers' rights, data privacy or job security in case of automation.

Resistance to Change and Legal Reform

The various stakeholders, including business leaders, industry groups, and political agencies, may resist the legal structures encouraging sustainable HR practices. Businesses may resist legal reforms they can comfortably label costly or expensive, considering that sometimes they usually require significant changes in long-established HR policies or processes of operation. Industry groups may also object to the mandates on law due to sustainability grounds, as such a mandate is portrayed to add extraneous costs or price out competitiveness through their inefficiency in profitable enterprises.

Politically, effective legal frameworks can also be derailed by resistance. In this perspective, governments of certain countries might hesitate to enact or implement labor and environmental laws that seem detrimental to economic growth or investor confidence. Thus, political interests may prop up short-term economic needs over long-term sustainability; legal reforms may be delayed or rolled back in an effort to ensure sustainable HR practices.

Such a resistance to change may hamper the adoption of sustainability-driven legal frameworks, particularly in industries where deep-rooted practices are in place or those where powerful lobby groups fight against regulatory intercession. Where there is a lack of political and business consensus, reforms made in law may lead only to limited results toward the target goal of sustainable labor practices, resulting in low momentum toward achieving more environmentally friendly practices.

While legal frameworks provide an important underpinning to promote sustainable HR practices, they are, at the same time, challenged and limited. Complexity and fragmentation of the legal systems, gaps in the chain of enforcement and tensions between business interests and compliance with the law all pose obstacles in implementing effective sustainability-driven HR policies. Such apparent ambiguities in legal definitions and resistance to legal reform further impede progress. To address these concerns, the government, corporate sector, and civil society need to come together to form clearer, more enforceable, and supportive frameworks that may foster long-term sustainability under an inescapable reality of economic constraints.

THE FUTURE OF LEGAL FRAMEWORKS IN SUSTAINABLE HR

Evolving Legal Standards and Regulations

Eminent legal standards will shape future legal frameworks in sustainable HR, achieving new standards and regulations with emphasis on sustainability and corporate responsibility. Because social and environmental matters are more intensely identified worldwide, governments-even international organizations-do recognize the necessity of better, all-inclusive legal frameworks that carry on to institute sustainable business practices. Along with these themes, regulations will be sterner and integrated, covering labor laws and HR practice considerations according to the perspective of sustainability principles.

In emerging trends, there is an acceptance of binding international agreements and national legislation with high sustainability goals, for instance, the Paris Agreement on climate change. Countries should strengthen their legal frameworks to address the emerging challenges on environmental degradation, labor rights, and social equity. This development is likely to be accompanied by stricter controls on pollution and waste as well as on working conditions (Trivedi et al., 2023). It will also be characterized by higher standards for workers in sectors most prone to exploitation.

Soon, new legal standards should be focused on diversity, equity, and inclusion (DEI) in the workplace. Societal attitudes toward corporate responsibility are in constant flux; the law will codify these changes such that organizations will be required to implement measurable DEI initiatives and report on their progress. As a result, the development of clear guidelines and metrics will be in demand to measure compliance and effectiveness in implementing sustainable HR practices.

Technology-Driven Legal Innovations

The future of sustainable HR legal frameworks will also be determined by technology innovations that make compliance more accessible and accountable. With technology increasingly becoming more integrated in the workflow, there will be an even greater need for HR departments to make sure that their legal frameworks are in step with innovations in this area. Among these are issues on data privacy and algorithmic bias as these bring to bear a significant impact on workers' rights in the face of automation and AI (Yadav et al., 2019).

One of the emerging technologies that can help address both these concerns is blockchain. Its applications can include tracking labor conditions in supply chains for compliance with labor laws and sustainability standards. Innovative legal frameworks might thus enhance both monitoring and enforcement of sustainable HR practices to make the business environment more transparent and ethical.

One of the added difficulties and opportunities from the horizon, sustainable HR brings forth through rising remote work and gig economy is in respect of how the legalities need to be maneuvered to accommodate these emergent demands. The key point here is that traditional employment models, no matter how gradually evolving they are, will continue to evolve. "Gig workers" need protection and rights equal to others for wages, benefits, and job security; hence innovations in legalities against them would be a determinant of equitable and sustainable HR practices in the future.

Integration of Sustainability into Corporate Governance

Sustainability will progressively become central in corporate governance. Then, the legal frameworks would increasingly force companies to form a greater intention toward embedding sustainability in their overall strategies and operations. This integration would take more than just HR practices but would include the wider corporate governance structures. The latter include board composition, stakeholder engagement, and reporting requirements.

The future legal frameworks may also establish the obligation of companies to have clear sustainability objectives and then incorporate them into the decision-making processes. This could be in form of imposing commitments on companies, such as requiring them to publicly declare their sustainability impacts, setting measurable targets, and reporting in respect of progress. Such legality will challenge organizations to give attention to sustainable HR practices as part of their bigger corporate strategy by embracing accountability and responsibility.

Second, stakeholders including investors, customers, and employees are increasingly demanding in what they expect regarding transparency and accountability related to the sustainability of the organization. Such legal frameworks will prompt firms to have more ambitious sustainability goals and ensure them as part of their human resources practices. This leads to performance measures, such as sustainability-linked performance measures, where executive compensations are based on how successfully sustainability objectives are met. This means further embedding sustainability into corporate governance.

Collaboration and Multi-Stakeholder Approaches

Greater coordination among governments, businesses, labor organizations, and civil society will be an integral part of the future of legal frameworks in sustainable HR. Multi-stakeholder approaches can help better develop and implement effective law frameworks in meeting complex social and environmental challenges.

Public-private partnerships, industry coalitions, and cross-sector initiatives have all been formed as means of promoting sustainable HR practices. Coalition through these different methods might provide an opportunity for diversity in perspective and expertise to come together around best practices, resources, and innovative solutions to common challenges (Yadav & Rangnekar, 2016).

As an increasing number of global supply chains become more interlinked, there will be an increasingly pressing demand for international cooperation to set up legal frameworks that promote sustainable development across borders. Examples include 'harmonizing regulations,' 'common enforcement mechanisms,' and mutual recognition of compliance standards between countries. Such cooperation can then serve to produce a more consistent and effective legal environment to promote sustainable HR practices around the world.

Therefore, future sustainable HR legal frameworks will find themselves at a point where the impact of change will be determined by how the law will evolve, new technologies will diffuse, and stakeholder requirements change. Organizations therefore must adapt to new regulations based on sustainability integrate new technologies into their practices work with a number of stakeholders in improving the workplace as more sustainable and equitable. Thus, the company would be improving not only the compliance of legal standards but also eventually be able to emerge as leaders in sustainability and create a better responsible and resilient global economy by embracing change.

CONCLUSION

Organizations are confronted with very pressing social and environmental challenges while urgency is on the increase. With the awareness of sustainable practices in HR today, it is pertinent that evolving labor laws and regulations be acknowledged by businesses as a step toward sustainable practices respecting the interests of employees, communities, and the environment. Governments can enforce comprehensive legal standards to channel organizations toward integrating sustainability into their core operations, thereby instilling a responsible and accountable culture.

However, this depends on various problems or issues that such legal frameworks face, such as complexity and fragmentation in legal systems, gaps in enforcement, and the normally conflicting interests between business and compliance. As the businesses face these problems, they have to be proactive about sustainability - an approach to compliance which is more of a chance for innovation and growth than a regulatory burden. So, integration of sustainability goals into HR practices could help organizations become more competitive and responsive in a conscience-driven market.

These will be in aspects of technology, multi-stakeholder collaboration in the succeeding stages of the future of legal frameworks on sustainable HR practices. The organizations need to embrace the needs of stakeholders for transparency and accountability in the actions of businesses toward society and the environment; therefore, a necessary integration of legal concerns in support of sustainable HR policies is required.

In conclusion, a holistic, sound legislative frame will define sustainable HR in the future, underpinning its ability to support an organization as it progresses toward sustainability. It's through proceeding toward legal, ethical, and operations contexts that businesses can truly make a difference that positively impacts workers and greater society. Now, how much it will cost depends on engagement, innovation, and cooperation, but payback in making things more sustainable and equitable has no price.

REFERENCES

Ahmad, S. (2015). Green human resource management: Policies and practices. *Cogent Business & Management*, *2*(1), 1–13.

Armstrong, M., & Taylor, S. (2020). *Armstrong's handbook of human resource management practice* (15th ed.). Kogan Page.

Brammer, S., Jackson, G., & Matten, D. (2012). Corporate social responsibility and institutional theory. *Socio-economic Review*, *10*(1), 3–28.

Choudhary, S., Yadav, M., & Srivastava, A. P. (2024). Cognitive biases among millennial Indian investors: Do personality and demographic factors matter? *FIIB Business Review*, *13*(1), 106–117.

De Stefano, F., Bagdadli, S., & Camuffo, A. (2018). HRM and performance in the digital era. *International Journal of Human Resource Management*, *29*(1), 1–22.

Eurofound. (2019). *Working conditions and sustainable work*. European Foundation for the Improvement of Living and Working Conditions.

European Commission. (2020). *The European Green Deal*. Publications Office of the European Union.

Gond, J. P., Igalens, J., Swaen, V., & El Akremi, A. (2011). Influence of CSR on HR management. *Journal of Business Ethics*, *98*(4), 507–525.

Guest, D. (2017). Human resource management and employee wellbeing. *Human Resource Management Journal*, *27*(1), 22–38.

International Labour Organization. (2016). *Non-standard forms of employment: Understanding challenges*. ILO.

International Labour Organization. (2019). *Work for a brighter future: Global Commission on the Future of Work*. ILO.

Kapoor, S., & Narayan, D. (2021). Legal frameworks in India supporting sustainability and HR reforms. *Indian Journal of Industrial Relations*, *56*(4), 625–642.

Kim, H., & Fernandez, S. (2017). Employee empowerment and sustainability. *Public Personnel Management*, *46*(1), 3–23.

Kramar, R. (2014). Beyond strategic human resource management: Sustainability orientation. *Human Resource Management Review*, *24*(2), 103–115.

Malik, A. (2018). Creating sustainable organizations through HRM. *Human Resource Management Review, 28*(3), 215–226.

OECD. (2020). *OECD guidelines for responsible business conduct*. OECD Publishing.

Paillé, P., Chen, Y., Boiral, O., & Jin, J. (2014). Green HRM and environmental citizenship. *Journal of Business Ethics, 121*(3), 1–15.

Pfeffer, J. (2010). Building sustainable organizations: HRM's role. *The Academy of Management Perspectives, 24*(1), 34–45.

Shen, J., & Benson, J. (2016). When CSR meets HRM: Bridging two fields. *International Journal of Human Resource Management, 27*(2), 1–21.

Tayal, R., Upadhyay, R. K., Yadav, M., & Singh, R. (2021). The development and validation of the organizational effectiveness scale using confirmatory factor analysis. *Global Business Review, 22*(3), 821–843.

Trivedi, S. K., Vishnu, S., Singh, A., & Yadav, M. (2023). Research trends in sustainable E-payment systems: A study using topic modeling approach. *IEEE Transactions on Engineering Management, 71*, 7511–7525.

Ulrich, D., Brockbank, W., & Johnson, D. (2020). *HR competencies for the future*. McGraw-Hill.

United Nations Global Compact. (2020). *Principles of responsible business*. United Nations.

World Economic Forum. (2022). *Future of jobs report*. World Economic Forum.

World Health Organization. (2021). *Mental health at work: Policy and practice recommendations*. WHO.

Wright, P. M., & McMahan, G. C. (2011). Exploring human capital: Toward a sustainable HRM theory. *International Journal of Human Resource Management, 22*(6), 1146–1160.

Yadav, M., & Rangnekar, S. (2016). Role clarity and organizational citizenship behaviour: Does tenure matter? A study on Indian power sector. *Global Business Review, 17*(3, suppl), 207S–224S.

Yadav, M., Rangnekar, S., & Srivastava, A. P. (2019). Demographic variables as moderators between QWL and OCB. *Industrial and Commercial Training, 51*(7/8), 396–408.

Zaid, A., Jaaron, A., & Bon, A. (2018). Green human resource management and sustainability performance. *Business Strategy and the Environment, 27*(8), 983–999.

Chapter 9
Compliance vs. Excellence:
HRM Legal Frameworks vs. HRM Biblical Principles

Mercia Selva Malar Justin
https://orcid.org/0000-0002-9721-1503
Christian Institute of Management, India

Perfecto G. Aquino
SouthStar Management Institute, Vietnam

Revenio Jalagat
https://orcid.org/0000-0002-8878-3825
Al-Zahra College for Women, Oman

ABSTRACT

This chapter examines the intersection between secular Human Resource Management (HRM) legal frameworks and Biblical principles. While legal systems, like India's four Labour Codes, establish a necessary institutional "floor" for safety and wages, they often suffer from a "compliance gap" where profit precedes personhood. Through a review of 23 articles, the research reveals that whereas secular HRM is transactional, a Biblical approach is covenantal, rooted in the concept of Imago Dei, which recognizes inherent dignity beyond economic value. The study highlights a synchronization between global standards, such as ILO conventions, and scriptural tenets, framing fair compensation as a modern codification of Biblical stewardship. Ultimately, while the law prevents exploitation, Biblical principles

DOI: 10.4018/979-8-3693-5390-5.ch009

provide the relational depth necessary for excellence. By shifting from compliance to sacred vocation, leaders can bridge the gap between "corner-cutting" and a flourishing culture.

1. INTRODUCTION

Human Resource Management in corporates is governed by various legal frameworks across the nations. In India the labour laws that were fragmented have been recently combined and presented as four labour codes. The HRM legal framework in any nation is to ensure that minimum standards of Human Resource Management are followed across the country and across the various sectors. The HRM legal framework serves as the basis for employee welfare and protection as well as organizational protection and sustainability. The HRM legal framework seeks compliance by corporates and sets the minimum standards. Yet, compliance is not whole heartedly fulfilled and most organizations finds shortcuts or corner cutting in compliance. The heart of organizations is not with employees but with the profits they need and want to make.

1.1. India's Legal Framework

India's HRM legal framework falls under the Concurrent list (covered by Central Government and State Government laws) and his extensive and complex. Recently efforts have been made to simplify and upgrade the HRM legal framework by replacing 29 central laws with just four labour codes. The four codes are: Code on Wages, 2019; Industrial Relations Code, 2020; Code on Social Security, 2020; Occupational Safety, Health and Working Conditions Code, 2020 (OSHWC Code). These labour codes are expected to establish all basic norms corporates must follow in HRM and employees are expected to adhere to.

1.2. HRM Legal Framework Scope

Labor codes are considered the legal floor as the motivation to comply is driven by the need to avoid fines, litigation, and regulatory punishment. Minimum wages legalised is to ensure that employees survive and avoid disparity. Employee value under the legal framework is determined by the economic value the employee brings in and is determined by contract and law. HRM legal frameworks works to ensure gender equality and non-discrimination. HRM legal framework works on how to justify retrenchment and not providing job security to employees. HRM legal framework mandates employee development through vocational and safety training. HRM legal framework demands that managers are compliant and adherent to the laws. HRM legal framework's goal is simplifying laws to attract investment and boost economic growth. Under the HRM legal framework grievance redressal/ conflict resolution is approached from a formal, process-driven mechanisms for dispute resolution. HRM legal framework on waste reduction insists on reducing administrative burden and improving productivity.

1.3. HRM Biblical principles Scope

On the contrary the HRM biblical principles are at the wholehearted interest of human beings who are created in the image of God. Employees who form part of the human resources are of different categories – whatever be the category, their wellbeing is important according to biblical principles. When the human resources are well taken care, they flourish and prosper and excellence flow out of their wellbeing. HRM biblical principles ensures that employers care for employees and their wellbeing, not out of compliance requirements and fear of punishment, but out of love and reverence for God (Deuteronomy 24:14). HRM biblical principles view employee as a person with unconditional worth, whose value is independent of their job role or productivity. (Genesis 1:27). HRM biblical principles focuses on stewardship of human resources ensuring they are sustained (James 4:5). HRM biblical principle is concerned about holistic development of employees through investment in the character, ethics, and life skills of the employee, seeing the job as a place for personal vocation (calling). (Ephesians 4:12). HRM biblical principles insists that manager's role is to serve, equip, mentor, and empower employees, prioritizing the follower's development over personal power. (Mark 10:45). HRM biblical principle emphasises to create ethical value for all stakeholders (employees, society, investors) through a lens of justice and responsibility. (Micah 6:8)

The biblical principles that govern HRM are man in God's image and stewardship, provides the motive, depth, and relational quality necessary to achieve true organizational excellence, which the law cannot mandate. HRM biblical principles are pursued by the urge to honour God by honouring the inherent dignity of the worker (Imago Dei). (Colossians 3:23). Biblical principles of just and living wages payment allows the employee and their family to flourish, save, and have dignity. HRM biblical principles mandates holistic equity, ensuring equal pay and opportunity, while adding moral requirements for protection, family support, and respect that go beyond the legal minimum safety measures. (Galatians 3:28). HRM biblical management's primary goal is to create ethical value for all stakeholders (employees, society, investors) through a lens of justice and responsibility. (Micah 6:8). HRM biblical principle is more relational enabling private, face-to-face reconciliation, seeking restoration and forgiveness before resorting to formal legalistic processes.

(Matthew 18:15). HRM biblical principles focuses on stewardship, which extends the concept of waste elimination to include waste of human potential (underutilization of gifts) and waste of natural resources (environmental stewardship). (John 6:12).

1.4. Chapter Objectives & Organization

The chapter explores the HRM legal frameworks and HRM biblical principles with the following objectives: A. To examine the importance of HRM legal frameworks and HRM biblical principles. B. To present the gap between the HRM legal frameworks and HRM biblical principles. C. To verify if HRM global standards synchronise with the biblical principles.

The chapter is purely literature based and 23 articles have been examined to arrive at the objectives. The chapter is organized as follows: Introduction, Review of literature, Discussion on the objectives and Conclusion. Introduction gives a preview of the HRM legal framework and HRM biblical principles. Review of literature examines 23 articles relevant to HRM legal framework and HRM biblical principles – floor and ceiling. The three objectives are discussed from the various HRM perspectives under the discussion on the objectives. The chapter is brought to close with the concluding remarks under conclusion.

2. REVIEW OF LITERATURE

2.1. The Legal and Strategic Foundations of Human Resource Management

The integration of legal frameworks into Human Resource Management (HRM) has evolved from a matter of simple compliance to a foundational pillar of strategic organizational success. This review synthesizes current research regarding the intersection of employment law, organizational culture, technological advancements, and ethical considerations.

Modern HRM research emphasizes that legal frameworks are no longer merely "checklists" but are transformative tools for building high-trust environments. Hasyim and Bakri (2023) demonstrate that rigorous adherence to safety and anti-discrimination laws fosters employee well-being and productivity. This is echoed by Gajenderan (2024), who argues that a proactive approach to compliance—using audits and training—mitigates risk while creating a fair and inclusive workplace. Erwin et al. (2025) further suggest that while some view regulations as restrictive, they actually drive innovation by forcing companies to improve operational standards to remain competitive.

The application of HRM policies varies significantly based on regional contexts and organizational structures. Murphy (2018) highlights how judicial rulings in the U.S. and EU distinguish between discriminatory practices and legitimate job-related requirements, influencing global standards. In the context of South-Eastern European SMEs, Psychogios et al. (2016) identified a "three-fold framework"—organizational size, industry sector, and internationalization—as the primary drivers for formalizing HR practices in post-communist economies.

A critical theme in recent literature is the disconnect between formal written policies and real-world execution. Gill and Meyer (2011) identify a "soft" language gap in Australian organizations, where supportive policy wording is not backed by action, leading to negative employee outcomes. Christopher (2019) notes that for policies to be effective, there must be a strong partnership of mutual respect where employers provide fair pay and training in exchange for employee adherence to conduct codes. Scheibmayr and Reichel (2023) suggest that HR professionals can close this gap by actively engaging with the law to set standards that exceed basic legal mandates, such as transparency in job advertisements.

The scope of HRM law extends into specialized domains like Human Resource Development (HRD) and Artificial Intelligence. Clardy (2003) provides a structured model for identifying legal mandates in training, including safety, drug education, and intellectual property. More recently, Gupta et al. (2025) address the "enormous disruption" caused by AI. While AI facilitates administrative efficiency and talent matching, it introduces significant ethical risks regarding privacy, bias, and transparency. The literature calls for robust legal and ethical frameworks to govern these technologies to ensure they benefit all stakeholders.

The literature indicates that the legal context of HRM is a dynamic force that shapes organizational legitimacy and efficiency. Effective HRM requires more than passive adherence to labor laws; it demands the proactive integration of legal standards into the very fabric of organizational culture and strategy. Research consistently shows that when organizations bridge the gap between formal policy and actual practice, and when they address emerging challenges like AI and regional economic shifts with structured legal frameworks, they achieve higher levels of employee loyalty, innovation, and long-term sustainability. Ultimately, the law acts not as a barrier, but as a catalyst for professionalizing the workplace and protecting the inherent rights of the global workforce.

2.2. Theological Foundations and Faith-Based Frameworks in HRM

The integration of religious principles and spiritual ethics into Human Resource Management (HRM) has emerged as a significant area of study, offering a moral counter-narrative to purely secular, profit-driven models. This review synthesizes research that bridges ancient scripture, denominational doctrines, and contemporary organizational science to define a "theology of work."

The literature suggests that many modern HRM concepts are not strictly 18th-century Western inventions but have ancient biblical roots. Thierry (2018) argues that the Old and New Testaments laid the groundwork for recruitment, fair wages, and performance appraisals centuries before the industrial revolution. Similarly, Van Buren III and Greenwood (2013) examine the Torah as a primary framework for employment ethics, utilizing its interpretive approach to resolve modern workplace dilemmas and promote social sustainability.

Central to a faith-based approach is the concept of Imago Dei—the belief that humans are created in the image of God. Busuttil and Van Weelden (2018) and Jonsen (2017) argue that this principle should fundamentally shape HR policies, shifting the focus from viewing employees as mere assets to treating them as individuals with inherent dignity. This theological foundation supports Roberts' (2014) "Servant Leader Human Resource Management" (SLHRM) model, which emphasizes that leaders must act as moral guardians and "doers" who prioritize service and accountability over the exercise of power.

The deliberate embedding of faith into business is explored through frameworks like "Kingdom Integration." Sangwa and Mutabazi (2025) identify stewardship, integrity, and compassion as essential drivers for professional success, arguing that this alignment fosters higher trust and social impact. Pambour (2022) further demonstrates that Christian ethics can be transformed into universal workplace policies that enhance the productivity and performance of both Christian and non-Christian employees alike.

The application of these principles varies by organizational type. McCutchen (2025) notes that in Protestant churches, factors such as age, size, and denomination influence how formal an HRM strategy becomes. In the Catholic tradition, Zigarelli (1993) extracts principles from social encyclicals, highlighting worker dignity and family economic security as non-negotiable mandates that may constrain traditional profit motivations in favor of societal welfare.

Beyond ethical codes, research focuses on the internal resources of the individual. Dhiraj et al. (2020) bridge a gap in management theory by proposing a model for systematic "character building" as a route to business sustainability. Miner and Bickerton (2020) advance this by applying the "Job Demands–Resources" model to Trinitarian theology, suggesting that a leader's secure relationship with God provides the spiritual resources necessary to reduce turnover and increase work engagement.

The body of literature presented here demonstrates that faith-based HRM is a robust and multidimensional field that offers a holistic alternative to secular management. By rooting HR practices in principles like Imago Dei, servant leadership, and biblical stewardship, organizations can move beyond administrative efficiency to create environments of profound moral and spiritual integrity. The research consistently finds that when organizations—whether churches, nonprofits, or secular firms—align their management strategies with these ancient ethical foundations, they see improved organizational health, employee satisfaction, and a more resilient moral climate. Ultimately, integrating faith into HRM does not hinder growth; rather, it provides a sustainable framework for honouring human nature while effectively achieving organizational missions.

3. GAP BETWEEN HRM LEGAL FRAMEWORK & HRM BIBLICAL PRINCIPLES

There is a distinct body of literature that seeks to bridge the gap between secular legal mandates (which focus on compliance and rights) and biblical principles (which focus on moral stewardship and inherent dignity).

While many secular studies treat the law as a "floor" for behaviour, the biblical studies you cited often argue that scripture provides a higher "ceiling" for ethical conduct.

3.1. Compliance vs. Covenant

Secular law (e.g., Hasyim & Bakri, 2023; Gajenderan, 2024) focuses on avoiding litigation and meeting regulatory standards. In contrast, the biblical perspective (e.g., Jonsen, 2017; Busuttil & Van Weelden, 2018) focuses on Imago Dei, where the "legal" treatment of a worker is rooted in their status as an image-bearer of God rather than just a contract holder. This distinction highlights that while secular law creates a transactional contract designed to mitigate risk and ensure procedural fairness, the biblical approach establishes a moral covenant where the employer acts as a steward of a person's divine potential. Consequently, this shift transforms HR policies from a set of restrictive rules to be navigated into an aspirational framework that actively seeks to help individuals flourish within their sacred vocation.

3.2. Strategic Evolution

McCutchen (2025) specifically compares how Protestant churches navigate the tension between "standard business practices" (legal/strategic) and "biblical principles" (spiritual), finding that size and denomination dictate which framework takes precedence. Larger or more institutionalized congregations often lean toward formal business structures to manage complexity and ensure legal compliance, while smaller churches typically rely on informal, relationally driven spiritual tenets. This suggests that as a religious organization grows, it must intentionally design a "strategic bridge" to professionalize its operations without diluting the core spiritual values that define its mission.

3.3. Historical Precedence

Thierry (2018) and Van Buren III & Greenwood (2013) argue that modern legal protections—such as fair wages and workplace safety—find their original "legal" framework in the Torah and the teachings of Jesus, suggesting the two are more integrated than often assumed. These authors contend that what we now perceive as progressive labour regulations are actually rooted in ancient covenants that mandated the prompt payment of labourers and the physical protection of the vulnerable. Consequently, viewing modern employment law through this lens allows practitioners to see legal compliance not as a secular burden, but as a continuation of a long-standing moral tradition of workplace stewardship.

4. HRM GLOBAL STANDARDS AND HRM BIBLICAL PRINCIPLES

The convergence of Global Human Resource Management (HRM) standards and Biblical principles begins with a shared foundational anthropology that recognizes the inherent dignity of every individual. While global frameworks like the United Nations Declaration of Human Rights view employees as rights-holders, the Biblical concept of Imago Dei (Image of God) provides a theological anchor for this status, suggesting that human value is intrinsic rather than granted by the state (Busuttil & Van Weelden, 2018). This synchronization is most evident in non-discrimination policies (ILO Convention 111), which align with the Biblical mandate for Divine Impartiality, where leadership is cautioned that "God does not show favouritism" (Romans 2:11; Roberts, 2014). This shared perspective extends to the protection of vulnerable groups, where the ILO's prohibition of child labour (Convention 182) codifies the scriptural imperative to protect the weak and ensure that no individual is treated as a mere commodity or economic tool (Pambour, 2022).

At the operational level, both frameworks emphasize justice, safety, and the holistic well-being of the workforce. The International Labour Organization (ILO) standards for fair wages (Convention 100) and the abolition of forced labor (Conventions 29 and 105) find their historical and moral precedents in the "worker's worth" and the prohibition of withheld wages found in Leviticus and the New Testament (Thierry, 2018; Van Buren III & Greenwood, 2013). Furthermore, modern Occupational Health and Safety (OHS) regulations (ILO Convention 155) sync with the Biblical principle of Stewardship of the Body, viewing life as a gift to be protected through proactive safety measures (Jonsen, 2017). Even the modern emphasis on work-life balance and mental health finds a direct parallel in the Sabbath Principle, which recognizes that human flourishing requires a rhythmic cycle of rest and renewal rather than constant mechanical output (Zigarelli, 1993). The UN's sustainable development goals align closely with the biblical concept of Sabbath-shalom, viewing environmental and human care as an integrated rhythm of rest, redemption, and covenantal relationship rooted in Creation. However, the study identifies a "fatal flaw" in the secular movement, suggesting that without these spiritual and covenantal roots, the journey toward true sustainability remains incomplete (Cafferky, 2015)

Finally, the governance and culture of an organization are transformed when global accountability standards are integrated with Biblical leadership models. The UN Guiding Principles on Business and Human Rights require "Due Diligence" from leaders, which converges with the Servant Leadership model where power is exercised as a stewardship to develop and equip others (Luke 22:26; Roberts, 2014). This synchronization is also seen in conflict resolution; while secular standards focus on grievance mechanisms and "Access to Remedy," the Biblical approach prioritizes Restorative Justice and face-to-face reconciliation to maintain organizational health (Matthew 18:15; Miner & Bickerton, 2020). Ultimately, modern ESG (Environmental, Social, and Governance) and sustainability goals sync with the mandate of Holistic Stewardship, viewing the management of an enterprise as a sacred responsibility to "tend the garden" for the benefit of both current stakeholders and future generations (Sangwa & Mutabazi, 2025).

5. CONCLUSION

The synthesis of research presented in this chapter underscores a fundamental distinction between the legal floor of human resource management and the biblical ceiling of organizational excellence. While the legal frameworks of nations—exemplified by India's transition to the four Labour Codes (2020)—are essential for establishing minimum standards of safety, social security, and fair wages, they primarily function through the lens of compliance and risk mitigation. These laws provide the necessary institutional "floor" that prevents exploitation and ensures basic survival; however, as the literature suggests, mere compliance often lacks the relational depth required to foster a truly flourishing workplace.

The Biblical principles of HRM offer a transformative alternative by shifting the focus from legal contracts to a covenant of stewardship. Rooted in the foundational concept of Imago Dei, this approach recognizes the unconditional worth of every employee as an image-bearer of God, independent of their economic productivity. This theological lens redefines the role of the manager from a supervisor of "human capital" to a servant leader dedicated to the holistic development of their followers. While the legal framework seeks to resolve disputes through formal, process-driven mechanisms, the Biblical model prioritizes restorative justice and reconciliation, seeking to maintain the moral and relational health of the organizational community.

Remarkably, the review reveals that global standards, such as those set by the ILO and UN, are not in conflict with Biblical ethics but are often a modern codification of them. The convergence on issues such as just wages, physical safety, and the "Sabbath-like" need for rest demonstrates that the "what" of ethical treatment is globally recognized, even if the "why" varies. Ultimately, organizations that integrate both frameworks move beyond a transactional relationship based on "corner-cutting" compliance. They embrace a transformational model where work is viewed as a sacred vocation. By grounding HR practices in these ancient yet enduring truths, leaders can build resilient, high-trust cultures that achieve organizational excellence while honouring the inherent dignity of the human person.

REFERENCES

Busuttil, L. R. G., & Van Weelden, S. J. (2018). Imago Dei and human resource management: How our understanding of the breath of God's Spirit shapes the way we manage people. *Journal of Biblical Integration in Business*, *21*(1).

Cafferky, M. E. (2015). Sabbath: The theological roots of sustainable development. *Journal of Biblical Integration in Business*, *18*(1).

Christopher, N. (2019). The effectiveness of HRM policies and practices. *The International Journal of Social Sciences (Islamabad)*, *2*(1), 24–32.

Clardy, A. (2003). The legal framework of human resource development: Overview, mandates, strictures, and financial implications. *Human Resource Development Review*, *2*(1), 26–53.

Dhiraj, A., Joshi, M., & Kumar, A. (2020). Human resource management and character building: Route to business sustainability. *International Journal of Business and Globalisation*, *25*(3), 332–348.

Erwin, E., Rauf, A., & Idy, M. Y. (2025). THE INFLUENCE OF LEGAL REGULATION ON HUMAN RESOURCE MANAGEMENT PRACTICES. *INJOSEDU: International Journal of Social and Education*, *2*(2), 443–445.

Gajenderan, N. (2024). Ensuring Hr Compliance: Strategies For Managing Legal And Regulatory Requirements. *Journal of Organizational Culture Communications and Conflict*, *28*(2), 1–3.

Gill, C., & Meyer, D. (2011). The role and impact of HRM policy. *The International Journal of Organizational Analysis*, *19*(1), 5–28.

Gupta, R., Kaur, H., & Raheja, S. (2025). Ethical and Legal Considerations in AI-Based HRM. In *Human Resource Management and Artificial Intelligence* (pp. 126–145). Routledge.

Hasyim, H., & Bakri, M. (2023). The Impact of Employment Law on Human Resource Practices: A Global Perspective. *The Journal of Business and Management Research*, *6*(1), 43–54.

Jonsen, R. H. (2017). Strategic person and organization development: Implications of Imago Dei for contemporary human resource management. *Journal of Biblical Integration in Business*, *20*(1).

. McCutchen, B. M. (2025). The Role of Standard Business and Biblical Principles in the Strategic Human Resource Management Practices of Contemporary Protestant Churches.

Miner, M., & Bickerton, G. (2020). A new model of Christian leadership: Insights from the job demands–resources model and Trinitarian theology. *Journal of Psychology and Theology*, *48*(4), 276–291.

Murphy, K. R. (2018). The legal context of the management of human resources. *Annual Review of Organizational Psychology and Organizational Behavior*, *5*(1), 157–182.

. Pambour, A. (2022). Christian Ethics and Employee Management systems. ADRRI Journal (Multidisciplinary), 31(3 (8) July-September), 31-49.

Psychogios, A., Szamosi, L. T., Prouska, R., & Brewster, C. (2016). A three-fold framework for understanding HRM practices in South-Eastern European SMEs. *Employee Relations*, *38*(3), 310–331.

Roberts, G. E. (2014). Principles of servant leader human resource management (SLHRM). In *Servant Leader Human Resource Management: A Moral and Spiritual Perspective* (pp. 1–38). Palgrave Macmillan US.

. Sangwa, S., & Mutabazi, P. (2025). Integrating Christian faith and ethics into global business: A biblical framework for leadership, culture, and decision-making. Open Journal of Business Theology, 5(2).

Scheibmayr, I., & Reichel, A. (2023). Beating the advertising drum for the employer: How legal context translates into good HRM practice. *Human Resource Management Journal*, *33*(1), 95–114.

Thierry, A. Z. (2018). HRM, ITS BIBLICAL ORIGINS AND PERSPECTIVES. *International Journal of Research Science and Management*, *5*(9), 10–20.

Van Buren, H. J.III, & Greenwood, M. (2013). The genesis of employment ethics. *Journal of Business Ethics*, *117*(4), 707–719.

Zigarelli, M. A. (1993). Catholic social teaching and the employment relationship: A model for managing human resources in accordance with Vatican doctrine. *Journal of Business Ethics*, *12*(1), 75–82.

Chapter 10
Employment Law and HRM Reform in India

Jeayaram Subramanian
Jindal Global Business School, O.P. Jindal Global University, India

Shivani Dhand
https://orcid.org/0000-0002-4809-1365
Lovely Professional University, India

Aayushi Pandey
https://orcid.org/0000-0001-7584-0520
Mittal School Of Business, India

Damith Gangodawilage
https://orcid.org/0000-0001-7968-6284
Qasim Ibrahim School of Business, Villa College, Maldives

Thi Minh Ngoc Luu
https://orcid.org/0000-0002-5972-7752
International School, Vietnam National University, Hanoi, Vietnam

ABSTRACT

Human Resource Management (HRM) reform has become a central policy and organizational concern in India as the country confronts economic liberalization, globalization, technological disruption, and significant demographic change. While mainstream strategic HRM scholarship often foregrounds managerial innovation, performance enhancement, and competitive advantage, this chapter argues that legal frameworks remain the most powerful institutional forces shaping employment relations and HRM practices. Focusing on the Indian context and informed by global comparative perspectives, the chapter examines the legal foundations of HRM reform

DOI: 10.4018/979-8-3693-5390-5.ch010

through a historical, institutional, and regulatory lens. It traces the evolution of Indian labour and employment law from colonial regulation and post-independence protectionism to contemporary reform initiatives, with particular emphasis on the consolidation of labour legislation into four labour codes.

1. INTRODUCTION

The human resource management (HRM) has experienced a radical change in the last few decades which has seen it change more into an administrative, record keeping and compliance based activity, rather than a strategic organizational competitiveness, innovation and sustainability driver. Early practices in personnel management were mostly reactive as they were based on payroll administration, compliance of labour regulations and maintenance of industrial discipline. By comparison, the modern HRM is becoming more theoretically understood as a strategic ally that helps to match the organizational capabilities with its goals, helps to innovate, manages human capital risks, and provides organizational resilience when faced with volatile economic conditions (Boxall and Purcell, 2016; Ulrich et al., 2012).Nevertheless, this change of HRM has not been done in a vacuum of institutions. Employment relations are legal constructs, influenced and limited by statutory obligations, regulatory provisions, judicial values and the institutions of enforcement which shape the rights and liabilities of the employer and employee (Budd, 2011; Deakin and Wilkinson, 2005). Labour and employment laws stipulate who qualifies as an employee, conditions in which the work is undertaken, wage rates, payable, how to settle disputes and how power is shared at the workplace. Therefore, HRM practices are entrenched in the scope, design, and implementation of the practices making the legal frameworks a core and not a periphery determinant of HRM reform.

The connection between law and HRM, in this case, is especially important in India because of the peculiar historical, constitutional, and socio-economic situation in the country. Historically, the labour law regime in India was typified by high volume of fragmented laws, protective orientation towards its workers in the organized sector and high volume of the state intervention in employment relations. This model was a product of post-independence constitutional pledge of social justice, equity and protection of workers as experienced in the Directive Principles of State Policy and initial industrial relations laws (Papola, 2012; Saini, 1995). The legislation of job security, the minimum wages, social security, and collective bargaining was very vital in ensuring the rights of the workers and the maintenance of a peaceful atmosphere in the industries within the first decades of nation-building.

Meanwhile, this safeguarding legal framework has also faced widespread criticism in promoting regulatory inflexibility, expensive compliance, legal incomprehensiveness, and non-uniform application across regions and sectors. It has been claimed that the proliferation of labour laws, the overlapping jurisdiction, and the procedural formalism posed great challenge to the employers, especially the small and medium enterprises, and did not provide adequate protection to the large informal workforce (Debroy et al., 2020; OECD, 2017). Consequently, there developed a widening gap between the formal legal regimes and the real practice of HRM, and the organizations increasingly relied on contractualization, delegation, and informality to gain flexibility, frequently tending to push towards the boundaries of legality (Shyam Sundar, 2017).

These strains became greater within the environment of globalization, economic liberalization, and change in technology. The integration process of India into the global markets, the development of the sphere of personal enterprise, and the rise of knowledge-intensive and service industries are fundamental to changing the character of work and employment relations in the country since the beginning of the 1990s. To withstand competition in the global value chains, employers have been put under pressure to embrace flexible staffing models, performance-based compensation systems, and technology-driven Hr processes (Boxall and Macky, 2014). Meanwhile policymakers have tried to make doing business easier at the expense of central labour protections spawning a long-standing debate on labour law reform and modernisation of HRM.

Indeed, responding to these structural pressures, India has embarked on one of the most ambitious labour law reform initiatives of the post-independence period with 29 central labour laws consolidated to become four comprehensive labour codes: the Code on Wages (2019), the Industrial Relations Code (2020), the Code on Social Security (2020) and the Occupational Safety, Health and Working Conditions Code (2020). These reforms are a radical change in the legal basis of HRM, the consequences of which can fully apply to the recruitment, employment relationships, remuneration, labour relations, social security, and workplace regulations (Debroy et al., 2020; Ministry of Labour and Employment, 2021). The labour codes aim to bring the legal frameworks closer to the modern-day HRM practices and labour market realities by rationalizing compliance criteria, redefining employment categories, and providing limited protections to gig and platform workers.Against this backdrop, this chapter scrutinizes the HRM reform in India in terms of law-institutional approach. The chapter not only views legal frameworks as restrictions on managerial action, but conceptualizes them as proactive institutions that design, scope, and strategic orientation of HRM systems (Budd and Bhave, 2008; Deakin, 2013). The chapter in particular discusses four questions that are connected. To begin with, what has been the historical impact of the Indian legislation in labour law and how it has developed the HRM practices and employment relations. Second, what are the fundamental legal areas, including employment contracts and wages, social security, occupational safety and collective relations, which seem to be central to HRM reform in India today? Third, what are the changes in the balance between labour market flexibility, worker protection and managerial autonomy under the new labour law reforms? Fourth, what are the emerging legal issues and opportunities in HRM under the conditions of the digitalization, platform work, artificial intelligence, and data-driven people management?The chapter is a part of the increasing body of interdisciplinary literature at the boundary of HRM, labour law, and employment relations. It pursues the thesis that the Indian HRM reform cannot be done by managerial innovation or by imitating world best practices alone but instead must be based on a consistent, legal and progressive legal frameworks. Meanwhile, by contextualizing the Indian experience, the chapter places it in the context of wider world of labour market regulation, flexibility, and decent work, which can inform practitioners, scholars and policy makers in emerging and developed economies alike in thinking about the future of work..

2. HISTORICAL EVOLUTION OF LABOUR LAW AND HRM IN INDIA

2.1 Colonial Foundations and Early Regulation

The foundations of Indian labour law were laid during the colonial period, primarily as instruments to regulate industrial employment in sectors that were strategically important to the colonial economy, such as plantations, factories, mines, railways, and ports. The primary objective of early labour regulation was not the protection of workers' rights in a normative or welfare-oriented sense, but rather the maintenance of industrial discipline, productivity, and social order necessary for colonial economic extraction (Saini, 1995; Chandrasekhar, 2016). As a result, labour legislation during this period reflected a narrow and instrumental approach to employment regulation.

Early statutes such as the Factories Act, 1881—later amended in 1891, 1911, and 1934—introduced limited protections relating to working hours, sanitation, ventilation, and the employment of women and children. These interventions were largely reactive and shaped by external pressures, including criticism from British social reform movements and international scrutiny over exploitative labour practices in colonial industries (Hepple, 2014). Importantly, these laws applied only to a small segment of the workforce employed in registered industrial establishments, leaving the vast majority of workers in agriculture, domestic service, and informal activities entirely outside the scope of legal protection.

The colonial labour regime was also characterized by a strong emphasis on control rather than participation. Laws governing labour relations prioritized managerial authority and public order, often restricting workers' ability to organize and protest. Trade union activity was initially viewed with suspicion, and collective bargaining rights were either weak or absent until the enactment of the Trade Unions Act, 1926, which granted limited legal recognition to unions but imposed significant constraints on their functioning (Sen, 1977). Consequently, early employment relations were marked by asymmetric power relations, with employers exercising substantial discretion over hiring, discipline, and termination.Personnel management practices during the colonial era were correspondingly rudimentary and compliance-driven. Employers' primary concern was adherence to statutory minimum standards and avoidance of legal penalties, rather than the systematic development of workforce capabilities or employee welfare. Labour unrest, which periodically erupted in the form of strikes and protests, was typically addressed through coercive state intervention, policing, or ad hoc negotiations rather than institutionalized dispute resolution mechanisms (Chakrabarty, 2004). The absence of structured grievance redressal systems, formalized job classifications, or participatory HR practices limited the evolution of personnel management as a professional or strategic function.From an HRM perspective, the colonial period established a legacy of legal formalism combined with weak enforcement and limited coverage. Employment law functioned as an external constraint imposed by the state rather than as an integrated framework shaping organizational HR policies. This legacy would continue to influence post-independence labour regulation and HRM practices, particularly the tendency to equate HRM with legal compliance rather than strategic workforce management (Sundar, 2011).

The HRM practices were permanently marked by these legal developments. The human-resource activities during the period had been saturated by industrial-relations management, statutory regulation as well as trade union negotiation. Employment arrangements were characterised by severe castes of permanence, temporaryity and causality; standard wage rates; promotion regimes based on seniority and limited performance based rewards. Keep in mind that although these arrangements have strengthened job security and secured employees, they have also subdued organisational flexibility and adaptability to market dynamics (Papola, 2012; Sundar, 2017).Moreover, the protective labour regime was characterised by a high level of coverage unevenness. Safeguarding and the complex HR systems was rich in workers of the organised sector, whereas the large majority part of the labour force in India was still in the informal sector, where they were not subject to statutory labour legislation or formal labour practices. This two-sided reality created a divided labour market, where protection and HR acumen was concentrated in a small privileged niche, which makes aspects of equity, efficiency and inclusivity remain permanent issues (Chen, 2012).In the perspective of reform, the post-independence era entrenched a compliance-based model of HRM, in which liability to labour laws and industrial conflict management were of primary concern, rather than strategic talent development or optimisation of performance. Although it accords with the developmental and redistributive needs of the state, this paradigm planted long-term conflicts between protection and flexibility, finally leading to demands of labour law and HRM reform in the liberalisation period (OECD, 2017).

2.3 Liberalization and Reform Pressures

The economic liberalization initiated in 1991 marked a turning point in India's labour and HRM landscape. Increased exposure to global competition, foreign investment, and technological change intensified demands for labour market flexibility and productivity enhancement. Employers and policymakers increasingly viewed existing labour laws as fragmented, complex, and misaligned with contemporary business needs (OECD, 2017).

HRM practices began to shift toward performance-based pay, flexible staffing, outsourcing, and contractual employment, often operating at the margins of existing legal frameworks. This divergence between law and practice highlighted the need for comprehensive legal reform to realign HRM with economic realities.

3. CORE LEGAL DOMAINS SHAPING HRM REFORM IN INDIA

3.1 Employment Contracts, Recruitment, and Termination

Employment contracts form the legal foundation of HRM. Indian labour law traditionally distinguished sharply between permanent workers and contract or casual labour, with significant implications for job security and managerial discretion. The Industrial Disputes Act imposed stringent conditions on retrenchment and closure in larger establishments, shaping conservative HR staffing strategies (Shyam Sundar, 2017).

Recent reforms under the Industrial Relations Code, 2020 seek to rationalize these provisions by redefining thresholds, introducing fixed-term employment, and simplifying dispute resolution mechanisms. From an HRM perspective, these changes expand the scope for flexible hiring while retaining statutory protections related to notice, compensation, and due process.

Recruitment and selection practices are also influenced by constitutional and statutory principles of equality and non-discrimination. While private-sector employment is not directly subject to constitutional equality provisions, judicial interpretations and social norms increasingly require fair and transparent HR practices (Bhandari, 2019).

3.2 Wages, Compensation, and Social Security

Wage regulation has traditionally been the major pillar of Indian labour law and one of the main devices on which the state tries to foster distributive justice, mitigate income inequality, and to protect vulnerable workers. The Indian wage governance was until the recent reforms defined by disaggregation in a myriad of acts: the Minimum Wages Act, 1948; the Payment of Wages Act, 1936; the Payment of Bonus Act, 1965; and the Equal Remuneration Act, 1976. This multiplicity introduced the problems of definitional ambiguity, complexity of compliance, and inconsistency across sectors and states, which is a significant challenge to human-resources compensation management (Papola, 2012; Debroy et al., 2020).The adoption of the Code on Wages, 2019 is a sharp shift in the direction of standardisation and simplification of wage regulation. The legislation, which has unified four key wage-related laws into one code, proposes a common understanding of the word wages that can be applied in all laws and also covers minimum-wage to all workers regardless of industry, and regardless of the wage rate. This reform has extensive HRM consequences of how organisations design their compensation; organisations have been forced to re-engineer the pay elements by ensuring that core wage principles meet statutory percentages and exclusions are strictly limited (Ministry of Labour and Employment, 2021).To the HR managers, the compliance with the Code on Wages requires a thorough analysis of compensation schemes, payroll systems and incentive schemes. Companies require realigning the basic remuneration, allowances and variable elements to align with the legal provisions in maintaining internal equity and external competitiveness. Besides, the Code reinforces the principles of pay equity and non-discrimination by reinforcing equal pay between men and women and increasing the transparency of wage determination, making employers institutionalise the fair and auditable compensation practices (Rani and Belser, 2012; Rubery and Grimshaw, 2016).

Social-security reform also increases the transformational effect of wage regulation to HRM. The Code on Social Security, 2020 pulls together the existing regulations in the field of provident funds, employee state insurance, gratuity, maternity benefits and employment-injury compensation, but greatly extends the field of influence. It is important to note that the Code presents a statutory status of gig workers, platform workers and unorganised workers, which marks a paradigmatic change in the protection of the Indian labour force (ILO, 2021). Though the modalities of contribution and benefit delivery are still subject to rule-making and implementation, the presence of non-standard workers undermines traditional HRM conjectures about the social-security liability of having a formal employment relationship.To employers and HR professionals, these reforms will necessitate the work involving larger conceptions of work responsibility beyond permanent employees to include multiple and changeable ways of work. HRM systems need to incorporate more social-security compliance, workforce classification and data management in their strategic decision-making. In this respect, wage and social-security changes not only reform the administration of the compensation but also reestablish the ethical and institutional framework of HRM in the changing labour market in India (De Stefano, 2016; Budd, 2011)..

3.3 Working Time, Occupational Health, and Welfare

The regulation of working hours, occupational health and employee welfare has formed a basic pillar of Indian labour law over many decades as it reflects the determination of the state towards protecting workers against physical harm, excessive workload and hazardous working conditions. The introduction of the Occupational Safety, Health and Working Conditions (OSHWC) Code in 2020 is a breakthrough towards the rationalisation and modernisation of this legal framework, as it brings together a plethora of industry-specific laws that previously regulated factories, mines, plantations, construction sites, and contract labour. By harmonisation of standards in these varied sectors, the Code purports to reduce regulatory fragmentation, as well as spreading protective coverage to a broader range of establishments and workers (Ministry of Labour and Employment, 2021).The OSHWC Code extends the focus of the issue of occupational health and safety beyond traditional scope of occupational health and safety to include welfare facilities, controlled working hours, leave, and faculty working conditions. In the HRM view, this combined practice highlights a paradigm shift in the comprehensive employee welfare and work sustainable design. The work-life balance, alleviation of work-related stress, and the development of psychologically safe work environments are becoming the major concerns of the modern HRM reforms, contributing to the alignment of the statutory compliance with the overall organisational well-being tactics (Walters et al., 2011; ILO, 2021).One of the milestones in the Code is the actual acknowledgment of the night work of women, under the condition of the safety requirements. This provision is the reflection of the social mores, the increased female involvement in various spheres and advanced HR practices which are aimed at the inclusion of genders. However, it also presents further obligations to employers and HR managers who should guarantee proper safety controls, safe transportation, proper redressing of grievances, and powerful risk evaluation systems. The adherence to the OSHWC standards, in turn, requires active systems of HR, training, involvement of employees, and monitoring using technology, thus pushing the HR into the realm of HR beyond the reactive compliance to the preventive and participatory model of governance (Quinlan et al., 2015).

3.4 Industrial Relations and Collective Voice

The institutionalised collective voice of workers and the existence of industrial relations have over the decades been one of the pillars of the human resource management architecture in the organised sector in India. The state institutionalized a pluralist paradigm of employment relations through the Trade Unions Act, 1926 and the industrial Disputes Act, 1947, which codified the existence of collective representation, collective bargaining and dispute resolution through state mediation, making trade union an important stakeholder in the corporate governance systems. This legal framework permanently etched itself on the HRM praxis, especially in the public-sector institutions and giant manufacturing companies, where practices like negotiation, consultation and industrial relations management became the primary role of the human-resource functions (Papola, 2012).

The Industrial Relations Code of 2020, however, aims to rationalise and modernise that legacy through simplification of the union-recognition processes, control of the practices of strikes, and formalisation of alternative dispute-resolution processes - conciliation and arbitration. When viewed through a reformist prism, the actions are supposed to suppress industrial hostility, increase predictability and ease the entrepreneurial climate. To the HR manager, the Code allegedly streamlines the daily running of the industrial relations, and at the same time promotes the anticipatory settlement of conflicts using institutionalized expressways (Debroy et al., 2020). Despite these changes, critics express concerns that the newly promulgated thresholds and strike-squashing laws are going to undermine the strength of the collective bargaining and the collective voice of the workers. In an HRM-reform agenda, these concerns reflect a light into the relative fragility of the efficient-needs balance and the maintenance of participatory, inclusive working relationships. Academic research has been adamant in indicating that strong employee-voice structures, be it within the framework of a union or not within non-union frameworks, play a decisive role in fostering organisational trust, legitimacy, and a longer-term performance (Budd and Bhave, 2008; Wilkinson et al., 2020). Therefore, any Indian HRM reforms should combine statutory requirements with the participatory voice practices that maintain the constructive labour-management relationships in the changing regulatory environment.

4. JUDICIAL INTERPRETATION AND ENFORCEMENT IN THE INDIAN CONTEXT

Indian judiciary has been in the centre and active stage of influencing the labour law, and Human Resource Management (HRM) practices by making broad interpretations of constitutional guarantees and statutory provisions. In contrast to a more textual approach to labour law, Indian courts have long taken a purposive and rights-based approach to interpretation, relying on some of the major constitutional principles of equality, freedom of association, and rights to life with dignity. The judicial system has used this jurisprudence to incorporate the principles of natural justice, fairness, and proportionality into the employment relations and, in the process, exerts an overwhelming impact on the organisational HRM systems (Baxi, 2000; Srivastava, 2021).

Judicial principles in regard to due process, reasonableness and procedural fairness have had far reaching impact on organisational practices in the disciplinary action, termination, transfer, suspension and grievance redressal. The managerial prerogative should be used in a manner that is seen to be within the efforts of fairness and legality, this has been reinforced in the courts and employers have been urged to remember that they have the obligation to engage in transparent procedures and give the employee the chance to be heard before making adverse decisions.

4.1 The Judicial Activism and Procedural Fairness in HRM.

Cases that pioneered courts have given an understanding of how an employer should carry out home investigations, misconduct judgment and discipline reprimands. Courts have been demanding that principles of natural justice are followed such as giving notice, fair inquiry and rational decision making and it has restricted arbitrary managerial action and helped to enhance procedural legitimacy of HRM systems (Baxi, 2000). This has forced organisations to institutionalise codes of discipline, documentation procedures and internal grievance policies.

On the part of HRM, this judicial activism has helped in the professionalisation of HR activities and especially in large organisations and in those run by the government. Misconduct investigation, disciplinary hearing and appeal standard operating procedures have become part of the HR governance that minimise legal risk whilst increasing the legitimacy of the organisation.

4.2 Extending the Concept of Employment Relationships.

The Indian courts have equally been instrumental when it comes to expanding the scope of defining employment relationships past the confines of contracts. Where there is contract labour, sham contracts and unfair labour practices, courts have examined the realities behind the contract because the contracts made are not always the terms of real control, supervision and economic reliance (Deakin and Wilkinson, 2005). This has been critical especially in safeguarding employees against the misleading employment relationships intended to avoid the statutory requirements.

In case of HRM reforming, this jurisprudence stresses the importance of a meticulous workforce segmentation, evident contracting and the alignment between formal HR policies and real practices at the workplace. Employers cannot afford to use contractual labels to only determine the work of employment, particularly when dealing with outsourcing, fixed-term contract and work mediated by a platform.

4.3 Implementation Lapses and Institutional Limitations.

Although the judiciary interpretation is strong, labour laws are still applied in an irregular fashion in India. This can be in cases of small enterprises, informal establishments and geographically dispersed workplaces that are usually not effectively under regulatory control. The ability of labour inspectorates to act as a deterrent to regulation is often limited by the lack of staffing, technical capacity and jurisdictional complexity (Papola, 2012).Administrative and financial compliance costs are also a sources of extra challenges, especially when it comes to small and medium enterprises that do not have dedicated HR or law knowledge. Such limitations are the source of selective compliance and informal HRM practices, which only exacerbate the discrepancies between legal standards and the actual situation in the workplace (Gunningham et al., 2003).

4.4 Implications for HRM Reform

The ultimate reform of HRM in India is therefore not just about the clarity of law and progressive judicial interpretation, but also about enhancing the enforcement institutions, the coordination of regulations and the legal awareness of the employers and workers. The role of the HR professionals will have to be more of an interplay between law and practice, converting the principles of the law to organisational processes, training courses and compliance regulations.

It is in this sense that judicial interpretation can act to correct, as well as provide a normative direction towards reforming HRM. Though courts ensure protection against unreasonable employment practices, the ultimate solution to this problem lies on institutional capacity building and proactive HR governance that facilitates the internalization of legal principles by managers to make daily managerial decisions..

5. INDIA IN COMPARATIVE AND GLOBAL PERSPECTIVE

The legal reforms of HRM in India are a symbolic representation of an international trend towards consolidation, simplification and increased labour market flexibility, and at the same time, maintain a unique normative focus on social justice and worker protection. Similar patterns of reform can be identified in both developed and developing economies; governments in those countries have strived to rationalise labour regulation due to the pressures of globalization, technological transformation, and shifting patterns of employment (OECD, 2017). However, the Indian experience of reform is also intricately influenced by its special socio-economic environment, although the most striking is the long-standing existence of a huge informal sector which swallows most of the labour force.

The labour market in India is highly dualistic unlike most of the developed economies, where formal employment relationships and institutionalised HRM systems are the order of the day. The formal legal safeguards, as well as advanced HRM, are mostly limited to a relatively small organised segment, and informal workers have only a marginal access to the realm of labour regulation and social insurance (Chen, 2012). This structural fact limits the effectiveness of the traditional change strategies in HRM reform and forces to consider the new legal and policy responses to the various conditions of employment.Conformity to the international work standards, especially those issued by International Labour Organisation (ILO), is a critical aspect of international interactions of India. India ratified some of the core ILO conventions on forced labour, child labour and non-discrimination and these ratifications have indicated its binding of the basic labour rights. However, there are still loopholes between the official ratification and a real realization, particularly in the fields of the freedom of association and collective bargaining (ILO, 2019). The only way of filling these gaps is through continual legal change, institutionalization and the smooth connection between international standards and the local practice of HRM.

6. DIGITALIZATION, ARTIFICIAL INTELLIGENCE, AND HRM LAW IN INDIA

There is a fast rate of digitalization, which has changed the way organizations recruit, manage, evaluate, and retain employees in India, making Human Resource Management (HRM) fundamentally transform. The rise in the use of online recruitment platforms, HR analytics, artificial intelligence (AI) -based screening tools and algorithmic performance management systems has also facilitated increased efficiency, scalability, and data-driven decision-making. Such technologies enable organizations to handle high volumes of applicant and employee data, determine the trends in performance and attrition, and automate many of their routine HR processes (Stone and Deadrick, 2015; Kellogg et al., 2020).Meanwhile, the digital revolution of HRM comes with complicated legal and ethical issues that the current employment and labour law models were not initially intended to address. Issues of data safety, employee confidentiality, algorithm prejudice, transparency and responsibility have become even more relevant in digitally mediated workplace settings (Ajunwa, 2020; De Stefano and Taes, 2021). Recruiting and evaluating systems based on AI can replicate or exaggerate discrimination practiced in historical data and opaque algorithms do not provide the employee with the opportunity to know, challenge, or claim redress against any unfavorable decision.

6.1 Data Protection, Privacy and Employer Obligations

The new norms of data protection in the Indian scenario have vastly increased employer obligations with regard to dealing with employee data. The more HRM systems handle sensitive personal data, such as biometric identifiers, health data, behavioural metrics and performance analytics, the more employers are placed in the role of data fiduciary with an augmented responsibility of care. This threat of abuse, unauthorized monitoring and discriminatory profiling is especially sharp in the digitally-intense HR settings (Ajunwa, 2020; ILO, 2023).The legal aspect of this area demands that HR managers include privacy-as-a-design concepts within the digital HR designs. This involves having a legitimate purpose to collect data, informed consent, data storage and having a clear protocol to access and retain data. Open dialogue with the employees on the process of collection, use and analysis of their data has become a key factor in the legal and ethical HRM practice (De Stefano and Taes, 2021).

6.2 Algorithmic Management, Fairness, and Accountability

The growing application of AI in the recruitment, promotion and performance appraisal also puts pressure on the conventional legal frameworks that rely on human decision-making. The way that algorithmic systems are designed is not always explainable and thus it is more challenging to determine whether a decision was made based on the set principles of fairness, proportionality, and non-discrimination. The problem of information asymmetry between employers and employees is also exacerbated by the fact that algorithmic logic is secured as a proprietary or trade-secret information type (Kellogg et al., 2020; European Commission, 2021).

According to an HRM reform point of view, this has required the creation of governance systems that guarantee algorithmic accountability. These can be in form of human-in-the-loop decision models, periodic bias audit, impact assessment and readily available grievance redressal systems. The absence of such protection will make digital HRM a threat to trust, legitimacy and legal compliance in employment relations.

6.3 HRM Reform Implication in India

Digitisation of HRM therefore demands legal innovation to move forward with the technology adoption. The question of digital surveillance and automated decision-making and algorithmic fairness will have to gain increased interest in Indian labour and employment law in order to stay pertinent in a data-intensive workplace. This means that as an HR practitioner, one is prone to the move towards a more integrative role of being technologically literate and competent in matters of law and ethics.

HRM reform in India should therefore be able to assure that digital transformation would improve, instead of undermine, decent work, equality and lawful employment relations. The difficulty consists in seizing the economic benefits of AI and analytics and introducing effective legal provisions that safeguard the rights of employees and enhance work transparency in the future..

7. PLATFORM WORK, GIG ECONOMY, AND EMPLOYMENT STATUS

The rapid expansion of platform-based and gig work in India represents one of the most significant transformations in contemporary employment relations. Sectors such as ride-hailing, food delivery, logistics, home services, and e-commerce have witnessed large-scale workforce reconfiguration through digital labour platforms. These platforms reorganize work through algorithmic management, data-driven task allocation, and customer rating systems rather than traditional hierarchical supervision. As a consequence, conventional legal distinctions between "employees" and "independent contractors" have become increasingly contested and blurred (De Stefano, 2016; International Labour Organization [ILO], 2021).

From an HRM perspective, platform work challenges foundational assumptions regarding workforce management, control, accountability, and responsibility. Platform firms typically classify workers as independent contractors, thereby limiting obligations related to minimum wages, social security contributions, working-time regulation, occupational safety, and collective representation. However, the high degree of economic dependence, algorithmic surveillance, and unilateral control exercised by platforms has prompted scholars, regulators, and courts worldwide to question the adequacy of existing legal categories and employment tests (Supiot, 2001; Stewart & Stanford, 2017).

7.1 Algorithmic Management and HRM Control Mechanisms

One of the defining features of platform work is the replacement of human supervision with algorithmic management systems. Algorithms determine task allocation, pricing, performance evaluation, and deactivation decisions, often with limited transparency or opportunity for worker contestation. This form of control challenges traditional HRM notions of managerial discretion, procedural fairness, and accountability, as decision-making authority is embedded within opaque technological systems rather than identifiable managers (Ajunwa, 2020; Kellogg et al., 2020).

For HRM reform, algorithmic management raises critical legal and ethical questions regarding due process, bias, and explainability. The absence of clear grievance redressal mechanisms and human oversight undermines established principles of natural justice, necessitating new regulatory and HRM responses that ensure transparency, auditability, and worker voice in algorithm-driven workplaces.

7.2 Employment Classification and Regulatory Ambiguity

Employment classification remains the central legal issue in the regulation of platform work. Traditional tests of employment—such as control, integration, and economic dependence—produce ambiguous outcomes when applied to platform-mediated work arrangements. While platforms claim to function as intermediaries, the operational realities of pricing control, performance monitoring, and unilateral rule-setting suggest a degree of employer-like authority (De Stefano, 2016; Stewart & Stanford, 2017).

In India, judicial engagement with platform work is still evolving, resulting in regulatory uncertainty for HR practitioners and platform firms alike. This ambiguity complicates workforce planning, compliance strategies, and the design of HRM systems capable of balancing flexibility with protection.

7.3 Social Security Expansion under the Code on Social Security, 2020

The Code on Social Security, 2020 represents a significant legal innovation in the Indian context by explicitly recognizing gig workers and platform workers as distinct categories and extending the possibility of social security coverage beyond standard employment relationships. Although the Code does not reclassify platform workers as employees, it signals a conceptual shift toward a more inclusive understanding of labour protection that moves beyond rigid binary classifications (ILO, 2021).

From an HRM reform standpoint, this development requires new approaches to workforce categorization, contribution mechanisms, data management, and regulatory compliance. Platform firms and aggregators are increasingly expected to participate in social security financing frameworks, raising strategic questions regarding cost-sharing, sustainability, and long-term workforce engagement (De Stefano, 2016).

7.4 Collective Voice, Representation, and Platform Workers

Platform work also challenges traditional models of collective representation and employee voice. The individualized and dispersed nature of platform labour weakens conventional trade union structures and collective bargaining mechanisms. Nevertheless, emerging forms of collective action—such as digital organizing, worker associations, and platform-specific unions—indicate growing demand for voice and representation among gig workers (Budd & Bhave, 2008; ILO, 2021).

HRM reform in this domain must explore alternative and hybrid voice mechanisms that can operate alongside flexible work arrangements. Failure to address representation concerns risks exacerbating power asymmetries and undermining the legitimacy of platform-based employment models.

7.5 Ethical Governance and the Future of Platform HRM

As platform work becomes a durable feature of India's labour market, HR officials and platform firms must increasingly engage with questions of ethical workforce governance, algorithmic transparency, and sustainable flexibility. Issues of income volatility, work intensity, safety, and social protection are central to debates on equity and inclusion in platform-mediated employment (Supiot, 2001; Ajunwa, 2020).

Platform work regulation thus represents a strategic frontier in India's HRM reform agenda. The manner in which legal frameworks, HRM systems, and organizational practices evolve in response to platform work will significantly influence the future of employment relations, social security, and decent work in the digital economy.

8. PERSISTENT CHALLENGES IN IMPLEMENTING HRM LEGAL REFORM

Despite the ambition and scope of recent labour law reforms, significant challenges remain in translating legal change into effective HRM practice. One of the most pressing issues is delayed and uneven implementation of the labour codes, as several provisions remain contingent on state-level rule-making and administrative capacity. This has created regulatory uncertainty for employers and HR professionals, complicating workforce planning and compliance strategies (Debroy et al., 2020).Resistance from multiple stakeholders also continues to shape the reform landscape. Trade unions have expressed concerns regarding dilution of job security and collective bargaining rights, while employers—particularly small and medium enterprises (SMEs)—face difficulties in understanding and adapting to new compliance requirements. Compliance costs, limited access to legal expertise, and weak digital infrastructure pose particular challenges for SMEs, which often lack formal HR departments (Gunningham et al., 2003; Papola, 2012). Enforcement deficits further undermine the effectiveness of HRM legal reform. Labour inspectorates and adjudicatory institutions frequently face capacity constraints, leading to inconsistent enforcement and prolonged dispute resolution. As a result, a gap persists between formal legal frameworks and actual workplace practices, particularly in the informal and semi-formal segments of the economy (Chen, 2012). Bridging this gap between law and practice remains a central and unresolved task for HRM reform in India.

9. FUTURE-ORIENTED LEGAL AND HRM REFORM AGENDA FOR INDIA

In the future, the HRM reform in India requires the advice of a progressive legal agenda, which aligns employment regulation with the goals of inclusive growth, skill advancement, technological accommodation, and sustainability. The digital platforms that reduce the complexity of the compliance process, unification of central and state-level regulations, and the capacity-building of enforcement agencies are essential priorities towards the effectiveness of the labour law reform (OECD, 2017; ILO, 2019).HRM systems need to change at the organisational level to incorporate legal compliance with the strategic planning of the workforce, ongoing skill development, and employee welfare. The ethical application of digital technologies, such as HR analytics, AI-powered recruitment, and algorithmic performance management, requires strong legal protection to tackle the problem of privacy, preference, and transparency (Ajunwa, 2020). Therefore, the law should be able to balance between innovation and the safeguarding of basic labour rights.This changes the situation so that HR professionals are gaining more and more responsibilities to operate as legal-strategic partners in organisations. In addition to compliance on the part of the administration, HR leaders have to decipher rather challenging legal regulations, foresee regulatory transformation, and transform acts of statutory provisions into practical and ethical HR practices. This is a role necessary in ensuring that the HRM reform can not only lead to the efficiency of the organisation but also to social legitimacy and sustainable development in the new world of work in India (Budd, 2011; Boxall and Purcell, 2016).

10. CONCLUSION

The issue of Human Resource Management reformation in India is incomplete without the appreciation of the key position the law systems play in defining the employment relations, organization practices, and the end results of labor force. Instead of acting as the external constraints, labour laws form the institutional framework of the HRM strategies conception, implementation, and contention. As revealed in this chapter, the direction that HRM reform in India has taken cannot be analyzed in isolation of the way the previous the historical development of employment control has led to its current reorganization.With a history of colonial labour regulation, followed by the nationalist era of protective law, the chapter puts the focus on the legal systems that have steadily intermediated the interaction between economic transformation and workplace regulation. The labour codes represent an important effort to streamline regulation, lessen the fragmentation, and to make the employment law consistent with the dynamics of a diversified and more flexible labour market. They have significant implications on HRM, that is they influence how the workforce will be structured, remunerating wages, social safeguarding, industrial connections, and work safety. Meanwhile, the application of these reforms is unequal, uncertainity of the regulations and enforcement restrictions continue to limit the transformative nature of these reforms.The analysis also highlights how the reform of the HRM in India continues to be unresolved as the tensions at its core are still unresolved flexibility and protection, efficiency and equity, and managerial discretion and worker security. The new types of work relating to digital platforms, algorithmic management, and non-standard employment increase the strength of these tensions as they problematize traditional legal categories and existing models of HRM. To deal with such developments, legal frameworks must be not only adaptive and responsive, but also based on fundamental principles of fairness, accountability and decent work.The implications of this chapter on HR professionals concern the redefined role, which is far beyond procedural compliance. Legal environments can become more complex and dynamic, this makes HRM have to be more of a legal-strategic operation, with the ability to interpret regulatory change, to integrate legal norms within the organization, and to balance business and social responsibility. HRM in this respect comes out as a very important institutional mediator between law, markets and society.Policy wise, the future of HRM reform in India lies in the success of operationalisation of labour codes, augmentation of enforcement capacity, prolonged social dialogue and enhanced involvement with international labour standards. An effective and rational legal system that promotes innovation and protects the rights of the workers can allow the Indian organizations to compete on the international level and to enhance the inclusive growth and sustainable employment. The success of the HRM reform will depend ultimately on the legislative intent, but the level of its realization in the day-in, day-out organizational practice and lived work experiences.

REFERENCES

Ajunwa, I. (2020). The paradox of automation as anti-bias intervention. *Cardozo Law Review, 41*(4), 1671–1740.

Baxi, U. (2000). *The avatars of Indian judicial activism. Explorations in the Geography of Justice*. Oxford University Press.

Bhandari, V. (2019). Labour law reforms in India: A critical analysis. *The Indian Journal of Labour Economics : the Quarterly Journal of the Indian Society of Labour Economics, 62*(3), 421–437. DOI: 10.1007/s41027-019-00193-4

Boxall, P., & Macky, K. (2014). High-involvement work processes, work intensification and employee well-being. *Work, Employment and Society, 28*(6), 963–984. DOI: 10.1177/0950017013512714

Boxall, P., & Purcell, J. (2016). *Strategy and human resource management* (4th ed.). Palgrave Macmillan.

Budd, J. W. (2011). *The thought of work.* Cornell University Press.

Budd, J. W., & Bhave, D. (2008). Values, ideologies, and frames of reference in employment relations. *Industrial Relations, 47*(1), 92–112.

Chen, M. A. (2012). *The informal economy: Definitions, theories and policies* (WIEGO Working Paper No. 1). WIEGO.

De Stefano, V., & Taes, S. (2021). Algorithmic management and collective bargaining. *International Labour Review, 160*(3), 419–438. DOI: 10.1111/ilr.12205

Deakin, S. (2013). Addressing labour market segmentation: The role of labour law. *International Labour Review, 152*(2), 211–232. DOI: 10.1111/j.1564-913X.2013.00178.x

Deakin, S., & Wilkinson, F. (2005). *The law of the labour market: Industrialization, employment and legal evolution.* Oxford University Press.

Debroy, B., Bhandari, L., & Santhanam, A. (2020). *Labour law reforms in India.* Penguin Random House India.

European Commission. (2021). Proposal for a regulation laying down harmonised rules on artificial intelligence (Artificial Intelligence Act). *European Union.*

Gunningham, N., Kagan, R. A., & Thornton, D. (2003). *Shades of green: Business, regulation, and environment.* Stanford University Press.

International Labour Organization. (2019). *Work for a brighter future: Global Commission on the Future of Work*. ILO.

International Labour Organization. (2023). *Artificial intelligence and the future of work*. ILO.

Kellogg, K. C., Valentine, M. A., & Christin, A. (2020). Algorithms at work: The new contested terrain of control. *The Academy of Management Annals*, *14*(1), 366–410. DOI: 10.5465/annals.2018.0174

Ministry of Labour and Employment. (2021). *Code on wages, 2019: An overview*. Government of India.

Ministry of Labour and Employment. (2021). *Occupational Safety, Health and Working Conditions Code, 2020: An overview*. Government of India.

OECD. (2017). *OECD economic surveys: India 2017*. OECD Publishing. https://doi.org/DOI: 10.1787/eco_surveys-ind-2017-en

Papola, T. S. (2012). Labour regulation in India. *The Indian Journal of Labour Economics : the Quarterly Journal of the Indian Society of Labour Economics*, *55*(3), 401–416.

Quinlan, M., Bohle, P., & Lamm, F. (2015). Managing occupational health and safety in precarious employment. *Policy and Practice in Health and Safety*, *13*(1), 3–22.

Rani, U., & Belser, P. (2012). The effectiveness of minimum wages in developing countries. *International Labour Review*, *151*(1–2), 81–112. DOI: 10.1111/j.1564-913X.2012.00149.x

Rubery, J., & Grimshaw, D. (2016). The 40-year pursuit of equal pay. *Cambridge Journal of Economics*, *40*(2), 319–343. DOI: 10.1093/cje/bev046

Saini, D. S. (1995). *Labour law and industrial relations in India*. Oxford University Press.

Shyam Sundar, K. R. (2017). Labour reforms and flexibility. *Economic and Political Weekly*, *52*(38), 49–58.

Srivastava, R. (2021). Employment relations and labour law in India. *Indian Journal of Industrial Relations*, *56*(4), 555–570.

Stewart, A., & Stanford, J. (2017). Regulating work in the gig economy. *Economic and Labour Relations Review*, *28*(3), 420–437.

Stone, D. L., & Deadrick, D. L. (2015). Challenges and opportunities affecting the future of human resource management. *Human Resource Management Review, 25*(2), 139–150. DOI: 10.1016/j.hrmr.2015.01.003

Supiot, A. (2001). *Beyond employment: Changes in work and the future of labour law*. Oxford University Press.

Supiot, A. (2001). *Beyond employment: Changes in work and the future of labour law*. Oxford University Press.

Ulrich, D., Younger, J., Brockbank, W., & Ulrich, M. (2012). *HR from the outside in: Six competencies for the future of human resources*. McGraw-Hill.

Walters, D., Wadsworth, E., & Quinlan, M. (2011). *Regulating workplace risks: A comparative study of inspection regimes in times of change*. Edward Elgar Publishing.

Wilkinson, A., Donaghey, J., Dundon, T., & Freeman, R. B. (2020). *Handbook of research on employee voice*. Edward Elgar Publishing.

Chapter 11
HR Management Reform Mediation in the Civil Service Operation's Effect on Decision-Making Effectiveness

Shashi Kant
https://orcid.org/0000-0003-4722-5736
DMI-St. Eugene University, Lusaka, Zambia

Rituraj Singh
https://orcid.org/0009-0008-0452-9303
O.P. Jindal Global University, India

ABSTRACT

This research discusses the function of HR management reform as a mediating variable in the operations of civil service by analysing its impact on the effectiveness of decision making process in community based administration as a whole. It particularly explores how Reforms in HRM, related with strategic use of IT capabilities and adoption of AI based outcomes, to deliver a more flexible as well as efficient civil service workforce that would be able to solve complex community based problems. The infoldment goes along with into how AI-powered tools can delineate HR processes related with recruitment as well as sustainability appraisal to augment organisational efficiency as well as sustainability in community based sector entities. As well as, the along with of AI, within HRM through management

DOI: 10.4018/979-8-3693-5390-5.ch011

information operations, optimises the decision-making process by making operations more precise and founded on information, leading to augmented recruitment, better long lasting operation and increased infoldment of staff.

INTRODUCTION

This chapter discussions about the complex link between Reforms in HRM in civil service operations along with follow-up effect on the efficiency of the decision making processes. It probes the mediating function of Reforms in HRM in pertaining to the effects of the civil service operation on decision-making outcomes, matter-oring in the complexity brought forward by the legacies of centralised operation of governance and politicised dimension of HRM which often hamper the efforts of professionalisation. The infoldment bases on the way different kinds of reform policies, from selection processes that works on merit to long standing operations, is meant to formulate a more neutral and impartial bureaucracy, capable to serve the community based interest (Irvianda and Masdupi 2025). However, existing bureaucratic cultures and low professionalisation of HRM functions are often huge barriers to the practical implementation of these reform policies (Poljasevic et al., 2025). As an output, there frequently exist historical legacies and imperative resistance to prevent successful implementation thus require an in-depth investigate into the adaptive behaviours as well as strategic choice needed to overpower like basic outcomes (Alnofeli et al. 2025; Poljasevic et al. 2025). This mediation is very crucial as HRM play a pivotal function in enhancing growth by optimising human capital, inspiring members of team competencies and members of team competent to match to strategic in organisational goals and innovation (Poljasevic et al., 2025).

In post-socialist European countries, like basic reforms are especially imperative and are aimed at overcoming imperative inertia and the influence of political actors that has weaken efficient community based administration over the past. The reforms aim at long lasting transparency, meritocracy along with regular efficiency in community based institutions, even in the face of much resistance to change and imperative inertia. However, the immediate impression of these reforms on the effectiveness of taking the decision can typically be indirect, through mediators related with higher infoldment of staff and amendment of information management dimensions (Polimerou & Spais, 2025). The effectiveness of these reforms often relied upon on their ability to promote organisational adaptability that allows them to respond quickly to changing demands and, in the end, to increase sustainability at a business level (Alnofeli et al., 2025).

Overcoming these operations assimilates a multi-pronged strategy that would combine the mechanisms of legal frameworks along with operations safeguards to combat risks and confirm that the AI foundations in HRM are governed by democratic values and human rights. Overcoming these operations calls for a multi-pronged operation that would incorporate both the mechanisms of legal frameworks as well as the safeguards of technology to combat them and confirm that the AI foundations in HRM are subject to democratic values and human rights (Sani & Mandina, 2024). The growing along with of AI under HRM also demands an extra level of information quality awareness as for efficient AI functionality, information is based upon high quality information input (Nawaz et al., 2024). Poor quality information may output in biased algorithms and inaccurate predictions, thus compromising the very goals of using AI to augment the effectiveness of taking the decision in community based administration. As like basic, information governance, related with smart information governance and security of information protocols to maintain integrity along with norm basedity in the use of HR information in AI-generated machines, takes on a high priority (Alnofeli, et al., 2025). As well as, the along with of AI under HR processes presents certain outcomes like skill voids in the workforce, which means baseed training programmes need to be put in place in order for the HR staff to manage and use these sophisticated technologies effectively. These training schemes will play an imperative function in closing the void between the existing HR capabilities and these demands within an AI augmented periphery to fully realise the transformational potential that AI offers rather than hinder its efficacy due to deficit of internal expertise (Madanchian and Taherdoost, 2025). Norm based considerations of AI under HRM - in terms of transparency, secrecy and answerability - are of prime importance and demand proactive governance to confirm fairness and eliminate potential bias linked to AI based augmented taking the answerability (Yanamala, 2024). This type of holistic operation can confirm that even though AI optimises HR functions, it is done within the framework of respecting individual rights and maintaining community based trust (Alnofeli et al., 2025; Shah et al., 2024).

BACKGROUND OF STUDY

The following section examines the available body of literature on the interaction between Reforms in HRM, the civil service operations and decision-making effectiveness including identification of imperative theoretical frameworks of infoldment and empirical voids. This review explains a critical evaluation of matter that AI founded tools, although they can efficiently used in augment decision-making processes present complex norm based and legal dilemmas in HR domain particularly regarding security of information and algorithmic bias (Du, 2024; Lutfi, & Mohammadi, 2025). The pervasive along with of Artificial intelligence under Human Resources

Management (HRM) poses a need of thorough deliberation on how organisations can navigate operations of fairness, transparency and answerability for upholding norm based standards (Saura et al., 2024a; Yanamala, 2024). Like very significant considering the matter that AI foundations, if built over biased informationsets will not only perpetuate but also magnify existing societal biases outputting in unequal outcomes of hiring etc. in HR (Shah et al., 2024). This risk suggests the need of developing sound norm based frameworks and governance mechanism to ensure the responsible use of artificial intelligence technologies in HRM (Yanamala, 2024). The strategic application of AI under the ambit of HRM though hold greater prospects of improving functions such as efficiency coupled with the personalisation of the HRM, also need to be cognizant of the serious operation of information security and set up proper ethics to prevent misuse and provide trust to the team members and stakeholders (Benabou & Touhami, 2025; Spais & Chryssochoidis, 2025).

This issue entails working in certifications for norm based use of AI for clients, and by extension, team members, to have clear signs of adherence to secrecy along with norm based norms (Saura et al., 2024). Along with, the spread of AI that deal with the secrecy of the user and the transparency of information are of the highest importance. These concerns makes it imperative to enact strong regulatory frameworks which specifically address AI founded dimensions - that go beyond the usual information protection laws, and address the unique outcomes that come with using advanced AI - imperative technologies (Saura et al., 2024). As well as, it is imperative to have pragmatic legal along with norm based frameworks that specifically govern the development and deployment of AI under HRM which in order to mitigate these risks and confirm that it is equitable (Shah et al., 2024). The norm based foundation of AI under HRM is along with complicated by considerations of secrecy and information security, which assimilates the gathering along with norm based of an objective worth of personal members of team information by AI foundations that presents a considerable threat to the rights of individual team members and a need for strict information protection protocols (Saura et al., 2024; Shah et al., 2024). This critical need translates to the development of transparent AI governance structures that clearly define answerability for algorithmic decisions as an outcome in order to create more trust and to assuage that AI foundations are being applied in a responsible way within civil service operations.

The inclusion of "secrecy-by-default" as well as "secrecy-by-design" foundations in like basic frameworks can along with embed secrecy considerations along developmental stages of AI technologies in advance of any problematic outcomes posed by information analytics and personalised HR strategies (Saura, _et al., 2024). Crucially, the knowledge building considerations for chasing the direction of the agenda require the building of strong norm based frameworks, as well as investments in capacity building for the HR practitioners in order to confirm human oversight in the AI imperative processes to mitigate possible risks (Mwita & Kitole, 2025). This assimilates developing certifications for norm based use of AI so clients, and by extension, team members, have clear indicators as to the use of secrecy along with norm based norms. Conversely, deficit of transparency in AI algorithms can debilitate trust and hence demands clear communication to the clients and team members alike in complex aspects about the information sources and matterors influencing the decision algorithm. The imperative for answerability extends also in the perspective of AI structures, especially seeing as most of their proprietary algorithms are often silent and make it difficult for the community based to question them and, even more difficult, assign responsibility for the outcome of toxic and/or material. The imperative for answerability extends along with even to AI structures given the often in opaque nature of their proprietary algorithms (Shah et al. 2024). As well as, a robust framework is necessary to nurture HR managers norm basedly govern the HRM processes which are augmented by AI thus providing transparency, secrecy and answerability (Yanamala, 2024).

STATEMENT OF PROBLEM

Despite the recognised transformative potential of AI under improving the effectiveness of HRM, significant outcomes remain, especially in regards to security of information, algorithmic transparency and the potential for perpetuating adherence to biases in civil service operations (Alnofeli et al., 2025; Ardichvili, 2022; Saura et al., 2024). These difficulties are also exacerbated by the norm based outcomes faced by developers of AI when complex and commercial imperatives outweigh norm based operations which formulates a need for a practical framework that would allow HR practitioners to assess the use of AI under their companies (Rodgers et al., 2022). This is a particularly imperative issue, considering that the unnorm based AI dimensions can formulate distrust between the clients and the platform they are using. As well as, the deficit of strong norm based guidelines could lead to organisational secrecy failures like information leakage and inappropriate profiling which impressions the confidence of stakeholders (Labib, 2024). The matter that cannot be recognised by AI decision-making processes and are often stationary the process of answerability and correction of bias and formulates a need for a clear algorithmic transparency framework (Alnofeli et al., 2025; Shah et al., 2024).

The reactors of its AI governance becomes along with acted by the demand for express directive about information and consent, especially in the face of current digital dimensions which habitually capture personal information without express authorisation of users and thus formulate a significant void between client perception and procedural information handling (Saura et al, 2024; Shah et al., 2024). Requirement makes it necessary for a holistic regulatory operation that will not only quantize norm based AI development but also put in place clear mechanisms for redress and overview, particularly in this sensitive area of community based sector HRM. In that sense, this study aims at bridging this void by proposing pragmatic structure of integrating norm based considerations regulatory compliance within the AI imperative HRM framework that is relevant for civil service perspectives (Rodgers et al., 2022). This along with is necessary in order to confirm that advances in technology in HRM are balanced against community based service values of fairness, equity and answerability so as to maximize effectiveness in taking the decision without violating basic norm based foundations. The structure will in particular be dealing with the nuances of operations in the civil service, where community based trust and answerability is parworth and being various from applications in the private sector.

As well as, the research looks at the ways robust Reforms in HRM can mediate the effects of Civil service operations in enhancing taking the decision effectiveness by incorporating norm based AI dimensions, making the community based sector more accountable and transparent (Rodgers et al., 2022; Sony et al., 2025). This study will dig even further into the imperative function of intelligible AI under making trust and satismatterion among users with these community based sector applications under compliance to norm based guidelines and regulatory bodies. The base of the investigation will be on the mechanisms through which Reforms in HRM, especially those involving AI can nurture positively affect the effectiveness of taking the decision operations in civil service frameworks through ensuring norm based governance of information and algorithmic transparency. This means analysing how Reforms in HRM to nurture address the potential negative impressions of AI on decision-making in order to confirm that AI tools augments rather than replaces with respect to human judgement and answerability. Thus, this research paper aims to analyse the complex linkage between the implementation of AI imperative Reforms in HRM and its mediating requests linked to taking the decision effectiveness within the civil service subject to the critical dimensions of transparency, norm based governance and answerability.

The research will examine the effects of explainable AI structures beyond trust on users and regulatory compliance, especially in the perspective of HR functions. Additionally, it will examine the workings of organisational capabilities in the along with of AI underto HR dimensions, especially in light of norm based dimensions and responsible action in ensuring the securement of members of team information and secrecy within these operations, (Labib, 2024). The research will also explain how proactive measures in norm based AI dimensions can nurture augment client loyalty and trust; thereby contributing to the final success and acceptance of AI powered - HRs management outcomes (HRM) in the community based sector.

THEORETICAL FRAMEWORK

This section outlines theoretical underpinnings through which the investigation of AI under HRM in civil service perspective is described, using established theories of technology adoption, organisational behaviour and community based administration. To be specific, it blends understanding from AI enhanced HRM assimilation processes, AI mediated social exchange and judgement and choice literature in order to provide an overarching analytical lens (Rodgers et al., 2022). The framework makes it easier to understand the ways that AI affects HR outcomes, specifically, the intelligibility as well as responsible nature of AI-generated decision-making in the community based sector. It also assimilates the Technology-Organisation-Periphery (TOE) framework which gives a rich operation to understanding the multiple dimensions affecting technology adoption including AI under HRM, (Mwita and Kitole, 2025). Building upon this, this framework takes theories of anthropomorphism to comprehend how the human like features of AI under HRM may influence users perception and users engagement making some comparisons with client's interaction with AI under marketing.

The incorporation of algorithmic norm based positions along with augments the proposed framework along with importance in the ability to select HRM strategy and achieve better outcomes in terms of intelligibility and answerability for the AI-generated decisions in the community based sector settings (Rodgers et al., 2022). This multiple layered theoretical lens is a must have, in an effort to ensure a thorough infoldment of this complex interaction between operational developments, organisational functioning along with normative based operations in the successful application of AI to community based sector HRM. The pragmatic operation ensures the strict examination of the potential and the consequences that the along with of AI can provide, which go way beyond discreet perspectives and are complex in terms of its effect on human capital and governance. As well as, it nurtures in the deeper understanding of the impression of AI on the members of team well-beings through various mechanisms related with transparency, job security and personalisation mediated by organisational perspective (Anjumanwarshaik et al., 2025).

Along with, the framework incorporates learnings from dynamic capabilities theory to show case how, community based sector organisations can adapt and reconfigure their resources to effectively harness the capabilities of AI under HRM to confirm sustained and resilience amid a rapidly changing operational foundation (Alnofeli et al., 2025). Specifically, this assimilates analysing the contributions of micro foundations to the creation of dynamic capabilities (especially in the areas of opportunity identification and reconfiguration of resources in order to integrate AI). This holistic way of understanding provide the methodological framework, in the evaluation the effectiveness of AI-imperative Reforms in HRM in intermediating the civil service decision-making, a particular emphasis on ethics and acceptance of users (Alnofeli et al., 2025; Polimerou & Spais, 2025; Rodgers et al., 2022). The framework is along with sub structureed by the Technology Acceptance Structure that emphasize the importance of perceived ease of use and usefulness in determining the success of AI adoption and along with within HRM (Faustine & Rachmawati, 2024). Additionally, the along with of the unified theory of acceptance and use of technology extends this understanding by adding social influence, condition facilitating, as well as sustainability expectancy as critical matterors in determining AI assimilation in the community based sector HR functions. This theoretical synthesis is imperative in addressing AI resistance and providing a powerful lens through which to understand the experiences of team members as well as develop strategies to alleviate related tensions (Golgeci et al., 2024).

LITERATURE REVIEW

Present study entailed infoldment of the effect of AI on the psychosocial dynamics infoldment of staff and acceptance and draws similarity with client behavior in the AI imperative marketing context (Labib, 2024). Apart from that, outputs about the function of artificial intelligence under optimizing perform the answerability through useful predictive infoldment and founded on information insights are introduced (Labib, 2024; Saura et al., 2024; Asmoro 2025; Spais & Chryssochoidis, 2025). The review assesses the impression of AI under operation efficiency and cost effectiveness of HR functions and how organizations make use of AI under improving talent matching and long lasting recruitment productivity (Abaza & Eltobgy, 2024).

The along with of AI under HRM provides a wonderful opportunity for efficiency, process optimization, based on the information insights and will fundamentally alter the way of making decisions for the organizations [26]. This transformation assimilates the whole HR life cycle from optimizing recruitment as well as long lasting operation to improving infoldment of staff and retention strategies (Madanchian, 2024). However, iterative and successful implementation of AI under HRM require resolution of major outcomes relating with resistance to change, norm based operations, and legal risks especially in the point of view of the sector of the community based. A deep understanding of these outcomes, as well as clear communication of the potential of AI is fundamental to successful strategies for adoption in community based sector HRM (Boussebaa, 2019; Fenwick et al., 2024).

The part tends to critically examine the ever-changing base of the application of AI under HRM by looking at how organizations can benefit from these technologies and incorporate them to formulate a more agile, responsive, and informed operation to human capital management. It assimilates in-depth investigation on the ability of AI to redefine the traditional HR functions through the use of highly analytical tools that run predictive structure for workforce planning and talent development (Mostafa, 2025). Along with, AI-imperative outcomes can significantly augment the accuracy and fairness of sustainability appraisal operations, by incorporating infoldment of diverse information sets, and so reducing any subjective bias and facilitate merit-based progressions (Benabou & Touhami, 2025). AI also leads to personalized learning and development pathways equivalent to the storage of information in one's online profile, adaptation of learning to the individual member of team needs and aspirations that makes for better skill development and job satismatterion. The use of AI under HRM goes beyond task automation and also assimilates strategic planning in building a skilled and top-notch motivated workforce (Zawada, 2024).

Implementation of AI spreads to the optimization of team members engagement through individualized communication techniques and proactive identification of potential risks of attrition will output in stable and productive work periphery (Ziobrowska & Starostka-Patyk, 2025). Realizing these benefits requires a general consideration of outcomes related with ensuring security of information, addressing algorithmic bias and the norm based implications of deploying AI (Zawada, 2024). Unaddressed, these outcomes could threat community based trust along significant legal and reputational risks outputing in the need for pragmatic governance frameworks along with a continual governance (Guvva, 2025).

Consequently, the current chapter aims to fill up the existing gap and empirically seeks into the mediating impact of Reforms in HRM in the respective ship between the civil service operations and taking the decision effectiveness in an AI-augmented periphery (Femwick et al, 2024). The examination into how AI and particularly objective language structures could impress the effectiveness along with strategic abilities of the HR functions inside the civil service functions would be checked in line with the calls for much more awareness and upskilling in this area (Smith et al., 2024). This investigation ties in with findings on the impression of AI on Management Information Operations (MIS), as it just as well enables AI to enhance information imperative decision-making process in HRM drastically as it offers more accurate, on time and objective outputs (Ashrafuzzaman et al., 2025).

The study also answers the norm based implications and impressions of the society into the incorporation of AI under civil service HRM especially in issues relating to transparency and answerability and the possibilities of job displacement - critical operations to be considered in view of a sustainable implementation. It seeks to explain the ways in which the AI tools, related with Objective Language Structures, can act as the active co-team members in improving the management of HRs processes, going beyond the mere automation to sub structureing the sophisticated analytical along with strategic tasks (Estevez et al., 2025). The efficiency of the combination of like basic advanced AI relied upon on reducing skill voids in HR departments and creating strong infrastructure for controlling norm based operations and inherent biases (Estevez et al., 2025.).

Thus, an overall infoldment of the along with of AI underto HRM entails the balancing act between a recognition of the potentially transformative potential of AI and an acknowledgement of both existing limitations and the need for continued human oversight along with norm based governability. This way, the AI is made augmentative and a complement, to be implemented sub structureing but not replacing the human expertise, thus promoting a more effective and equitable decision-making periphery in the community based sector (Fenwick et al., 2024).

The chapter specifically evaluates the mediating function of the Reforms in HRM in the pertaining ship between the civil service operations and taking the decision effectiveness; especially when supplemented by AI (Prikshat et al., 2023). The research along with examines the matters of ethics, organizational culture, and readiness to adopt AI for the sustainability of HRM dimensions in this AI-imperative setting (Mahade et al., 2025). This analytical framework is of great importance for grasping the function of human-centric taking the decision in the organization by leveraging the power of AI. as HRM plays a huge function in the AI digital transformation (Fenwick et al., 2024).

METHODOLOGY

This part of the report outlines the methodological strategy used to explore the pertaining ships under examination; it covers the research design, the information collection methods, and the analytical methods taken advantage of in order to answer research questions using methodological rigor. A stringent quantitative operation, using survey questionnaires, was followed to obtain primary information from a heterogeneous set of HR professionals working in civil service organisations (Mahade et al. 2025; Nawaz et al. 2024). The survey instrument was carefully designed to reflect perceptions and experiences related to innovative along with by diffusion of AI, organizations transform HRM and decision-making effectiveness that formulates security of measurements (content validity) and a proven and still effective reliability using widely recognized psychometric methods (Polimerou & Spais, 2025). The process of validation consists of a pilot study for survey items and validation checks of clarity followed by an extensive phase of information collection in several civil service entities to confirm generalisability (Arora et al., 2024). The obtained information was then put under a robust statistical infoldment, both descriptive and inferential, in order to find some patterns, trends and causal pertaining ships among a set of variables.

Specifically, structural equation structureling was used in order to examine the hypothesised mediating effects, and to determine the direct and indirect impressions of AI-augmented HRM on decision-making effectiveness within the perspective of the civil service (Mollah et al., 2024). AI founded sustainability monitoring operations can formulate significant enhancements to responsiveness and predicted sustainability but due to operations related with information along with and skill voids, their implementation is not straightforward (Alapini, 2025). The adoption of Analytics of HR and positive sentiment towards AI significantly impression on the taking the decision process (Arora et al., 2024) where matterors related with accuracy and computing capabilities and personalisation, play a vital function to achieve time savings and cost reduction (Nawaz et al., 2024). Corporatizing analyses, more specifically using the Spearman - Rho coefficient, were used to analyze the strength and direction of the pertaining ships between these variables; this is a method that is optimised for nonparametric information. Additional statistical methods related with regression infoldment were used in order to along with examine the predictive value of AI adoption along with Reforms in HRM in taking the decision effectiveness in order to determine potential drivers for successful implementation in civil service operations (Nawaz et al., 2024).

Mediation infoldment, especially using bootstrapping, was then used to unravel the interconnections between certain variables and assess the importance and robustness of the mediating effects. Indeed, sound information governance frameworks are necessary to nurture implement the adoption of and optimise information imperative taking the decision in HRM, ensuring norm based use of information and compliance with regulations (Tuli et al., 2018). These frameworks play instrumental functions in handling security operations and compliance adherence which are very crucial in fruitful along with of AI under HR functions. This strategic along with also requires a keen alignment with organisational goals in order to maximise the utilisation of AI under reshaping modern workforce strategies (Madhuri & Kumar, 2025; Spais & Chryssochoidis, 2025).

OUTPUTS

This section outlines the empirical outputs that output from the above infoldment methods while baseing on the statistically significant corporatising's and mediating effects that were found among the variables. The preliminary analyses proved the validity of the measurement instruments, as high internal consistency scores were identified for major constructs, and the accurate scores of the derived variables were achieved (Polimerou & Spais, 2025). Subsequent descriptive statistics were used to offer an overview of the distribution of the information, which assimilated central tendencies and variability in AI adoption rates, reform implementation in HRM and taking the decision effectiveness in the civil service entities surveyed. Additional inferential statistical analyses, related with regression and mediation structures, revealed significant pathways of contribution that AI-imperative Analytics of HR have on augmented decision-making effectiveness, even when controlling for various confounding matterors (Madhuri & Kumar, 2025; Polimerou & Spais, 2025). Specifically, organisations that leverage the powers of AI-imperative Analytics of HR have been shown to have higher levels of efficiency in talent management and have augmented levels of infoldment of staff and consequently, enhance workforce retention (Madhuri & Kumar, 2025).

These findings show case the strategic importance of transition to combine Analytics of HR and digital tools to optimise decision-making and take business outcomes to the next level. This strategic necessity for enterprises in the modern world that aspire to develop a strong and high-performing workforce is reinforced by discoveries that emphasise AI-imperative HRM as an integral component in managing complexities in the digital age (Selvamohana, 2025). Along with, the along with of AI-powered Analytics of HR significantly changes the optimisation of workforce and decision-making with machine learning structures for talent acquisition, retention and personalised members of team strategies (Ayanponle et al., 2022). These enhanced analytic capabilities are empowering organisations to move away from the traditional reactive HR functions, towards proactive and information informed strategic initiatives.

DISCUSSION

The findings show case the critical function of Analytics of HR in the development of a information imperative paradigm for the assessment of members of team's sustainability along with strategic decisions. (Arora et al., 2024; Madhuri & Kumar, 2025). Incorporating AI managed information operations offers significant possibilities to refine HR taking the decision thereby outputing in a better sustainability of the organization and explaining its competitiveness (Ashrafuzzaman et al, 2025). As well as, employed usage of AI under the HRM sector to not only supply the planet for the best talent, employments, and enhanced success. As well as, strategic deployment of AI within HRM does not only optimize talent management and contributes to reinforced overall organizational efficiency through the application of predictive analytics regarding workforce planning and development (Madhuri, & Kumar, 2025; Selvamohana, 2025).

The strategic use of AI along with Analytics of HR nurtures the HR practitioners to determine the preparedness of an organization for like basic technologies and as well as nurtures in developing a future-proof workforce with the rightful competencies (Arora et al., 2024). Like basic foresight confirms that organizations are capable of adapting themselves to new evolving demands along with operations amenities as well as developing a workforce capable of metering the outcomes that may be in the foreseen course ahead. Additionally, having a full understanding of the micro-foundations of information management capabilities is essential to harnessing the potential of information - imperative taking the decision, including implementing strong information governance frameworks to insure information integrity and compliance (Alnofeli et al., 2025). This strict operation to information management along with norm based considerations is especially imperative in the face of the growing reliance on algorithmic HRM and the use of like basic information for strategic taking the decision and achievement of competitive advantage.

Indeed, the use of algorithmic HRM wields a powerful impression on strategic HR decision-details of firms by allowing them to develop a competitive advantage by long lasting the use of founded on information decisions (Alabdali et al., 2024). Along with evidence seems to sub structure the premise that the along with of AI under HRM. Especially through MIS.

CONCLUSION

In this discussion, I try to discuss how AI can actually change the practices of HRM in general and civil service decision making practices in general. At the same time, there is no doubt that we need strong ethics and transparent implementation in order to build trust and make these organizations sustainable. It is this: identifying in advance members of the team who may be benefiting from special development programs, and gaining a handle on the cultural norms that govern the individuals and the organization. Because AI is everywhere, we have to keep re-evaluating its effects, especially when it comes to the norms governing the way we use information and risk of algorithmic bias in HR. Finding solutions to these norm-based issues is key to building client trust and ensuring AI in HR really helps to deliver better outcomes. So, there's a push to establish some solid regulatory bodies and certification processes because there needs to be some form of AI strategies that are compliant with ethical lines, and that are transparent. Regular audits are also important - basic ones can be helpful to confirm accountability and support the responsible implementation of AI, particularly when we're assessing sustainability for team members in HR. Despite the obvious benefits of AI - such as higher efficiency and lower bias - there are still concerns surrounding norm-based decisions and data security, and the need to preserve the human touch.

However, many of us still have limited knowledge on how AI is really part of HRM decision-making, including these norms and values, despite its fact that it is increasing. Researchers highlight that AI tools can and should be used to work on the side of human roles and, to ensure the best outcomes, a balance between these norm-based concerns should be practiced. The strategy is about augmentation rather than replacement of human judgement in complex HRM situations such as talent management and organizational development, particularly in touchy areas. For all these reasons adopting a balanced approach to AI in HRM is vital to unlocking the potential of AI to benefit substantialising of humanistic values and create a fairer, more effective workforce. Khair et al., 2020; Du, 2024; Shah et al., 2024). Along with, creating an inrelied uponent ethics committee or review board can nurture in providing an extra layer of scrutiny for AI foundations used in HRM in order to offer guidance on complex norm based dilemmas and confirm adherence to societal values and legal mandates (Alnofeli et al., 2025).

LIMITATIONS

This study, while pragmatic, is based mostly on a qualitative synthesis of existing literature, which has inherent limitations on the generalisability of its findings because of potential biases and voids in the existing literature. This is a methodological relied uponence; that is, the conclusions arrive under relied uponence on the quality and extent of the works previously published-hence, there is a risk of falling short of an emerging trend or perspectiveual nuances not yet fully described. As well as, since the AI technologies are evolving quickly, some of the ethics as well as practical aspects discussed may become outdated due to the new advancements in AI technology that may be seen as a problem for maintaining the long-term relevance of the recommendations (Rusdi et al., 2024). Additionally, the deficit of empirical information from direct organisational implementations makes it impossible to quantitatively analyse the actual effectiveness of the proposed frameworks in addressing norm based risks and ultimately in improving taking the decision in real world HRM scenarios. Future research should as well as assimilate empirical studies, related with case studies and controlled experiments, to validate the effectiveness of proposed frameworks for ethics in AI under various organisational perspectives and to try to quantify the impression of like basic frameworks on critical HRM outcomes.

Along with, longitudinal studies are a must to see the long-term impressions of AI along with on members of team morale, organisational culture and overall strategic human capital development. Like basic researches would also be complemented by studying the intersection of AI ethics and diverse regulatory peripherys, with a view to how diverse legal and cultural peripherys impression the practical implementation and acceptance of AI under HRM (Bankins, 2021). An additional limitation arises from the emphasis on norm based frameworks for decision-making, with some of the practical outcomes of integrating AI underto existing HRM operations or financial and resource constraints of organisations left unexamined (Rodgers et al., 2022). Finally, the main use of self-reported information in the reviewed literature outputs in a possible response bias in the study, which influences the degree of objectivity and accuracy of the obtained insights. As well as, future investigations should base more on empirical methodologies (related with direct observation, quantitative infoldment of AI foundation sustainability in real world HRM perspectives) to offer more robust along with regularisable insight into the effectiveness of norm based AI frameworks. As well as, the base of this study under base on the existing literature associated with AI under HRM has an inherent limitation in that future research should base beyond the specific applications of AI to the assessment of wider applications of technology and perspective.

FUTURE DIRECTIONS

Future scholarship should also strive to differ its purview to consider a broader range of AI-powered operations across current HRM applications to determine the generalizability of these findings in disparate organizational functions and impostures of various operational maturities. Research would also be enriched with the study of the impression of the along with of operations with AI-related and psychological contract of the team members from the community based sector towards their employers, particularly in terms of job security and perceived fairness of the HR processes. Investigations into the sociological impression of AI under the community based sector HRM are of key importance to the understanding of the transformations in organisational culture along with norm based of staff that AI drives. As well as, the success of AI along with, in community based sector's HRM, relied upon on addressing operations regarding security of information and security as indicated by the rising incidence of information breaches that occurred in both community based and private sectors.

REFERENCES

Abaza, W. A., & Eltobgy, A. E. (2024). Examining the Intention to use AI under Recruitment and Selection within *Human Resource* Management: A Case Study of Egyptian Tourism and Travel Agencies. *Journal of Association of Arab Universities for Tourism and Hospitality*, *28*(1), 83. DOI: 10.21608/jaauth.2025.394785

Alabdali, M. A., Khan, S. A., Yaqub, M. Z., & Alshahrani, M. A. (2024). Harnessing the Power of Algorithmic *Human Resource* Management along with HR Strategic Decision-Making for Achieving Organizational Success: An Empirical Infoldment. *Sustainability*, *16*(11), 4854. DOI: 10.3390/su16114854

Alapini, O. (2025). Implementing AI-Imperative Sustainability Monitoring for Enhanced Decision-Making. *International Journal of Scientific Research and Modern Technology.*, *85*. Advance online publication. DOI: 10.38124/ijsrmt.v4i5.551

Alnofeli, K. K., Akter, S., & Yanamandram, V. (2025). Unlocking the power of AI under CRM: A pragmatic multidimensional exploration. *Journal of Innovation & Knowledge*, *10*(3), 100731. DOI: 10.1016/j.jik.2025.100731

Anjumanwarshaik, Shaikh, S., Desai, P. S., & YM, G. (2025). AI under *Human Resource* management and members of team well-being. *International Journal of Applied Research*, *11*(10), 219. DOI: 10.22271/allresearch.2025.v11.i10c.12943

Ardichvili, A. (2022). The Impression of AI on Expertise Development: Implications for HRD. *Advances in Developing HRs*, *24*(2), 78. DOI: 10.1177/15234223221077304

Arora, S., Chaudhary, P., & Singh, R. K. (2024). Adoption of Analytics of HR for future-proof taking the decision: function of attitude toward AI as a moderator. *International Journal of Organizational Infoldment*. https://doi.org/DOI: 10.1108/ijoa-03-2024-4392

Ashrafuzzaman, M., Prince, K. B., & Rahman, A. (2025). Integrating AI under HRM: The Function of Management Information Operations in Enhancing Decision-Making Processes. SSRN *Electronic Journal*. https://doi.org/DOI: 10.2139/ssrn.5031919

Asmoro, R. D. (2025). The function of AI under transforming defense *Human Resource* management: Adaptive efforts toward global strategic dynamics. *International Journal of Multidisciplinary Trends*, *7*(6), 32. DOI: 10.22271/multi.2025.v7.i6a.703

Ayanponle, L., Okatta, C. G., & Ajiga, D. (2022). AI-powered Analytics of HR: Transforming workforce optimization and decision-making. *International Journal of Science and Research Archive*, *5*(2), 338. DOI: 10.30574/ijsra.2022.5.2.0057

Bankins, S. (2021). The norm based use of AI under Human resource management: A decision-making framework. *Ethics and Information Technology, 23*(4), 841. DOI: 10.1007/s10676-021-09619-6

Benabou, A., & Touhami, F. (2025). AI under Human Resource Management: A PRISMA-based Operationatic Review. *Acta Informatica Pragensia, 14*(3), 489. DOI: 10.18267/j.aip.264

Boussebaa, M. (2019). In the shadow of empire: Global Britain and the UK business school. *Organization, 27*(3), 483. DOI: 10.1177/1350508419855700

Du, J. (2024). Norm based and Legal Outcomes of AI under Human Resource Management. *Journal of Computing and Electronic Information Management, 13*(2), 71. DOI: 10.54097/83j64ub9

Estévez, M., Ballestar, M. T., & Sáinz, J. (2025). Market research and knowledge using Generative AI: The power of Objective Language Structures. *Journal of Innovation & Knowledge, 10*(5), 100796. DOI: 10.1016/j.jik.2025.100796

Faustine, P., & Rachmawati, R. (2024). AI Adoption Determinants and Its Impressions on HRM Effectiveness within MES in Tanzania. *Open Journal of Business and Management, 12*(4), 2532. DOI: 10.4236/ojbm.2024.124131

Fenwick, A., Molnár, G., & Frangos, P. (2024a). Revisiting the function of HR in the age of AI: bringing humans along with artificials closer together in the workplace [Review of *Revisiting the function of HR in the age of AI: bringing humans along with artificials closer together in the workplace*]. *Frontiers in AI, 6*, 1272823. Frontiers Media. https://doi.org/DOI: 10.3389/frai.2023.1272823

Fenwick, A., Molnár, G., & Frangos, P. (2024b). The critical function of HRM in AI-imperative digital transformation: A paradigm shift to enable firms to move from AI implementation to human-centric adoption. *Discover AI, 4*(1). Advance online publication. DOI: 10.1007/s44163-024-00125-4

Guvva, S. (2025). *A Study on AI Implementation and Automation With AI under Business Marketing and Transformation.*

Irvianda, I., & Masdupi, E. (2025). The Effect of the Selection Process on Merit Operation Outcomes in Civil Servants of Padang City: The Mediating Function of Merit Criteria and the Moderating Function of Demographic Matterors. In *Advances in economics, business and management research/Advances in Economics, Business and Management Research* (p. 1715). Atlantis Press. https://doi.org/DOI: 10.2991/978-94-6463-839-4_134

Khair, M. A., Mahadasa, R., Tuli, F. A., & Ande, J. R. P. K. (2020). Beyond Human Judgment: Exploring the Impression of AI on HR Decision-Making Efficiency and Fairness. *Global Disclosure of Economics and Business*, *9*(2), 163. DOI: 10.18034/gdeb.v9i2.730

Labib, E. (2024). AI under marketing: Exploring current and future trends. *Cogent Business & Management*, *11*(1). Advance online publication. DOI: 10.1080/23311975.2024.2348728

Lutfi, L., & Mohammadi, A. (2025). Outcomes of Implementation AI under HRs Management. *International Journal of Academic Research in Business & Social Sciences*, *15*(4). Advance online publication. DOI: 10.6007/ijarbss/v15-i4/24796

Madanchian, M. (2024). From Recruitment to Retention: AI Tools for HR Decision-Making. *Applied Sciences (Basel, Switzerland)*, *14*(24), 11750. DOI: 10.3390/app142411750

Madanchian, M., & Taherdoost, H. (2025). Barriers and Enablers of AI Adoption in Human Resource Management: A Critical Infoldment of Organizational along with operations Matterors. *Information (Basel)*, *16*(1), 51. DOI: 10.3390/info16010051

Madhuri, A., & Kumar, B. (2025). Analytics of HR and Decision-Making: A Founded on information Operation to Members of team Long lasting operation. *Journal of Neonatal Surgery*, *14*, 409. DOI: 10.52783/jns.v14.2425

Mahade, A., Elmahi, A., Alomari, K. M., & Abdalla, A. A. (2025). Leveraging AI-imperative insights to enhance sustainable Human Resource management sustainability: moderated mediation structure: evidence from UAE higher education. *Discover Sustainability*, *6*(1). Advance online publication. DOI: 10.1007/s43621-025-01114-y

Mollah, Md. A., Rana, M., Amin, M. B., Sony, M. M. A. A. M., Rahaman, Md. A., & Fenyves, V. (2024). Examining the Function of AI-Augmented HRM for Sustainable Sustainability: Key Determinants for Digital Culture and Organizational Strategy. *Sustainability*, *16*(24), 10843. DOI: 10.3390/su162410843

Mostafa, M. A. (2025). *Transforming Human Resource Management: The Function of AI under Enhancing Employer Branding, Members of team Experience, and Beyond*. https://doi.org/DOI: 10.2139/ssrn.5117973

Mwita, K., & Kitole, F. A. (2025). Potential benefits and outcomes of AI under *Human Resource* management in community based institutions. *Discover Global Society*, *3*(1). Advance online publication. DOI: 10.1007/s44282-025-00175-8

Nawaz, N., Arunachalam, H., Pathi, B. K., & Gajenderan, V. (2024). The adoption of AI under HRs management dimensions. *International Journal of Information Management Information Insights*, *4*(1), 100208. DOI: 10.1016/j.jjimei.2023.100208

Polimerou, R., & Spais, G. S. (2025). Establishing pertainingships between brands and customers via strategic social media chatbots for telecom goods and services. *Journal of Marketing Analytics*. https://doi.org/DOI: 10.1057/s41270-025-00396-5

Prikshat, V., Islam, M., Patel, P., Malik, A., Budhwar, P., & Gupta, S. (2023). AI-Augmented HRM: Literature review and a proposed multilevel framework for future research [Review of *AI-Augmented HRM: Literature review and a proposed multilevel framework for future research*]. *Operational Forecasting and Social Change, 193*, 122645. Elsevier BV. https://doi.org/DOI: 10.1016/j.techfore.2023.122645

Rodgers, W., Murray, J. M., Stefanidis, A., Degbey, W. Y., & Tarba, S. Y. (2022). An AI algorithmic operation to norm based decision-making in *Human Resource* management processes. *Human Resource Management Review*, *33*(1), 100925. DOI: 10.1016/j.hrmr.2022.100925

Rusdi, S. D., Ismail, I. R., & Isa, R. M. (2024). Unravelling Smart HRM 4.0: A Narrative Review of Progressive 4.0 Technology Along with in *Human Resource* Management [Review of *Unravelling Smart HRM 4.0: A Narrative Review of Progressive 4.0 Technology Along with in Human Resource Management*]. *Information Management and Business Review, 16*, 415. International Foundation for Research and Development. https://doi.org/DOI: 10.22610/imbr.v16i3(i)s.4070

Sani, S., & Mandina, S. P. (2024). Examining the Outcomes of Adopting Modern Technologies in Community based Sector *Human Resource* Management. In *Advances in HRs management and organizational development book series* (p. 63). IGI Global., DOI: 10.4018/979-8-3693-2889-7.ch004

Saura, J. R., Škare, V., & Došen, Đ. O. (2024). Is AI founded digital marketing norm based? Assessing a new security of information paradox. *Journal of Innovation & Knowledge*, *9*(4), 100597. DOI: 10.1016/j.jik.2024.100597

Selvamohana, K. (2025). From Analytics of HR to AI-Imperative HRM: Enhancing Workforce Productivity and Engagement. *Journal of Information Operations Engineering & Management, 10*, 578. DOI: 10.52783/jisem.v10i21s.3395

Shah, E. A., Raiz, A., & Rashid, M. (2024). *Norm based Considerations in Use of AI under Digital Marketing*. https://doi.org/DOI: 10.36968/JPDC-V08-I02-25

Smith, M. H., Prabhakar, G., Nisar, T. M., & Tseng, H. (2024). Adoption of AI by the HR function in the civil service. *Members of team Pertainings, 47*(1), 104. https://doi.org/DOI: 10.1108/er-02-2024-0096

Sony, M. M. A. A. M., Amin, M. B., Ashraf, A., Islam, K. M. A., Debnath, N. C., & Debnath, G. C. (2025). Bias in AI-imperative HRM operations: Investigating discrimination risks embedded in AI recruitment tools along with Analytics of HR. *Social Sciences & Humanities Open, 12*, 102082. DOI: 10.1016/j.ssaho.2025.102082

Spais, G. S., & Chryssochoidis, G. (2025). Trends and future of AI, machine learning (ML) algorithms, and information analytics along with applications and implications for digital marketing and digital promotions. *Journal of Marketing Analytics*. https://doi.org/DOI: 10.1057/s41270-025-00406-6

Tuli, F. A., Varghese, A., & Ande, J. R. P. K. (2018). Founded on information Taking the decision: A Framework for Integrating Workforce Analytics and Predictive HR Metrics in Digitalized Peripherys. *Global Disclosure of Economics and Business, 7*(2), 109. DOI: 10.18034/gdeb.v7i2.724

Yanamala, K. K. R. (2024). Transparency, Secrecy, and Answerability in AI-Enhanced HR Processes. *Journal of Advanced Computing Operations, 3*(3), 10. DOI: 10.69987/jacs.2023.30302

Zawada, M. (2024). The Impression of AI on *Human Resource* Management: Outcomes, Opportunities, and Future Directions. *Operation Safety Human - Complex Facility - Periphery, 6*(1). https://doi.org/DOI: 10.2478/czoto-2024-0026

Ziobrowska, A., & Starostka-Patyk, M. (2025). Exploring the AI Revolution in *Human Resource* Management: Key Insights and Case Studies. In *Springer proceedings in business and economics* (p. 885). Springer International Publishing. https://doi.org/DOI: 10.1007/978-981-96-4116-1_56

Compilation of References

. McCutchen, B. M. (2025). The Role of Standard Business and Biblical Principles in the Strategic Human Resource Management Practices of Contemporary Protestant Churches.

. Pambour, A. (2022). Christian Ethics and Employee Management systems. ADRRI Journal (Multidisciplinary), 31(3 (8) July-September), 31-49.

. Sangwa, S., & Mutabazi, P. (2025). Integrating Christian faith and ethics into global business: A biblical framework for leadership, culture, and decision-making. Open Journal of Business Theology, 5(2).

Aaskoven, L. (2019). Redistributing under fiscal constraint: Partisanship, debt, inequality and labour market regulation. *Journal of Public Policy*, *39*(3), 423–441. DOI: 10.1017/S0143814X18000193

Abaza, W. A., & Eltobgy, A. E. (2024). Examining the Intention to use AI under Recruitment and Selection within *Human Resource* Management: A Case Study of Egyptian Tourism and Travel Agencies. *Journal of Association of Arab Universities for Tourism and Hospitality*, *28*(1), 83. DOI: 10.21608/jaauth.2025.394785

Acker, J. (1990). Hierarchies, jobs, bodies: A theory of gendered organizations. *Gender & Society*, *4*(2), 139–158.

Adikaram, A., Naotunna, N., & Priyankara, H. (2021). Battling covid-19 with human resource management bundling. *Employee Relations*, *43*(6), 1269–1289. DOI: 10.1108/er-08-2020-0390

Aghion, P., Burgess, R., Redding, S., & Zilibotti, F. (2008). The unequal effects of liberalization: Evidence from dismantling the license raj in india. *The American Economic Review*, *98*(4), 1397–1412. DOI: 10.1257/aer.98.4.1397

Ahmad, S. (2015). Green human resource management: Policies and practices. *Cogent Business & Management*, *2*(1), 1–13.

Ajunwa, I. (2018). Algorithms at work: Productivity monitoring applications and wearable technology as the new data-centric research agenda for employment and labor law. *Louis ULJ*, *63*, 21.

Ajunwa, I. (2020). The paradox of automation as anti-bias intervention. *Cardozo Law Review*, *41*(4), 1671–1740.

Ajunwa, I. (2020). *The quantified worker: Law and technology in the modern workplace*. Cambridge University Press.

Akbar, M. S. (2025). Governance transformation through institutional conversion: From Section 42 company to authority. *Review of Education. Administration & Law*, *8*(2), 401–414.

Al Ariss, A., Cascio, W. F., & Paauwe, J. (2014). Talent management: Current theories and future research directions. Journal of World Business, 49(2), 173–179. (Stahl et al., 2012)

Alabdali, M. A., Khan, S. A., Yaqub, M. Z., & Alshahrani, M. A. (2024). Harnessing the Power of Algorithmic *Human Resource* Management along with HR Strategic Decision-Making for Achieving Organizational Success: An Empirical Infoldment. *Sustainability*, *16*(11), 4854. DOI: 10.3390/su16114854

Alapini, O. (2025). Implementing AI-Imperative Sustainability Monitoring for Enhanced Decision-Making. *International Journal of Scientific Research and Modern Technology.*, *85*. Advance online publication. DOI: 10.38124/ijsrmt.v4i5.551

Alnofeli, K. K., Akter, S., & Yanamandram, V. (2025). Unlocking the power of AI under CRM: A pragmatic multidimensional exploration. *Journal of Innovation & Knowledge*, *10*(3), 100731. DOI: 10.1016/j.jik.2025.100731

Amin, M. (2009). Labor regulation and employment in india's retail stores. *Journal of Comparative Economics*, *37*(1), 47–61. DOI: 10.1016/j.jce.2008.07.001

Anjanappa, J. (2025). Balancing Growth and Safety: Occupational Health Risks, Policy Gaps, and Inclusive Frameworks in India's Renewable Energy Transition. *Policy Gaps, and Inclusive Frameworks in India's Renewable Energy Transition (May 07, 2025).*

Anjumanwarshaik, Shaikh, S., Desai, P. S., & YM, G. (2025). AI under *Human Resource* management and members of team well-being. *International Journal of Applied Research*, *11*(10), 219. DOI: 10.22271/allresearch.2025.v11.i10c.12943

Anner, M. (2020). Squeezing workers' rights in global supply chains: Purchasing practices in the Bangladesh garment export sector in comparative perspective. *Review of International Political Economy, 27*(2), 320–347.

Ardichvili, A. (2022). The Impression of AI on Expertise Development: Implications for HRD. *Advances in Developing HRs, 24*(2), 78. DOI: 10.1177/15234223221077304

Armstrong, M., & Taylor, S. (2020). *Armstrong's handbook of human resource management practice* (15th ed.). Kogan Page.

Arora, S., Chaudhary, P., & Singh, R. K. (2024). Adoption of Analytics of HR for future-proof taking the decision: function of attitude toward AI as a moderator. *International Journal of Organizational Infoldment*. https://doi.org/DOI: 10.1108/ijoa-03-2024-4392

Arslan, A., Cooper, C., Khan, Z., Golgeci, I., & Ali, I. (2022). Artificial intelligence and human workers interaction at team level: A conceptual assessment of the challenges and potential HRM strategies. *International Journal of Manpower, 43*(1), 75–88.

Ashrafuzzaman, M., Prince, K. B., & Rahman, A. (2025). Integrating AI under HRM: The Function of Management Information Operations in Enhancing Decision-Making Processes. SSRN *Electronic Journal*. https://doi.org/DOI: 10.2139/ssrn.5031919

Asmoro, R. D. (2025). The function of AI under transforming defense *Human Resource* management: Adaptive efforts toward global strategic dynamics. *International Journal of Multidisciplinary Trends, 7*(6), 32. DOI: 10.22271/multi.2025.v7.i6a.703

Ayanponle, L., Okatta, C. G., & Ajiga, D. (2022). AI-powered Analytics of HR: Transforming workforce optimization and decision-making. *International Journal of Science and Research Archive, 5*(2), 338. DOI: 10.30574/ijsra.2022.5.2.0057

Bakkar, Y., Durst, S., & Gerstlberger, W. (2021). The Impact of Institutional Dimensions on Entrepreneurial Intentions of Students—International Evidence. *Journal of Risk and Financial Management, 14*(4). Advance online publication. DOI: 10.3390/jrfm14040174

Bakshi, P. (2024). Language, religion, and workplace discrimination: Intersectional microaggressions in India. *Asian Ethnicity, 25*(2), 185–214.

Ball, K. (2021). *Surveillance, work and technology: New directions in workplace monitoring*. Routledge.

Bamberger, K. A., & Mulligan, D. K. (2019). *Privacy on the ground: Driving corporate behavior in the United States and Europe*. MIT Press.

Bankins, S. (2021). The norm based use of AI under Human resource management: A decision-making framework. *Ethics and Information Technology*, *23*(4), 841. DOI: 10.1007/s10676-021-09619-6

Bapuji, H., Chrispal, S., Attri, P. S., Ertug, G., & Soundararajan, V. (2024). An integrative review of management research on caste: Broadening our horizons. *The Academy of Management Annals*, *18*(2), 506–549.

Basu, S., Majumdar, B., Mukherjee, K., Munjal, S., & Palaksha, C. (2023). Artificial intelligence–HRM interactions and outcomes: A systematic review and causal configurational explanation. *Human Resource Management Review*, *33*(1), 100893.

Baxi, U. (2000). *The avatars of Indian judicial activism. Explorations in the Geography of Justice*. Oxford University Press.

Benabou, A., & Touhami, F. (2025). AI under Human Resource Management: A PRISMA-based Operationatic Review. *Acta Informatica Pragensia*, *14*(3), 489. DOI: 10.18267/j.aip.264

Benjamin, R. (2019). *Race After Technology: Abolitionist Tools for the New Jim Code* (1st ed.). Polity.

Bennett, C. J., & Raab, C. D. (2020). *The governance of privacy: Policy instruments in the digital age* (3rd ed.). MIT Press.

Bhandari, V. (2019). Labour law reforms in India: A critical analysis. *The Indian Journal of Labour Economics : the Quarterly Journal of the Indian Society of Labour Economics*, *62*(3), 421–437. DOI: 10.1007/s41027-019-00193-4

Bharadwaj, V., Sharma, V., & Bhatnagar, A. (2022). Covid-19 and manufacturing industries in india and role of human resources management. *Business and Management Research*, *11*(1), 15. DOI: 10.5430/bmr.v11n1p15

Boes, A., Kämpf, T., Langes, B., Lühr, T., & Ziegler, A. (2017). Cloud & crowd: New challenges for labour in the digital society. *TripleC*, *15*(1), 132–147. DOI: 10.31269/triplec.v15i1.760

Boni, A. (2023). Towards mandatory human rights due diligence: the European Corporate Sustainability Due Diligence Directive.

Bonsay, J., Cruz, A., Firozi, H., & Camaro, A. (2021). Artificial intelligence and labor productivity paradox: The economic impact of ai in china, india, japan, and singapore. *Journal of Economics Finance and Accounting Studies*, *3*(2), 120–139. DOI: 10.32996/jefas.2021.3.2.13

Boussebaa, M. (2019). In the shadow of empire: Global Britain and the UK business school. *Organization, 27*(3), 483. DOI: 10.1177/1350508419855700

Boxall, P., & Macky, K. (2014). High-involvement work processes, work intensification and employee well-being. *Work, Employment and Society, 28*(6), 963–984. DOI: 10.1177/0950017013512714

Boxall, P., & Purcell, J. (2016). *Strategy and human resource management* (4th ed.). Palgrave Macmillan.

Brammer, S., Jackson, G., & Matten, D. (2012). Corporate social responsibility and institutional theory. *Socio-economic Review, 10*(1), 3–28.

Brewster, C., Sparrow, P., Vernon, G., & Houldsworth, E. (2016). International human resource management (4th ed.). Kogan Page. (Stone et al., 2015)

Britton, D. M. (2017). Beyond the chilly climate: The salience of gender in women's academic careers. *Gender & Society, 31*(1), 5–27.

Brown, G. D. (2021). Women garment workers face huge inequities in global supply chain factories made worse by COVID-19. *New Solutions, 31*(2), 113–124. PMID: 33966528

Budd, J. W. (2011). *The thought of work.* Cornell University Press.

Budd, J. W., & Bhave, D. (2008). Values, ideologies, and frames of reference in employment relations. *Industrial Relations, 47*(1), 92–112.

Budhwar, P., & Debrah, Y. (Eds.). (2013). Human resource management in developing countries. Routledge. (Ulrich et al., 2012)

Budhwar, P. S., & Varma, A. (2011). Emerging HR management trends in India and the way forward. *Organizational Dynamics, 40*(4), 317–325.

Budhwar, P., Malik, A., De Silva, M. T., & Thevisuthan, P. (2022). Artificial intelligence–challenges and opportunities for international HRM: A review and research agenda. *International Journal of Human Resource Management, 33*(6), 1065–1097.

Bustamante, A. R. (2017). Labor Relations Reform in 21st Century. *Latinskaia Amerika = América Latina.*

Busuttil, L. R. G., & Van Weelden, S. J. (2018). Imago Dei and human resource management: How our understanding of the breath of God's Spirit shapes the way we manage people. *Journal of Biblical Integration in Business, 21*(1).

Cafferky, M. E. (2015). Sabbath: The theological roots of sustainable development. *Journal of Biblical Integration in Business, 18*(1).

Cárdenas, L. (2023). Trajectories of Labour Market Liberalisation in Spain: An Empirical Approach to the Historical Evolution of Institutional Change. *Revista Española de Investigaciones Sociológicas*, *183*, 121–132. DOI: 10.5477/cis/reis.183.121

Cascio, W. F., & Boudreau, J. W. (2016). The search for global competence: From international HR to talent management. SHRM Foundation. (Al Ariss et al., 2014)

Castilla, E. J. (2025). *The Meritocracy Paradox: Where Talent Management Strategies Go Wrong and How to Fix Them*. Columbia University Press.

Cavoukian, A. (2011). *Privacy by design: The 7 foundational principles*. Information and Privacy Commissioner of Ontario.

Chaudhary, T., & Remesh, B. (2021). Changing scenario of Indian labour and new labour codes: A critical analysis. *Christ ULJ*, *10*, 1.

Chen, M. A. (2012). *The informal economy: Definitions, theories and policies* (WIEGO Working Paper No. 1). WIEGO.

Chhibber, A. (2021). India's demographic dividend or disaster? mismanaged factors of production—Land, labor, infrastructure, cities. *Journal of Infrastructure Policy and Development*, *5*(1), 1253. DOI: 10.24294/jipd.v5i1.1253

Chigater, S. (2021). Labour Law Reforms and Women's Work in India: Assessing the New Labour Codes From a Gender Lens. *Available at SSRN* 3947175.

Choudhary, S., Yadav, M., & Srivastava, A. P. (2021). Cognitive Biases Among Millennial Indian Investors: Do Personality and Demographic Factors Matter? *FIIB Business Review*, *13*(1), 106–117. DOI: 10.1177/23197145211057343

Choudhary, S., Yadav, M., & Srivastava, A. P. (2024). Cognitive biases among millennial Indian investors: Do personality and demographic factors matter? *FIIB Business Review*, *13*(1), 106–117.

Chowdhury, S., Dey, P., Joel-Edgar, S., Bhattacharya, S., Rodriguez-Espindola, O., Abadie, A., & Truong, L. (2023). Unlocking the value of artificial intelligence in human resource management through AI capability framework. *Human Resource Management Review*, *33*(1), 100899.

Christopher, N. (2019). The effectiveness of HRM policies and practices. *The International Journal of Social Sciences (Islamabad)*, *2*(1), 24–32.

Clardy, A. (2003). The legal framework of human resource development: Overview, mandates, strictures, and financial implications. *Human Resource Development Review*, *2*(1), 26–53.

Clarke, R. (2019). Regulatory alternatives for AI. *Computer Law & Security Review, 35*(4), 398–409.

Collings, D. G., & Mellahi, K. (2009). Strategic talent management: A review and research agenda. Human Resource Management Review, 19(4), 304–313. (Brewster et al., 2016)

Collins, P. H. (2000). Patricia Hill Collins. *Intersectionality and Matrix of Domination, 28.*

Cooke, F., & Saini, D. (2015). From legalism to strategic hrm in india? grievance management in transition. *Asia Pacific Journal of Management, 32*(3), 619–643. DOI: 10.1007/s10490-015-9417-0

Custers, B., van der Hof, S., & Schermer, B. (2019). *Privacy, data protection and cybersecurity in Europe*. Springer.

Dabrowski, W. (2019). Applying PIPEDA in the workplace. *Canadian Labour & Employment Law, 23*(2), 145–167.

Darwish, T., Singh, S., Batsakis, G., & Potočnik, K. (2023). Cross-country analysis of hrm parameters in emerging markets: An assessment of measurement invariance. *British Journal of Management, 35*(2), 692–705. DOI: 10.1111/1467-8551.12730

Das, S., Raychaudhuri, A., & Roy, S. (2014). Trade and labor demand in an emerging market economy: An analysis for indian manufacturing during 1991–2010. *Journal of Developing Areas, 48*(3), 353–379. DOI: 10.1353/jda.2014.0043

Davis, G. (2020). Digital workplaces and organizational transformation. *Journal of Management Innovation, 14*(3), 45–62.

De Stefano, F., Bagdadli, S., & Camuffo, A. (2018). HRM and performance in the digital era. *International Journal of Human Resource Management, 29*(1), 1–22.

De Stefano, V., & Taes, S. (2021). Algorithmic management and collective bargaining. *International Labour Review, 160*(3), 419–438. DOI: 10.1111/ilr.12205

Deakin, S. (2013). Addressing labour market segmentation: The role of labour law. *International Labour Review, 152*(2), 211–232. DOI: 10.1111/j.1564-913X.2013.00178.x

Deakin, S., & Wilkinson, F. (2005). *The law of the labour market: Industrialization, employment and legal evolution*. Oxford University Press.

Debroy, B., Bhandari, L., & Santhanam, A. (2020). *Labour law reforms in India*. Penguin Random House India.

Deci, E. L., & Ryan, R. M. (2000). The "what" and "why" of goal pursuit: Human needs and self-determination. *Psychological Inquiry*, *11*(4), 227–268.

Demmke, C. (2020). Governance reforms, individualization of human resource management (HRM), and impact on workplace behavior—A black box? *Public Integrity*, *22*(3), 268–279.

DeNisi, A. S., & Murphy, K. R. (2017). Performance appraisal and performance management: 100 years of progress? Journal of Applied Psychology, 102(3), 421–433. (Budhwar & Debrah, 2013)

Desai, V., Conte, A. H., Nguyen, V. T., Shin, P., Sudol, N. T., Hobbs, J., & Qiu, C. (2023). Veiled harm: Impacts of microaggressions on psychological safety and physician burnout. *The Permanente Journal*, *27*(2), 169. PMID: 37292028

Dhiraj, A., Joshi, M., & Kumar, A. (2020). Human resource management and character building: Route to business sustainability. *International Journal of Business and Globalisation*, *25*(3), 332–348.

Dibben, P., Brewster, C., Brookes, M., Cunha, R., Webster, E., & Wood, G. (2017). Institutional legacies and HRM: Similarities and differences in HRM practices in Portugal and Mozambique. *International Journal of Human Resource Management*, *28*(18), 2519–2537.

Dougherty, S., Robles, V., & Krishna, K. (2011). Employment protection legislation and plant-level productivity in india.. https://doi.org/DOI: 10.3386/w17693

Dougherty, S. (2009). Labour regulation and employment dynamics at the state level in india. *Review of Market Integration*, *1*(3), 295–337. DOI: 10.1177/097492921000100303

Dowling, P. J., Festing, M., & Engle, A. (2017). International human resource management (7th ed.). Cengage Learning. (Cascio & Boudreau, 2016)

Drubel, J., & Mende, J. (2023). The hidden contestation of norms: Decent work in the International Labour Organization and the United Nations. *Global Constitutionalism*, *12*(2), 246–268. DOI: 10.1017/S2045381722000259

Du, J. (2024). Norm based and Legal Outcomes of AI under Human Resource Management. *Journal of Computing and Electronic Information Management*, *13*(2), 71. DOI: 10.54097/83j64ub9

Erwin, E., Rauf, A., & Idy, M. Y. (2025). THE INFLUENCE OF LEGAL REGULATION ON HUMAN RESOURCE MANAGEMENT PRACTICES. *INJOSEDU: International Journal of Social and Education*, *2*(2), 443–445.

Estévez, M., Ballestar, M. T., & Sáinz, J. (2025). Market research and knowledge using Generative AI: The power of Objective Language Structures. *Journal of Innovation & Knowledge, 10*(5), 100796. DOI: 10.1016/j.jik.2025.100796

Eurofound. (2019). *Working conditions and sustainable work.* European Foundation for the Improvement of Living and Working Conditions.

European Commission. (2020). *The European Green Deal.* Publications Office of the European Union.

European Commission. (2021). Proposal for a regulation laying down harmonised rules on artificial intelligence (Artificial Intelligence Act). *European Union.*

Fagernäs, S. (2010). Labor law, judicial efficiency, and informal employment in india. *Journal of Empirical Legal Studies, 7*(2), 282–321. DOI: 10.1111/j.1740-1461.2010.01179.x

Farndale, E., Scullion, H., & Sparrow, P. (2010). The role of the corporate HR function in global talent management. Journal of World Business, 45(2), 161–168. (Collings & Mellahi, 2009)

Faustine, P., & Rachmawati, R. (2024). AI Adoption Determinants and Its Impressions on HRM Effectiveness within MES in Tanzania. *Open Journal of Business and Management, 12*(4), 2532. DOI: 10.4236/ojbm.2024.124131

Fenwick, A., Molnár, G., & Frangos, P. (2024a). Revisiting the function of HR in the age of AI: bringing humans along with artificials closer together in the workplace [Review of *Revisiting the function of HR in the age of AI: bringing humans along with artificials closer together in the workplace*]. *Frontiers in AI, 6*, 1272823. Frontiers Media. https://doi.org/DOI: 10.3389/frai.2023.1272823

Fenwick, A., Molnár, G., & Frangos, P. (2024b). The critical function of HRM in AI-imperative digital transformation: A paradigm shift to enable firms to move from AI implementation to human-centric adoption. *Discover AI, 4*(1). Advance online publication. DOI: 10.1007/s44163-024-00125-4

Fernandes, A. and Pakes, A. (2008). Factor utilization in indian manufacturing: a look at the world bank investment climate surveys data.. https://doi.org/DOI: 10.3386/w14178

Friedman, T. L. (2014). The world is flat: A brief history of the twenty-first century (3rd ed.). Picador. (DeNisi & Murphy, 2017)

Fuenzalida, J., & Riccucci, N. M. (2019). The effects of politicization on performance: The mediating role of HRM practices. *Review of Public Personnel Administration, 39*(4), 544–569.

Gajenderan, N. (2024). Ensuring Hr Compliance: Strategies For Managing Legal And Regulatory Requirements. *Journal of Organizational Culture Communications and Conflict, 28*(2), 1–3.

GDPR, G. D. P. R. (2016). General data protection regulation. *Regulation (EU) 2016/679 of the European Parliament and of the Council of 27 April 2016 on the protection of natural persons with regard to the processing of personal data and on the free movement of such data, and repealing Directive 95/46/EC.*

Geetika, G., Ghosh, P., Rai, A., Joshi, J., & Singh, P. (2014). Measuring workers' satisfaction with grievance-handling procedure: Study of a power distribution major in india. *Asian Journal of Management Cases, 11*(2), 139–157. DOI: 10.1177/0972820114538347

Ghemawat, P. (2016). The laws of globalization and business applications. Cambridge University Press. (Dowling et al., 2017)

Ghosh, J. (Ed.). (2021). *Informal women workers in the Global South: Policies and practices for the formalisation of women's employment in developing economies.* Routledge.

Gill, C., & Meyer, D. (2011). The role and impact of HRM policy. *The International Journal of Organizational Analysis, 19*(1), 5–28.

Goldar, B., & Aggarwal, S. (2012). Informalization of industrial labor in india: Effects of labor market rigidities and import competition. *The Developing Economies, 50*(2), 141–169. DOI: 10.1111/j.1746-1049.2012.00162.x

Gond, J. P., Igalens, J., Swaen, V., & El Akremi, A. (2011). Influence of CSR on HR management. *Journal of Business Ethics, 98*(4), 507–525.

Guest, D. (2017). Human resource management and employee wellbeing. *Human Resource Management Journal, 27*(1), 22–38.

Gunningham, N., Kagan, R. A., & Thornton, D. (2003). *Shades of green: Business, regulation, and environment.* Stanford University Press.

Gupta, P. and Kumar, U. (2012). Performance of indian manufacturing in the postreform period., 225-252. https://doi.org/DOI: 10.1093/oxfordhb/9780199734580.013.0008

Gupta, P., & Kumar, U. (2010). Performance of indian manufacturing in the post reform period. SSRN Electronic Journal. https://doi.org/DOI: 10.2139/ssrn.1608663

Gupta, R. (2024). Impact of Artificial Intelligence (AI) on Human Resource Management (HRM). *International Journal For Multidisciplinary Research, doi, 10.*

Gupta, R., Kaur, H., & Raheja, S. (2025). Ethical and Legal Considerations in AI-Based HRM. In *Human Resource Management and Artificial Intelligence* (pp. 126–145). Routledge.

Guvva, S. (2025). *A Study on AI Implementation and Automation With AI under Business Marketing and Transformation.*

Harding, E. L., Vanto, J. J., Clark, R., Hannah Ji, L., & Ainsworth, S. C. (2019). Understanding the scope and impact of the california consumer privacy act of 2018. *Journal of Data Protection & Privacy*, *2*(3), 234–253.

Hart, C. G. (2021). Trajectory guarding: Managing unwanted, ambiguously sexual interactions at work. *American Sociological Review*, *86*(2), 256–278.

Hasan, R., Mitra, D., & Ramaswamy, K. (2003). Trade reforms, labor regulations and labor-demand elasticities: empirical evidence from india.. https://doi.org/DOI: 10.3386/w9879

Hasnas, J. (2002). Equal opportunity, affirmative action, and the anti-discrimination principle: The philosophical basis for the legal prohibition of discrimination. *Fordham Law Review*, *71*, 423.

Hasyim, H., & Bakri, M. (2023). The Impact of Employment Law on Human Resource Practices: A Global Perspective. *The Journal of Business and Management Research*, *6*(1), 43–54.

Hmoud, B. (2021). The adoption of artificial intelligence in human resource management and the role of human resources. [). Wydawnictwo Naukowe Akademii WSB.]. *Forum Scientiae Oeconomia*, *9*(1), 105–118.

Hoang, D. (2019). Labour standards in the global supply chain: Workers' agency and reciprocal exchange perspective. *Societies (Basel, Switzerland)*, *9*(2). Advance online publication. DOI: 10.3390/soc9020038

Hochschild, A., Irwin, N., & Ptashne, M. (1983). Repressor structure and the mechanism of positive control. *Cell*, *32*(2), 319–325. PMID: 6218886

Hofstede, G., Hofstede, G. J., & Minkov, M. (2010). Cultures and organizations: Software of the mind (3rd ed.). McGraw-Hill. (Farndale et al., 2010)

Hunt, A., & Samman, E. (2020). Domestic work and the GIG economy in South Africa: Old wine in new bottles? *Anti-Trafficking Review*, *2020*(15), 102–121. DOI: 10.14197/atr.201220156

International Labour Organization. (2016). *Non-standard forms of employment: Understanding challenges*. ILO.

International Labour Organization. (2019). *Work for a brighter future: Global Commission on the Future of Work*. ILO.

International Labour Organization. (2020). Global employment trends. ILO Publications. (Friedman, 2014)

International Labour Organization. (2023). *Artificial intelligence and the future of work*. ILO.

Irvianda, I., & Masdupi, E. (2025). The Effect of the Selection Process on Merit Operation Outcomes in Civil Servants of Padang City: The Mediating Function of Merit Criteria and the Moderating Function of Demographic Matterors. In *Advances in economics, business and management research/Advances in Economics, Business and Management Research* (p. 1715). Atlantis Press. https://doi.org/DOI: 10.2991/978-94-6463-839-4_134

Jackson, S. E., & Ruderman, M. (Eds.). (2018). Diversity in work teams: Research paradigms for a changing workplace. American Psychological Association. (Ghemawat, 2016)

Jadhav, S., & Kulkarni, S. (2020). Sexual Harassment of Women at Workplace in India: A Review of the POSH Act 2013. *Journal of Real Estate. Construction Manager*, *35*(4), 36–43.

Jalón Aymerich, F. B., & Herce, J. A. (2020). Countercyclical labor productivity: The case of Spain. *Cuadernos de Economía (Santiago, Chile)*, *43*(122), 105–118. DOI: 10.32826/cude.v42i122.194

Jamali, D. (2010). MNCs and international accountability standards through an institutional lens: Evidence of symbolic conformity or decoupling. *Journal of Business Ethics*, *95*(4), 617–640.

James, K. (2011). India's demographic change: Opportunities and challenges. *Science*, *333*(6042), 576–580. DOI: 10.1126/science.1207969 PMID: 21798938

Janssens, M., & Steyaert, C. (2019). A practice-based view of diversity management. Academy of Management Annals, 13(1), 1–49. (Hofstede et al., 2010)

Jonsen, R. H. (2017). Strategic person and organization development: Implications of Imago Dei for contemporary human resource management. *Journal of Biblical Integration in Business*, *20*(1).

Kanskar, S., & Pal, D. (2021). Reconceptualizing Sexual Harassment: Extending the POSH Act, 2013. *Jus Corpus LJ*, *2*, 467.

Kanter, R. M. (1977). *Men and women of the corporation.*

Kapoor, S., & Narayan, D. (2021). Legal frameworks in India supporting sustainability and HR reforms. *Indian Journal of Industrial Relations*, *56*(4), 625–642.

Kaushal, N., Kaurav, R. P. S., Sivathanu, B., & Kaushik, N. (2023). Artificial intelligence and HRM: Identifying future research Agenda using systematic literature review and bibliometric analysis. *Management Review Quarterly*, *73*(2), 455–493.

Kellogg, K. C., Valentine, M. A., & Christin, A. (2020). Algorithms at work: The new contested terrain of control. *The Academy of Management Annals*, *14*(1), 366–410. DOI: 10.5465/annals.2018.0174

Kerswell, T., & Pratap, S. (2015). Informality in automobile value chains in india. *Working USA*, *18*(4), 533–553. DOI: 10.1111/wusa.12211

Khair, M. A., Mahadasa, R., Tuli, F. A., & Ande, J. R. P. K. (2020). Beyond Human Judgment: Exploring the Impact of Artificial Intelligence on HR Decision-Making Efficiency and Fairness. *Global Disclosure of Economics and Business*, *9*(2), 163–176.

Khair, M. A., Mahadasa, R., Tuli, F. A., & Ande, J. R. P. K. (2020). Beyond Human Judgment: Exploring the Impression of AI on HR Decision-Making Efficiency and Fairness. *Global Disclosure of Economics and Business*, *9*(2), 163. DOI: 10.18034/gdeb.v9i2.730

Khaled, A. F. M., & Ansar, A. (2024). Bangladesh's ready-made garments sector rebound: Revisiting gendered labor precarity and dependency. *Asian Jorunal of Comparitive Politics*, *9*(2), 218–237.

Khamzina, Z., Buribayev, Y., Taitorina, B., Yessengazieva, A., & Kuttygalieva, A. (2022). Towards Nondiscrimination and Gender Equality: The Role of International Labor Standards. *Sustainability (Switzerland)*, *14*(9), 1–14. DOI: 10.3390/su14095349

Khan, Z. (2018). Transnational Labour Governance: A Critical Review of Proposals for Linkage through the Lens of the Rana Plaza Collapse in Bangladesh. *Canadian Journal of Law and Society*, *33*(2), 177–197. DOI: 10.1017/cls.2018.12

Kim, H., & Fernandez, S. (2017). Employee empowerment and sustainability. *Public Personnel Management*, *46*(1), 3–23.

Kim, N., & Cho, W. (2014). Agencification and performance: The impact of autonomy and result-control on the performance of executive agencies in Korea. *Public Performance & Management Review*, *38*(2), 214–233.

Kramar, R. (2014). Beyond strategic human resource management: Sustainability orientation. *Human Resource Management Review*, *24*(2), 103–115.

Kshetri, N. (2018). The emerging role of big data in key development issues: Opportunities, challenges, and concerns. Big Data for Development, 1(1), 1–20. (Jackson & Ruderman, 2018)

Kubasinski, S. and Sławińska, M. (2021). Research on corporate social responsibility (crs) in terms of work safety. European Research Studies Journal, XXIV(Special Issue 5), 626-636. https://doi.org/DOI: 10.35808/ersj/2755

Kumar, M., Dagar, M., Yadav, M., Choudhury, T., & Luu, T. M. N. (2025). Navigating the future: Challenges and opportunities in intelligent RPA implementation. In *Intelligent Robotic Process Automation: Development, Vulnerability and Applications* (pp. 393–420). IGI Global. https://doi.org/DOI: 10.4018/979-8-3693-4365-4.ch015

Kumar, M., Jain, A., Mittal, A., Gera, R., Biswal, S. K., Yadav, M., Hung, T. H., & Priya Srivastava, A. (2024). Inclusion of Neural Networks in Higher Education: A Systematic Review and Bibliometric Analysis. *2024 4th International Conference on Innovative Practices in Technology and Management (ICIPTM)*, 1–6. https://doi .org/DOI: 10.1109/ICIPTM59628.2024.10563852

Kumar, M., Nain, N., Dagar, M., Luu, T. M. N., & Kaur, K. (2025). Redefining work and outsourcing in the AI era: Challenges and opportunities. In *Global Work Arrangements and Outsourcing in the Age of AI*. IGI Global., DOI: 10.4018/979-8-3373-1270-5.ch021

Kumar, M., & Yadav, R., Sushma, & Yadav, M. (2025). Investigating the influence of digital and social media marketing on university brand equity: An in-depth literature review and bibliometric study. *Global Knowledge, Memory and Communication*, •••, 1–26. DOI: 10.1108/GKMC-07-2024-0426

Labib, E. (2024). AI under marketing: Exploring current and future trends. *Cogent Business & Management*, *11*(1). Advance online publication. DOI: 10.1080/23311975.2024.2348728

Lawler, J. J., & Elliot, R. (1993, June). Artificial intelligence in HRM: an experimental study of an expert system. In *Proceedings of the 1993 conference on Computer personnel research* (pp. 473-480).

Liukkunen, U. (2020). The ILO and transformation of labour law. In *International Labour Organization and Global Social Governance*. https://doi.org/DOI: 10.1007/978-3-030-55400-2_2

Lodder, A. and Zeleznikow, J. (2010). Enhanced dispute resolution through the use of information technology.. https://doi.org/DOI: 10.1017/cbo9780511777554

Lutfi, L., & Mohammadi, A. (2025). Outcomes of Implementation AI under HRs Management. *International Journal of Academic Research in Business & Social Sciences*, *15*(4). Advance online publication. DOI: 10.6007/ijarbss/v15-i4/24796

Madanchian, M. (2024). From Recruitment to Retention: AI Tools for HR Decision-Making. *Applied Sciences (Basel, Switzerland)*, *14*(24), 11750. DOI: 10.3390/app142411750

Madanchian, M., & Taherdoost, H. (2025). Barriers and Enablers of AI Adoption in Human Resource Management: A Critical Infoldment of Organizational along with operations Matterors. *Information (Basel)*, *16*(1), 51. DOI: 10.3390/info16010051

Madhuri, A., & Kumar, B. (2025). Analytics of HR and Decision-Making: A Founded on information Operation to Members of team Long lasting operation. *Journal of Neonatal Surgery*, *14*, 409. DOI: 10.52783/jns.v14.2425

Mahade, A., Elmahi, A., Alomari, K. M., & Abdalla, A. A. (2025). Leveraging AI-imperative insights to enhance sustainable Human Resource management sustainability: moderated mediation structure: evidence from UAE higher education. *Discover Sustainability*, *6*(1). Advance online publication. DOI: 10.1007/s43621-025-01114-y

Mahmoud, M. M. H., & Othman, R. (2024). Effects of new public management reforms on human resource practices: A case study in Jordan. *Management and Labour Studies*, *49*(1), 149–176.

Maiti, D. (2012). Precarious work in india. *The American Behavioral Scientist*, *57*(4), 507–530. DOI: 10.1177/0002764212466247

Malik, A., Srikanth, N. R., & Budhwar, P. (2020). Digitisation, artificial intelligence (AI) and HRM. *Human resource management: Strategic and international perspectives, 88*, 103.

Malik, A. (2018). Creating sustainable organizations through HRM. *Human Resource Management Review*, *28*(3), 215–226.

Malik, A., & Rai, G. C. (2022). Need Of Laws For Anti-Discrimination And Equal Opportunity. *Cosmos: An International Journal of Art and Higher Education*, *11*(2), 61–66.

Malik, D. (2024). *Sex-based Harassment in the World of Work: Examining Evolving Jurisprudence Under India's Posh Law*. Cambridge Scholars Publishing.

Martins, P. S. (2019). The Microeconomic Impacts of Employee Representatives: Evidence from Membership Thresholds. *Industrial Relations, 58*(4), 591–622.

Mateescu, A., & Nguyen, A. (2019). *Algorithmic management in the workplace.* Data & Society Research Institute.

Meijerink, J., & Keegan, A. (2019). Conceptualizing human resource management in the gig economy. *Journal of Managerial Psychology, 34*(4), 214–232. DOI: 10.1108/jmp-07-2018-0277

Melhem, M. (2024). Navigating hrm practices in the indian institutional context: Multinational vs domestic enterprises in comparative perspective. *Review of International Business and Strategy, 34*(4), 495–515. DOI: 10.1108/ribs-12-2023-0142

Meyer, K. E. (2017). International business and management in emerging economies. Journal of International Business Studies, 48(1), 1–17. (Janssens & Steyaert, 2019)

Mezzadri, A. (2017). *Sweatshop regimes in the Indian garment industry.* Cambridge University Press.

Mezzadri, A. (2021). Indias informal capitalism: social structures of accumulation, forms of exploitation and social reproduction in the Sweatshop Regime. In *Handbook on social structure of accumulation theory* (pp. 152–168). Edward Elgar Publishing.

Miner, M., & Bickerton, G. (2020). A new model of Christian leadership: Insights from the job demands–resources model and Trinitarian theology. *Journal of Psychology and Theology, 48*(4), 276–291.

Ministry of Labour and Employment. (2021). *Code on wages, 2019: An overview.* Government of India.

Ministry of Labour and Employment. (2021). *Occupational Safety, Health and Working Conditions Code, 2020: An overview.* Government of India.

Mishra, A., & Dwivedi, A. (2024). Labor laws in India: History, evolutions, and critical analysis. *Labor History, 65*(5), 678–698.

Mishra, A., Joseph, R., Gangadhara, M., & Lobo, R. (2023). Body as machine: Health vulnerability of women garment factory workers in India. *SSM. Qualitative Research in Health, 4*, 100301.

Mohammed, M. A. (2020). Ethical Implications of AI Adoption in HRM: Balancing Automation with Human Values. *NEXG AI Review of America, 1*(1), 1–15.

Mollah, Md. A., Rana, M., Amin, M. B., Sony, M. M. A. A. M., Rahaman, Md. A., & Fenyves, V. (2024). Examining the Function of AI-Augmented HRM for Sustainable Sustainability: Key Determinants for Digital Culture and Organizational Strategy. *Sustainability*, *16*(24), 10843. DOI: 10.3390/su162410843

Moore, P. V. (2022). *Employee surveillance and the new workplace*. Polity Press.

More, A. A., & Jadhav, S. (2023). Implications of the New Labour Codes in India: A Comprehensive Analysis. *Jus Corpus LJ*, *4*, 298.

Mostafa, M. A. (2025). *Transforming Human Resource Management: The Function of AI under Enhancing Employer Branding, Members of team Experience, and Beyond*. https://doi.org/DOI: 10.2139/ssrn.5117973

Murphy, K. R. (2018). The legal context of the management of human resources. *Annual Review of Organizational Psychology and Organizational Behavior*, *5*(1), 157–182.

Musakhonovich, M. M., Esirgapovich, E. A., Jaelani, A. K., Wan Khairuldin, W. M. K. F., & Luthviati, R. D. (2024). The Protection of Labor Rights on the Court System. *Journal of Human Rights. Culture and Legal System*, *4*(3), 742–764. DOI: 10.53955/jhcls.v4i1.115

Mwita, K., & Kitole, F. A. (2025). Potential benefits and outcomes of AI under *Human Resource* management in community based institutions. *Discover Global Society*, *3*(1). Advance online publication. DOI: 10.1007/s44282-025-00175-8

Nahar, H. L. (2024). *Addressing the silence: A study on the underreporting of sexual violence among female garment workers in Bangladesh* (No. 64). GLU Working Paper.

Nandan, S., Halkias, D., Thurman, P., Komodromos, M., Alserhan, B., Adendorff, C., & Seaman, C. (2018). Assessing cross-national invariance of the three-component model of organizational commitment. *EuroMed Journal of Business*, *13*(3), 254–279. DOI: 10.1108/emjb-09-2017-0031

Nathan, D., Kelkar, G., & Mehta, B. (2022). Platform economy, techno-nationalism, and gig workers in India. In *The Routledge Handbook of the Gig Economy* (pp. 374–391). Routledge.

Nawaz, N., Arunachalam, H., Pathi, B. K., & Gajenderan, V. (2024). The adoption of AI under HRs management dimensions. *International Journal of Information Management Information Insights*, *4*(1), 100208. DOI: 10.1016/j.jjimei.2023.100208

Nguyen, T. B., Kumar, M., Sahoo, D. K., Nain, N., Yadav, M., & Dadhich, V. (2025). Mapping the landscape of women entrepreneurs in micro and small enterprises: Trends, themes, and insights through systematic review and text mining. *F1000Research, 14*. https://doi.org/DOI: 10.12688/f1000research.163030.1

Nilsen, M., Kongsvik, T., & Antonsen, S. (2022). Taming Proteus: Challenges for Risk Regulation of Powerful Digital Labor Platforms. *International Journal of Environmental Research and Public Health, 19*(10). Advance online publication. DOI: 10.3390/ijerph19106196 PMID: 35627735

Nixon, R. (2011). *Slow Violence and the Environmentalism of the Poor*. Harvard University Press.

Noe, R. A., Hollenbeck, J. R., Gerhart, B., & Wright, P. M. (2021). Human resource management: Gaining a competitive advantage (12th ed.). McGraw-Hill. (Kaufman, 2014)

Ntoumanis, A. B., Jorge, S. O., Zagarese, E., Wunderlin, A., Stern, A. R., & Luiz, P. J. (2024). The Impact of Decree 70/2023 on Labor Regulation and Industrial Relations in Argentina: A Legal and Economic Analysis. *International Journal of Law and Public Policy, 6*(2), 77–84.

O'Neil, C. (2016). *Weapons of math destruction: How big data increases inequality and threatens democracy*. Crown.

OECD. (2017). *OECD economic surveys: India 2017*. OECD Publishing. https://doi.org/DOI: 10.1787/eco_surveys-ind-2017-en

OECD. (2020). *OECD guidelines for responsible business conduct*. OECD Publishing.

Oommen, S.S. (2023). The cost of silence: Examining the long-term impact of sexual exploitation on women in the workplace. *Issue 2 Indian JL & Legal Rsch, 5*,1.

Oosterom, M., Huq, L., Namuggala, V., Nazneen, S., Nankindu, P., Sultan, M., ... & Azim, F. (2022). The gendered price of precarity: Voicing and challenging workplace sexual harassment.

Oyewole, A. (2024). Human resource management strategies for safety and risk mitigation in the oil and gas industry: A review. *International Journal of Management & Entrepreneurship Research, 6*(3), 623–633. DOI: 10.51594/ijmer.v6i3.875

Paillé, P., Chen, Y., Boiral, O., & Jin, J. (2014). Green HRM and environmental citizenship. *Journal of Business Ethics, 121*(3), 1–15.

Pandey, S. K., & Spoorthi, B. (2023). Understanding the Social Consequences of Legal Developments in India. *Journal of Survey in Fisheries Sciences, 10*(1), 3095–3104.

Papola, T. S. (2012). Labour regulation in India. *The Indian Journal of Labour Economics : the Quarterly Journal of the Indian Society of Labour Economics, 55*(3), 401–416.

Parry, E., & Tyson, S. (2019). An introduction to HRM in the public sector. Taylor & Francis. (Kshetri, 2018)

Pérez, I., & Canevaro, S. (2016). Entre lo público y lo privado: Empleadores y trabajadoras domésticas frente al Tribunal del Trabajo Doméstico de la ciudad de Buenos Aires. *Politica y Sociedad, 53*(1), 169–186. DOI: 10.5209/rev_POSO.2016.v53.n1.45274

Pfeffer, J. (2010). Building sustainable organizations: HRM's role. *The Academy of Management Perspectives, 24*(1), 34–45.

Pillai, R., & Sivathanu, B. (2022). Measure what matters: Descriptive and predictive metrics of HRM-pathway toward organizational performance. *International Journal of Productivity and Performance Management, 71*(7), 3009–3029.

Policies, P. (2023). *Latin America and the Caribbean ' s Productivity : The Role of.*

Polimerou, R., & Spais, G. S. (2025). Establishing pertainingships between brands and customers via strategic social media chatbots for telecom goods and services. *Journal of Marketing Analytics*. https://doi.org/DOI: 10.1057/s41270-025-00396-5

Power, M. (1997). *The audit society: Rituals of verification*. OUP Oxford.

Power, M. (2021). Modelling the micro-foundations of the audit society: Organizations and the logic of the audit trail. *Academy of Management Review, 46*(1), 6–32.

Prikshat, V., Islam, M., Patel, P., Malik, A., Budhwar, P., & Gupta, S. (2023). AI-Augmented HRM: Literature review and a proposed multilevel framework for future research [Review of *AI-Augmented HRM: Literature review and a proposed multi-level framework for future research*]. *Operational Forecasting and Social Change, 193*, 122645. Elsevier BV. https://doi.org/DOI: 10.1016/j.techfore.2023.122645

Psychogios, A., Szamosi, L. T., Prouska, R., & Brewster, C. (2016). A three-fold framework for understanding HRM practices in South-Eastern European SMEs. *Employee Relations, 38*(3), 310–331.

Pulford, A., Thapa, A., Thomson, R. M., Guilding, A., Green, M. J., Leyland, A., Popham, F., & Katikireddi, S. V. (2022). Does persistent precarious employment affect health outcomes among working age adults? A systematic review and meta-analysis. *Journal of Epidemiology and Community Health, 76*(11), 909–917. DOI: 10.1136/jech-2022-219292 PMID: 36137738

Punnett, B. J. (2018). International perspectives on organizational behavior and human resource management. Routledge. (Meyer, 2017)

Purang, P., Dutta, A., & Biwalkar, S. (2025). You do not belong here: Experiences of microaggression among Indian women engineers. *Gender in Management*, *40*(7), 891–909.

Purba, Y. (2024). Implications of technological evolution on human resource management strategies and legal compliance. *Jurnal Minfo Polgan*, *12*(2), 2686–2692. DOI: 10.33395/jmp.v12i2.13337

Quinlan, M., Bohle, P., & Lamm, F. (2015). Managing occupational health and safety in precarious employment. *Policy and Practice in Health and Safety*, *13*(1), 3–22.

Raman, A. V., & Krishnan, L. R. K. (2021). Invisible Scars: Female Ready-made Garment Workers' Gendered Exploitation. *Indian Journal of Industrial Relations*, *56*(4).

Rani, A., Raman, K. J., Antony, S., & Thirumoorthy, A., & B, C. (2025). Microaggression and Its Impact on Lower Caste Women with Psychiatric Disorders in India. *Violence and Gender*, *12*(1), 35–42.

Rani, U., & Belser, P. (2012). The effectiveness of minimum wages in developing countries. *International Labour Review*, *151*(1–2), 81–112. DOI: 10.1111/j.1564-913X.2012.00149.x

Ringblom, L. (2022). "It is just a joke!" informal interaction and gendered processes underground. *NORA*, *30*(2), 94–107.

Roberts, G. E. (2014). Principles of servant leader human resource management (SLHRM). In *Servant Leader Human Resource Management: A Moral and Spiritual Perspective* (pp. 1–38). Palgrave Macmillan US.

Rodgers, W., Murray, J. M., Stefanidis, A., Degbey, W. Y., & Tarba, S. Y. (2022). An AI algorithmic operation to norm based decision-making in *Human Resource* management processes. *Human Resource Management Review*, *33*(1), 100925. DOI: 10.1016/j.hrmr.2022.100925

Rossi, E. S., Cacchiarelli, L., Severini, S., & Sorrentino, A. (2024). Consumers preferences and social sustainability: A discrete choice experiment on 'Quality Agricultural Work' ethical label in the Italian fruit sector. *Agricultural and Food Economics*, *12*(1). Advance online publication. DOI: 10.1186/s40100-024-00307-9

Rubery, J., & Grimshaw, D. (2016). The 40-year pursuit of equal pay. *Cambridge Journal of Economics*, *40*(2), 319–343. DOI: 10.1093/cje/bev046

Rusdi, S. D., Ismail, I. R., & Isa, R. M. (2024). Unravelling Smart HRM 4.0: A Narrative Review of Progressive 4.0 Technology Along with in *Human Resource* Management [Review of *Unravelling Smart HRM 4.0: A Narrative Review of Progressive 4.0 Technology Along with in Human Resource Management*]. *Information Management and Business Review, 16*, 415. International Foundation for Research and Development. https://doi.org/DOI: 10.22610/imbr.v16i3(i)s.4070

Sabil, S., Bangkara, B. A., Mogea, T., Niswan, E., & Timotius, E. (2023). Identification of HRM Improvement Strategy Using Artificial Intelligence in Modern Economic Development. *International Journal of Professional Business Review: Int. J. Prof. Bus. Rev.*, *8*(6), 10.

Saini, D. S. (1995). *Labour law and industrial relations in India*. Oxford University Press.

Salmon, U. (2024). "It's wicked hard to fight covert racism": The case of microaggressions in science research organizations. *Gender, Work and Organization*, *31*(3), 727–748.

Sanders, S. R., Cope, M. R., & Pulsipher, E. R. (2018). Do factory audits improve international labor standards? An examination of voluntary corporate labor regulations in global production networks. *Social Sciences*, *7*(6). Advance online publication. DOI: 10.3390/socsci7060084

Sani, S., & Mandina, S. P. (2024). Examining the Outcomes of Adopting Modern Technologies in Community based Sector *Human Resource* Management. In *Advances in HRs management and organizational development book series* (p. 63). IGI Global., DOI: 10.4018/979-8-3693-2889-7.ch004

Sapkal, R. S. (2016). Labour law, enforcement and the rise of temporary contract workers: Empirical evidence from India's organised manufacturing sector. *European Journal of Law and Economics*, *42*(1), 157–182. DOI: 10.1007/s10657-015-9514-z

Sapre, S. R. (2024). *Made in India: Contestation and Power Dynamics in Export-Oriented Garment Production in the Indian Context*. Michigan State University.

Satispi, E., Rajiani, I., Murod, M., & Andriansyah, A. (2023). Human Resources Information System (HRIS) to Enhance Civil Servants' Innovation Outcomes: Compulsory or Complimentary? *Administrative Sciences*, *13*(2). Advance online publication. DOI: 10.3390/admsci13020032

Saura, J. R., Škare, V., & Došen, Đ. O. (2024). Is AI founded digital marketing norm based? Assessing a new security of information paradox. *Journal of Innovation & Knowledge*, *9*(4), 100597. DOI: 10.1016/j.jik.2024.100597

Scheibmayr, I., & Reichel, A. (2023). Beating the advertising drum for the employer: How legal context translates into good HRM practice. *Human Resource Management Journal, 33*(1), 95–114.

Schuett, J., Anderljung, M., Carlier, A., Koessler, L., & Garfinkel, B. (2024). From principles to rules: A regulatory approach for frontier AI. *arXiv preprint arXiv:2407.07300.*

Schuler, R. S., Jackson, S. E., & Tarique, I. (2011). Global talent management and global talent challenges: Strategic opportunities for IHRM. Journal of World Business, 46(4), 506–516. (Parry & Tyson, 2019)

Schwartz, P. (1999). Privacy and democracy in cyberspace. *Vanderbilt Law Review, 52*(6), 1601–1647.

Selvamohana, K. (2025). From Analytics of HR to AI-Imperative HRM: Enhancing Workforce Productivity and Engagement. *Journal of Information Operations Engineering & Management, 10*, 578. DOI: 10.52783/jisem.v10i21s.3395

Sengupta, S., & Guchhait, S. K. (2021). Inequality in contemporary India: Does caste still matter? *Journal of Developing Societies, 37*(1), 57–82.

Shah, E. A., Raiz, A., & Rashid, M. (2024). *Norm based Considerations in Use of AI under Digital Marketing*. https://doi.org/DOI: 10.36968/JPDC-V08-I02-25

Sharma, B., & Geetha, K. A. (2021). Casteing gender: Intersectional oppression of Dalit women. *Journal of International Women's Studies, 22*(10), 1–7.

Shen, J., & Benson, J. (2016). When CSR meets HRM: Bridging two fields. *International Journal of Human Resource Management, 27*(2), 1–21.

Sheveleva, A., & Rogov, E. (2021). Organization of remote work in the context of digitalization. *E3S Web of Conferences, 273*. https://doi.org/DOI: 10.1051/e3sconf/202127312042

Shyam Sundar, K. R. (2017). Labour reforms and flexibility. *Economic and Political Weekly, 52*(38), 49–58.

Singh, A., & Chouhan, T. (2023). Artificial intelligence in HRM: role of emotional–social intelligence and future work skill. In *The Adoption and Effect of Artificial Intelligence on Human Resources Management, Part A* (pp. 175-196). Emerald Publishing Limited.

Singh, P., & Sarkar, S. (2022). Human resource metrics for enhancing organizational performance: Case of Indian State-owned enterprises. *Management and Labour Studies, 47*(2), 233–250.

Sipahi, E., & Artantaş, E. (2022). Artificial intelligence in HRM. *Handbook of Research on Innovative Management Using AI in Industry 5.0*, 1-18.

Smith, M. H., Prabhakar, G., Nisar, T. M., & Tseng, H. (2024). Adoption of AI by the HR function in the civil service. *Members of team Pertainings, 47*(1), 104. https://doi.org/DOI: 10.1108/er-02-2024-0096

Sony, M. M. A. A. M., Amin, M. B., Ashraf, A., Islam, K. M. A., Debnath, N. C., & Debnath, G. C. (2025). Bias in AI-imperative HRM operations: Investigating discrimination risks embedded in AI recruitment tools along with Analytics of HR. *Social Sciences & Humanities Open, 12*, 102082. DOI: 10.1016/j.ssaho.2025.102082

Spais, G. S., & Chryssochoidis, G. (2025). Trends and future of AI, machine learning (ML) algorithms, and information analytics along with applications and implications for digital marketing and digital promotions. *Journal of Marketing Analytics*. https://doi.org/DOI: 10.1057/s41270-025-00406-6

Sridevi, J. (2024). The implications of the covid-19 pandemic on hrm practices in indian manufacturing industry., 578-588. https://doi.org/DOI: 10.2991/978-94-6463-433-4_44

Srivastava, R. (2021). Employment relations and labour law in India. *Indian Journal of Industrial Relations, 56*(4), 555–570.

Stahl, G. K., Björkman, I., & Morris, S. (2012). Handbook of research in international human resource management. Edward Elgar. (Punnett, 2018)

Stankevičiute, Ž., & Savanevičiene, A. (2018). Designing sustainable HRM: The core characteristics of emerging field. *Sustainability (Switzerland), 10*(12). Advance online publication. DOI: 10.3390/su10124798

Stewart, A., & Stanford, J. (2017). Regulating work in the gig economy. *Economic and Labour Relations Review, 28*(3), 420–437.

Stone, D. L., Deadrick, D. L., Lukaszewski, K. M., & Johnson, R. (2015). The influence of technology on the future of human resource management. Human Resource Management Review, 25(2), 216–231. (Robbins & Judge, 2020)

Stone, D. L., & Deadrick, D. L. (2015). Challenges and opportunities affecting the future of human resource management. *Human Resource Management Review, 25*(2), 139–150. DOI: 10.1016/j.hrmr.2015.01.003

Stone, D., Deadrick, D., Lukaszewski, K., & Johnson, R. (2015). The influence of technology on the future of human resource management. *Human Resource Management Review, 25*(2), 216–231.

Strohmeier, S., & Piazza, F. (2015). Artificial intelligence techniques in human resource management—a conceptual exploration. *Intelligent Techniques in Engineering Management: Theory and Applications*, 149-172.

Sue, D. W., & Spanierman, L. (2020). *Microaggressions in everyday life*. John Wiley & Sons.

Sundar, K. S. (2021). The shaky foundation of the labour law reforms. *The Hindu.*

Supiot, A. (2001). *Beyond employment: Changes in work and the future of labour law*. Oxford University Press.

Tambe, P., Cappelli, P., & Yakubovich, V. (2019). Artificial intelligence in human resources management: Challenges and a path forward. *California Management Review*, *61*(4), 15–42.

Tayal, R., Upadhyay, R. K., Yadav, M., & Singh, R. (2021). The development and validation of the organizational effectiveness scale using confirmatory factor analysis. *Global Business Review*, *22*(3), 821–843.

Teltumbde, A. (2010). Globalization and caste. *Voice of Dalit*, *3*(2), 101–138.

Tewari, I., & Pant, M. (2020, December). Artificial intelligence reshaping human resource management: A review. In *2020 IEEE international conference on advent trends in multidisciplinary research and innovation (ICATMRI)* (pp. 1-4). IEEE.

Thakkar, S. (2024). Exploitation, harassment, and violence: Lived experiences of women paid domestic workers in India. *Journal of South Asian Development*, *19*(1), 44–60.

Thierry, A. Z. (2018). HRM, ITS BIBLICAL ORIGINS AND PERSPECTIVES. *International Journal of Research Science and Management*, *5*(9), 10–20.

Tripathi, G. (2022). A comprehensive study on sexual harassment in india and its impact on women well being and social dynamics.

Trivedi, S., Singh, A., Yadav, M., Kumar, A., & Srivastava, P. (2023). Intention to Use Social Media in Online and Blended Learning: Potential Predictors and Mediation of Collectivism. IEEE Transactions on Engineering Management, PP, 1–14. https://doi.org/DOI: 10.1109/TEM.2023.3257422

Trivedi, S. K., Vishnu, S., Singh, A., & Yadav, M. (2023). Research trends in sustainable E-payment systems: A study using topic modeling approach. *IEEE Transactions on Engineering Management*, *71*, 7511–7525.

Tuli, F. A., Varghese, A., & Ande, J. R. P. K. (2018). Founded on information Taking the decision: A Framework for Integrating Workforce Analytics and Predictive HR Metrics in Digitalized Peripherys. *Global Disclosure of Economics and Business, 7*(2), 109. DOI: 10.18034/gdeb.v7i2.724

Ulrich, D., Younger, J., Brockbank, W., & Ulrich, M. (2012). HR from the outside in: Six competencies for the future of human resources. McGraw-Hill. (Schuler et al., 2011)

Ulrich, D., Brockbank, W., & Johnson, D. (2020). *HR competencies for the future.* McGraw-Hill.

Ulrich, D., Younger, J., Brockbank, W., & Ulrich, M. (2012). *HR from the outside in: Six competencies for the future of human resources.* McGraw-Hill.

United Nations Global Compact. (2020). *Principles of responsible business.* United Nations.

Upender, M. (2011). Differential output elasticity of employment during post-economic reform period in the indian economy. *The Singapore Economic Review, 56*(02), 189–202. DOI: 10.1142/s0217590811004249

Valencia-Quintana, R., Milić, M., Bonassi, S., Ochoa-Ocaña, M. A., Campos-Peña, V., Tenorio-Arvide, M. G., Pérez-Flores, G. A., & Sánchez-Alarcón, J. (2023). Effect of Pesticide Exposure over DNA Damage in Farmers from Los Reyes, Michoacan in Mexico. *Toxics, 11*(2), 1–11. DOI: 10.3390/toxics11020122 PMID: 36850997

Van Buren, H. J.III, & Greenwood, M. (2013). The genesis of employment ethics. *Journal of Business Ethics, 117*(4), 707–719.

van der Straaten, K., Pisani, N., & Kolk, A. (2020). Unraveling the MNE wage premium. *Journal of International Business Studies, 51*(9), 1355–1390. DOI: 10.1057/s41267-019-00285-x

Van Landuyt, Y., Dewaelheyns, N., & Van Hulle, C. (2017). Employment Protection Legislation and SME Performance. *International Small Business Journal, 35*(3), Vermeeren, B., Steijn, B., Tummers, L., Lankhaar, M., Poerstamper, R. J., & Van Beek, S. (2014). HRM and its effect on employee, organizational and financial outcomes in health care organizations. *Human Resources for Health, 12*(1), 35. PMID: 28549434

Velluti, S. (2024). Labour standards in global garment supply chains and the proposed EU corporate sustainability due diligence directive. *European Labour Law Journal, 15*(4), 822–850.

Voigt, P., & Von dem Bussche, A. (2017). *The EU General Data Protection Regulation (GDPR): A practical guide*. Springer.

Vrontis, D., Christofi, M., Pereira, V., Tarba, S., Makrides, A., & Trichina, E. (2023). Artificial intelligence, robotics, advanced technologies and human resource management: a systematic review. *Artificial intelligence and international HRM*, 172-201.

Waas, B. (2021). The "S" in ESG and international labour standards. *International Journal of Disclosure and Governance*, *18*(4), 403–410. DOI: 10.1057/s41310-021-00121-5

Walters, D., Wadsworth, E., & Quinlan, M. (2011). *Regulating workplace risks: A comparative study of inspection regimes in times of change*. Edward Elgar Publishing.

Wang, J. (2021). Datafication and the future of digital work. *Information Systems Journal*, *31*(4), 637–660.

Wang, M., Zhu, C. J., Mayson, S., & Chen, W. (2019). Contextualizing performance appraisal practices in Chinese public sector organizations: The importance of context and areas for future study. *International Journal of Human Resource Management*, *30*(5), 902–919.

Wang, Q. (2023). The Impact of AI on Organizational Employees: A Literature Review. *Journal of Education. Humanities and Social Sciences*, *19*, 45–53.

Warhurst, C. (2016). From invisible work to invisible workers. *Invisible Labor: Hidden Work in the Contemporary World*, 214.

Wheeler, A. R., & Buckley, M. R. (2021). The current state of HRM with automation, artificial intelligence, and machine learning. In *HR without People?* (pp. 45–67). Emerald Publishing Limited.

Wilkinson, A., Donaghey, J., Dundon, T., & Freeman, R. B. (2020). *Handbook of research on employee voice*. Edward Elgar Publishing.

World Economic Forum. (2022). *Future of jobs report*. World Economic Forum.

World Health Organization. (2021). *Mental health at work: Policy and practice recommendations*. WHO.

Wright, D., & Kreissl, R. (2020). *Surveillance in Europe: A critical overview*. Routledge.

Wright, P. M., & McMahan, G. C. (2011). Exploring human capital: Toward a sustainable HRM theory. *International Journal of Human Resource Management*, *22*(6), 1146–1160.

Yadav, M., Mittal, S., Kumar, M., Sahoo, A., Jayarathne, P. G. S. A., Yadav, M., Mittal, S., Kumar, M., Sahoo, A., & Jayarathne, P. G. S. A. (2024). From Textbooks to Teamwork:The Importance of Collaboration Skills in Workforce Preparation. In https://services.igi-global.com/resolvedoi/resolve.aspx?doi=10.4018/979-8-3693-3856-8.ch011 (pp. 333–352). IGI Global Scientific Publishing. https://doi.org/ DOI: 10.4018/979-8-3693-3856-8.ch011

Yadav, M., Kumar, M., Alyousef, M. I., Dagar, M., Dewasiri, N. J., & Amoozegar, A. (2025). Mapping Research Trends on Gender Diversity, Work Stress, and Job Satisfaction in Higher Education: A Bibliometric Analysis. *International Journal of Learning. Teaching and Educational Research, 24*(8), 444–472. DOI: 10.26803/ijlter.24.8.19

Yadav, M., Kumar, M., Goswami, A., Tiwari, N. K., Amoozegar, A., & Rani, P. (2025). Innovating under constraints: A bibliometric and systematic review of frugal and inclusive innovations in start-up ecosystems. *International Journal of Business Innovation and Research, 38*(8), 31–55. DOI: 10.1504/IJBIR.2025.150148

Yadav, M., Kumar, M., Sahoo, A., & Rathnasiri, M. S. H. (2024). AI and the evolution of artistic expression: Impacts on society and culture. In *Transforming Cinema with Artificial Intelligence* (pp. 15–36). IGI Global., DOI: 10.4018/979-8-3693-3916-9.ch002

Yadav, M., & Rangnekar, S. (2016). Role clarity and organizational citizenship behaviour: Does tenure matter? A study on Indian power sector. *Global Business Review, 17*(3, suppl), 207S–224S.

Yadav, M., & Rangnekar, S. (2016). Role Clarity and Organizational Citizenship Behaviour: Does Tenure Matter? A Study on Indian Power Sector. *Global Business Review, 17*(3, suppl), 207S–224S. DOI: 10.1177/0972150916631216

Yadav, M., Rangnekar, S., & Srivastava, A. P. (2019). Demographic variables as moderators between QWL and OCB. *Industrial and Commercial Training, 51*(7/8), 396–408.

Yanamala, K. K. R. (2024). Transparency, Secrecy, and Answerability in AI-Enhanced HR Processes. *Journal of Advanced Computing Operations, 3*(3), 10. DOI: 10.69987/jacs.2023.30302

Yassi, A., Bryce, E., Breilh, J., Lavoie, M., Ndelu, L., Lockhart, K., & Spiegel, J. (2011). Collaboration between infection control and occupational health in three continents: A success story with international impact. *BMC International Health and Human Rights, 11*(S2). Advance online publication. DOI: 10.1186/1472-698x-11-s2-s8 PMID: 22166059

You, C., Qiu, H., Pi, Z., & Yu, M. (2023). Sustainable Enterprise Development in the Manufacturing Sector: Flexible Employment and Innovation in China. *Sustainability (Switzerland), 15*(10), 1–30. DOI: 10.3390/su15108180

Zaid, A., Jaaron, A., & Bon, A. (2018). Green human resource management and sustainability performance. *Business Strategy and the Environment, 27*(8), 983–999.

Zawada, M. (2024). The Impression of AI on *Human Resource* Management: Outcomes, Opportunities, and Future Directions. *Operation Safety Human - Complex Facility - Periphery, 6*(1). https://doi.org/DOI: 10.2478/czoto-2024-0026

Zigarelli, M. A. (1993). Catholic social teaching and the employment relationship: A model for managing human resources in accordance with Vatican doctrine. *Journal of Business Ethics, 12*(1), 75–82.

Ziobrowska, A., & Starostka-Patyk, M. (2025). Exploring the AI Revolution in *Human Resource* Management: Key Insights and Case Studies. In *Springer proceedings in business and economics* (p. 885). Springer International Publishing. https://doi.org/DOI: 10.1007/978-981-96-4116-1_56

Zolak Poljašević, B., Gričnik, A. M., & Šarotar Žižek, S. (2025). Human resource management in public administration: The ongoing tension between reform requirements and resistance to change. *Administrative Sciences, 15*(3), 94.

About the Contributors

Perfecto G. Aquino, Jr., was a former Director of the Center for Research and Creativity at the University of Cambodia and a Research Associate at Duy Tan University, Vietnam. He has taught at prestigious universities in Oman, Bahrain, UAE-Dubai, Vietnam, and Cambodia. He is a holder of PhD in Public Administration and Management at the Pontifical and Royal University of Santo Tomas, Manila, Philippines in 2001. Dr. Aquino is finishing his Post -Doctoral in Strategic Management and Leadership at an International Christian University.

Mercia Justin Is currently an Associate Professor at Xavier Institute of Management and Entrepreneurship in Bangalore, India. She was a former Dean at Emirates College of Management and Information Technology in Dubai, UAE. She has published books locally and internationally in the area of finance and business management.

Revenio Jalagat, Jr. is currently an Associate Professor at Al Zahra College of Oman. He has published several papers and books duly indexed in Scopus, Web of Science and Analytics indexed journals.

***

Narayanage Jayantha Dewasiri, Ph.D., is a Chartered Manager at the Chartered Management Institute, UK. He conducts research at the Open University of Sri Lanka and the Sri Lanka Institute of Marketing. He is the founding Editor-in-Chief of the South Asian Journal of Marketing. His research interests are in corporate social responsibility, corporate governance, marketing and sales, management, and finance. He is working as the Head of Field Force at the HMD Global Inc., Sri Lanka. He also serves as a senior lecturer at University of Sabaragamuwa, Sri Lanka. He can be reached at dnjay@ou.ac.lk

Shivani Dhand is an Associate Professor (14+ years of experience),a Certified SHRM (Society for Human Resource Management)faculty in the department of Mittal School of Business of Lovely Professional University.She is NLP(Neuro Linguistics Programming) Practioner She is also a member of the Indian Society for Training and Development (ISTD) and the Indian Society of Labour Economics. She is also a core committee member and Mentor of an NGO(Shalini Fellowship) Shivani Dhand has worked in an IT company as an HR. She has published 15 research papers in various journals which include Scopus-indexed, UGC care and peer-reviewed journals. She is a certified POSH trainer. She has worked with CPSC (Columbo Plan Staff College) Manila Philippines, and trained the faculty and Principals of various Institutions in Bhutan (2015). In 2016, She worked on one of the projects," Austria as an Innovation leader in EU in Austria and was awarded as best presentation and Excellent paper. Her research is situated in the field of Startups, HR Practices Human Resource Management, Entrepreneurship, and social entrepreneurship with a special focus on academic entrepreneurship.

Damith Gangodawilage serves as the Deputy Dean of the Qasim Ibrahim School of Business (QISB) and the Director of the Centre for Innovation and Entrepreneurship Development (CIED) at Villa College, Maldives. With deep expertise in entrepreneurship education, innovation management, and sustainable business practices, Dr. Damith plays a pivotal role in shaping entrepreneurial ecosystems in the Maldives and beyond. A driving force behind the VIgnite Business Incubator, Dr. Damith has led impactful collaborations with industry partners, government organizations, and startup networks in the Maldives and Sri Lanka. The incubator focuses on fostering innovation in key areas such as technopreneurship, social entrepreneurship, women entrepreneurship, and global entrepreneurship, providing aspiring entrepreneurs and students with the tools and networks to create meaningful solutions for global challenges. In his academic role, Dr. Damith has spearheaded the integration of Design Thinking into undergraduate programs and incubator projects. He actively engages in curriculum development and 'train-the-trainer' programs, empowering both students and staff to cultivate entrepreneurial mindsets. His work reflects a dedication to advancing entrepreneurship within Villa College and the broader community. As an accomplished researcher, Dr. Damith has published extensively in the fields of corporate sustainability, critical thinking, and sustainable reporting practices. His ongoing research bridges the gap between academic theory and practical applications, contributing valuable insights to the business and academic communities. His forthcoming book, "Corporate Sustainability and Reporting: Theory and Practices," offers new perspectives on sustainable business models and practices. Dr. Damith's leadership in entrepreneurship development aligns with his efforts to connect local and global entrepreneurial communities. His role in positioning the Maldives on the global entrepreneurship map, including ongoing efforts to make Villa College the national host for Global Entrepreneurship Week (GEW), underscores his commitment to collaboration and innovation. With a passion for empowering youth, enabling sustainable ventures, and fostering inclusive ecosystems, Dr. Damith Gangodawilage continues to drive innovation, entrepreneurship, and lifelong learning at Villa College and beyond.

Revenio Jalagat Jr. serves as the Associate Professor and Program Manager, Al-Zahra College for Women, Oman. He has Google Scholar Citations: 1,037, h-index= 12; i10-index = 12. He is External Reviewer Expert of MBA Program Institutional Applications submitted to the Ministry of Higher Education, Research and Innovation (MOHERI). He was awarded as Most Outstanding Researcher by Al Zahra College for Women, Oman (AY 2022-2023). He was also awarded the Certification from The Chartered Association of Business Schools (CABS) in the UK as "Certified Management and Business Educator" (CMBE).He serves as Editorial Member/Reviewer in different International Peer-Reviewed Journals and Publications such as Elseivier, Emerald, Taylor & Francis, Sage, IGI.

Nandan Kumar Jha is an accomplished academic and healthcare management professional, UGC-NET qualified, currently serving as an Assistant Professor at the Faculty of Commerce and Management, SGT University, Gurugram, India. He holds a B.Pharm degree and a postgraduate qualification in Healthcare Management, with expertise in hospital operations, hospital planning, healthcare policy, public health management, and quality standards. His professional exposure includes internships with PlasmIT Healthcare IT Vector, National Health Mission (NHM) Punjab, and Analystoserve, where he gained experience in healthcare IT requirement analysis, maternal and child health program evaluation, and healthcare market research. He possesses strong analytical, technical, and problem-solving skills, with proficiency in MS Office and data-driven decision-making, and is actively involved in teaching, mentoring, and academic development in healthcare management. His research interests focus on healthcare management and hospital administration.

Sneha Kadyan is a sociologist with demonstrated experience and performance at all organisations and institutes in academic and professional development across diverse social issues. Knowledge innovator with methodological proficiency in qualitative and quantitative skills and analysis. Unique perspective as a professor, scholar and researcher in global institutional environments. Excellent relationship builder -team worker with collaborative research across the globe. Presently she is working as Assistant Professor, Jindal Global Business School, O.P Jindal Global University, Haryana, India.

Preet Kanwal is an Associate Professor at the Mittal School of Business, Lovely Professional University, with over 22 years of academic and research experience in Human Resource Management. A Post-Doctoral Fellow from the University of Quebec in Montreal, she holds a PhD in HRM from I.K. Gujral Punjab Technical University. Her research interests include quality of work life, labour laws, industrial relations, organisational behaviour, and workforce well-being. She has published widely in Scopus-indexed and UGC-listed journals, authored books and numerous book chapters, and presented at several national and international conferences. She has taught internationally for Victoria University (Online), Australia, and Sunway University (Online), Malaysia. She recently completed an ICSSR-funded project as Co-Principal Investigator on empowering women artisans for Vision Viksit Bharat@ 2047 and is currently a Co-Investigator on an ongoing ICSSR-funded project on enhancing Social-Emotional Learning (SEL) in government schools across Punjab.

Mohan Kumar is an Assistant Professor in the Faculty of Commerce & Management at SGT University, Gurugram. He holds a Ph.D. in Management from Maharshi Dayanand University and has qualified UGC-NET/JRF multiple times in both Commerce and Management. His academic and research career spans a broad spectrum of themes including AI-driven business transformation, entrepreneurial behaviour, MSME finance, digital learning ecosystems, bibliometric analysis, and higher education research. Dr. Kumar has published extensively in Scopus-indexed and ABDC-listed journals, with contributions appearing in Emerald, Taylor & Francis, Inderscience, IEEE Xplore, and IGI Global. His scholarship includes systematic reviews, bibliometric studies, empirical analyses, and conceptual explorations focusing on technology, entrepreneurship, and organizational development. He has also authored two books and holds two published patents in the areas of AI-enabled fraud detection and machine-learning–based ERP optimization. In addition to his research contributions, Dr. Kumar plays an active academic leadership role as Program Coordinator for the Online BBA Program. He has supervised Ph.D. and postgraduate scholars, organized faculty development programmes and international conferences, and contributed to curriculum design, KRA–KPI policy frameworks, and digital pedagogy initiatives. His work reflects a strong commitment to impactful, interdisciplinary, and technology-enabled research.

Thi-Minh-Ngoc Luu is now working and teaching at International School VNU Hanoi, Vietnam. She received a Ph.D. degree in 2014 in Business Administration from the university of economics, Vietnam National University, Vietnam. She becomes an Associate professor in 2022. She is currently working and teaching in the areas of human resource management, business management, and International Business with many invitations to review papers from ISI and Scopus indices journals. She has published many papers in the research fields of human resource management, corporate governance, individual and organizational behavior, entrepreneurship, sustainable development, and so on in high-ranking journals (ISI and Scopus indices).

Firdous Ahmad Malik was born in India and is currently employed by the University of People as an Assistant Professor of Economics (instructor), Department of Management. Currently he is perceiving Post Doctoral research at Amity Dubai University. Before that, he was a research fellow at the National Institute of Public Finance and Policy (NIPFP) in Delhi, India. Prior to this, he was a senior research associate at the O.P. Jindal Global University in Sonipat, Haryana's Jindal Center for the Global South. From Babasaheb Bhimrao Ambedkar University in Lucknow, India, he received his Ph.D. He has a Master's in Economics from the University of Kashmir and an MPhil in Economics from Babasaheb Bhimrao Ambedkar University Lucknow. Microfinance, financial inclusion, and financial literacy are his main areas of study interest. He has articles in journals that are Scopus-indexed from Springer, Elsevier, Taylor Francis, and others. Moreover, he has published more than seven books.

Shashank Mittal has done his FPM in Organizational behavior and Human Resource from Indian Institute of Management Raipur. He holds B. Tech from I.E.T. Lucknow. His post FPM work experience includes almost five years of industry and academics exposures in multiple roles. Prior to joining FPM, he has over two years of industrial experience and three years of teaching experience in various organizations. He has published multiple papers in ABDC ranked and SSCI indexed journals of international repute such as Journal of Knowledge Management, Journal of Behavioral and Experimental Finance, International Journal of Conflict Management, Journal of Management and Organization and Current Psychology. His current research interest includes Social identity, Knowledge exchanges, Status, Proactive helping, Employer branding, Organizational justice, and Humanitarian relief management. He enjoys badminton and cycling during leisure time.

Mukhtaruddin is a senior lecturer in Accounting Department, Faculty of Economics, Universitas Sriwijaya. He finished his degree on accounting field in Accounting Department, Faculty of Economics Universitas Sriwijaya in 1992. His master degree finished 1997 on accounting field in Economics Faculty, Universitas Gadjahmada. I finished the doctoral degree in financial management in Faculty of

Economics, Universitas Sriwijaya, 2022. He was as reviewer some international journal and have published his research in some international journal, 20 articles have published in Scopus journal indexed (H-index 6). He has presented some papers in some international conferences. Some of job related to his competences are head of accounting professional education, secretary of accounting department, head of diploma accounting program study, vice dean for financial and employee affairs, vice rector for financial and employee affairs and vice director of postgraduate school of Universitas Sriwijaya

Ali Najeeb is the Vice Rector and Chief Operating Officer (COO) of Villa College (VC), Maldives and CEO of Bristol Institute of Business Management (BIBM), Sri-Lanka. He is also an Adjunct Associate Professor at the School of Hospitality, Tourism and Events, Taylor's University, Malaysia. He holds a PhD in Management and HR strategy at the University of Wollongong, Australia, a Master's Degree in Human Resource Management at the University of Newcastle, Australia, and BA in Business Studies from the University of the South Pacific, Fiji. He is a Chartered Professional Member of Chartered Institute of Personnel and Development (CIPD) and a Certified Professional Member of Australian Human Resource Institute (AHRI). Besides his official roles, he also holds several advisory roles and membership in local and international NGOs and professional bodies. His research interests include higher education leadership, governance and management, industrial relations, employment law and labour issues in small island states, migrant workers, HRM/ER in tourism and hospitality industry. He has published several research papers in refereed international journals, shared his experience in local and international panel discussions and presented his research work in international scholarly conferences. He is a recipient of the Emerald Literati Award for Excellence 2014 – the outstanding paper award. Dr Najeeb is a former school principal and worked as a Director of the Education and Development Centre in the Ministry of Education. He is also a former fulltime member of the Employment Tribunal, Maldives. Besides his administrative, teaching and research work, he is actively engaged in management and corporate consultancy and training.

Majdi Anwar Quttainah earned his Ph.D. degree in Management from Rensselaer Polytechnic Institute, Lally School of Management & Technology (USA); MBA degree with merits from the Business School & Entrepreneurship at Newcastle University (UK), and bachelor's degree in International Business from the American International University in London (UK). Dr. Quttainah is an associate professor of management in the College of Business Administration at Kuwait University. His research and teaching interests are corporate governance and strategies, entrepreneurship & small businesses, and organizational development. In addition, as a recognition of his research, he was awarded the Best Young Researcher academic year 2016/2017 Kuwait University. He is an active scholar, presently working as senior editor of FIIB Business Review (Scopus, WoS, Published by the Sage Publishing). His research won several recognition and awards including the Best Paper Award at the 76th Annual Meeting of the Academy of Management Anaheim, CA, the Best Paper Award at the AGBA's 12th Annual World Congress, Kuantan City (State of Pahang), Malaysia, and the Best Paper Award of the Gorontalo International Conference of Project Management (ICPM) – Gorontalo/Indonesia. Also, at the home country level the best paper award for the Kuwait Economic Researcher Award by the Central Bank of Kuwait; May 2019 and 2022.

Mananage Shanika Hansini Rathnasiri is a Senior Lecturer attached to the Department of Marketing Management, Faculty of Management Studies (FMS), Sabaragamuwa University of Sri Lanka (SUSL). Currently, she is pursuing her doctoral studies at the College of Society and Professions, London South Bank University (LSBU), London, United Kingdom. She serves as an Associate Editor cum Editorial Assistant of the South Asian Journal of Marketing, published by Emerald Publishing. She is also serving as an Editor of the book namely "Shaping Entrepreneurial Marketing: A South Asian Perspective," by Emerald Publishing. Furthermore, she contributes as an Editor of the Sri Lankan Marketer Magazine, published by the Sri Lanka Institute of Marketing.

Jeayaram Subramanian holds a PhD in OB & HR from Universite Paris Saclay, Paris, France. He's also a B.Tech (EEE) from Anna University, Chennai and an MBA from Amrita Vishwa Vidaypeetham University, Coimbatore. Jeayaram had a short stint in sales with 99acres.com before going for his PhD. Post PhD, he has been an Assistant Professor in OB & HR with Amrita Vishwa Vidyapeetham, School of Business, subsequently at International School of Business & Media at Pune, and Bharathidasan Institute of Management Trichy prior to joining the Jindal Global Business School in January 2024. His areas of interests for teaching & research span across Leadership, Personality, Psychological contract, Psychoanalytics, and the likes. Apart from this, Jeayaram is also an accomplished Carnatic classical vocalist for the past 23+ years. He has performed music concerts at various places across the world. Apart from music, Jeayaram maintains his own blog page titled "THE INDIAN DHARMA", where he tries to bring out modern-day leadership / management principles from our ancient scriptural texts. The blog page has so far attracted around 1.4 lakh viewers from across 115 countries around the globe.

Mohit Yadav is a Professor in the area of Human Resource Management at Jindal Global Business School (JGBS). He has a rich blend of work experience from both Academics as well as Industry. Prof. Mohit holds a Ph.D. from Department of Management Studies, Indian Institute of Technology Roorkee (IIT Roorkee) and has completed Master of Human Resource and Organizational Development (MHROD) from prestigious Delhi School of Economics, University of Delhi. He also holds a B.Com (Hons.) degree from University of Delhi and UGC-JRF scholarship. He has published various research papers and book chapters with reputed publishers like Springer, Sage, Emerald, Elsevier, Inderscience etc. and presented research papers in national and International conferences both in India and abroad. He has many best paper awards on his credit too. He is reviewer of various international journals like Computers in Human Behavior, Policing etc. His areas of interest are Organizational Behavior, HRM, Recruitment and Selection, Organizational Citizenship Behavior, Quality of work life and role.

Index

R

S

T

W

www.ingramcontent.com/pod-product-compliance
Lightning Source LLC
LaVergne TN
LVHW080857300926
849162LV00003B/452